CADEL EVANS
close to flying

CADEL EVANS

close to flying

with
Rob Arnold

Macquarie
Regional Library

hardie grant books
MELBOURNE · LONDON

Published in 2009
Hardie Grant Books
85 High Street
Prahran, Victoria 3181, Australia
www.hardiegrant.com.au

Cataloguing-in-Publication data is available from the
National Library of Australia.
Cadel Evans: Close to flying
ISBN 978 1 74066 667 1

Printed and bound in Australia by McPhersons Printing Group

10 9 8 7 6 5 4

Contents

Introduction

It's all about stages. In life they can be categorised in other terms: phases, moments, sequences or just the act of living. The single-parent upbringing, the discovery of cycling and his talents, the mountain bike years, the national team years, the successful debut as a professional road cyclist … and then there was that horse incident in his childhood when a kick to the head put Cadel in a coma for seven days; a scar from the brain surgery it necessitated remains clear even beneath a brush of hair. These are all stages of a life that eventually took Cadel to the Tour de France.

A professional bike rider like Cadel Evans learns to see things in stages: a race in stages; an annual summer pilgrimage that takes a peloton of the world's elite cyclists around Europe racing in stages. And it's because of the Tour de France that he has made his name. Cadel Evans is aware that his actions have contributed to people enjoying cycling, perhaps even for the first time, because of what he's doing. He races. People watch, and they care.

There's a lot that can be gained from riding a bike; the benefits of this rudimentary machine are plentiful. Those who ride realise that it is one of life's joys. It is good on so many levels: we ride for pleasure and practicality; some use the bike to get to work, others use it as exercise or to get a release from daily pressures.

It is a device with uses that extend it beyond the exact purpose for which it has been created: carrying someone from A to B.

But it becomes more than that.

I ride because I love it. And I follow cycling for the same reason. The opportunity to ride when, where and how I like is rare but I've had moments that are slotted into a happy part of my memory. Some of the best things in my life have come about because of the bike. It gives me enormous satisfaction. I've shared many journeys on my own and in the company of others riding a bike.

Of the cultures of cycling that litter the planet, racing is an element which can captivate even those who, for one reason or another, cannot – or just do not – ride. It evokes emotion and generates pride or admiration. Yet following it can be cruel. It's frustrating but exciting.

It's easy to suffer if you're passionate about cycling. If you ride, you know the pain that can come with hours in the saddle, pushing your body to its limits. If you watch those riding, it's easy to admire human physiology and its sheer vulnerability which is on display.

For Cadel it is simply achieving an objective that he has set himself. From 1992 until 2001 he was a cross-country rider, a mountain biker – off-road, up steep inclines, down spectacular trails, through forests and over barren landscapes dominated by rocks or mud or gravel or tree roots or any number of obstacles which tested handling ability and stamina alike. It was a solitary endeavour where although the rider is part of a team, it's only the individual who can lay claim to the result in a race. He was good at it and he won often. Consistency was one trait which endeared him to the best teams in the sport. After two victories in the World Cup series, he rode away from his first love and adopted a new passion: road cycling.

He waited until he finished in the under-23 category and then he went into some good-sized road races and it was those results that were the first stages of a path that led him to the Tour de France. The Mapei team he joined confirmed that they had scouts who had been watching him since 1997, and that's what opened the door for him to have a go as a full-time road cyclist. The fact that he enjoyed it and he was doing well and the team were happy to have him there going for results, was all part of a happy new equation. It was the flourishing of a career that had been blooming since the mid-1990s when cycling was changing dramatically. For a start, mountain biking had become an Olympic sport.

However by the beginning of the new millennium medicine became as important as decisions about the race route, more so in fact, because with the right elixir in the blood even mountains could fall, becoming little more than small hurdles for a rider charged beyond natural limits. This was the world Cadel was entering. It's impossible to ignore the implications of doping in cycling. This is one part of cycling that is not at all attractive, but cyclists have had to accept that those who break the rules will have their names denoted with asterisks in the sport's listings. World titles have been won, but with asterisks pointing out a retrospective change in the results. The reputations of Olympic champions have been brought into question because of bad blood. Even a Tour de France champion has lost his crown retrospectively because of doping, but his had nothing to do with blood; testosterone was the cause. Plenty of stages have been won when the second man over the line was indeed the best clean athlete on the day. If you've become a fan, you know that it's difficult to be confident that those you cheer are racing cleanly.

Cadel has raced cheats. He's beaten them in some races but probably lost to more of them. There's a list of positive doping tests for several cyclists who have beaten him at world championships over the years. And there are some still on the scene in the Tour de France. The techniques and products used by these cyclists have changed but thankfully detection methods have improved as well. Cadel knows what he is up against, but having to confront a challenge isn't anything new to him.

When you become a professional there is the risk that always comes with working in a field you're passionate about: the risk that it stops being fun and starts being just a job. But this has never been a problem for Cadel, and it still isn't. Cadel liked riding the bike and there has never been a separation between work and fun.

With help from him and the people he knows, this is Cadel.

Rob Arnold

I
Ride like you're flying

Joy of riding

The first international competition for Cadel was a watershed moment in his life:

I treasured that first trip overseas to race when I went to Vail, Colorado for the World Championships in 1994. The Hermosa Creek Trail was such a good place to ride. It allowed me to be free. The training days remain highlights of my time on the bike. It was exploration and exhilaration. A roller coaster, two wheels spinning over gravel, dirt and sand, showering a spray of dust in their wake. It was cycling bliss. Descending most of the way, pedalling as often as possible but having the option to freewheel. These were free riding hours. Race day would come but on Hermosa near Durango it was me, my bike, my mind and my body all feeling as one. It was all so simple: a front-wheel lift to clear a rock, a shift of the body to absorb some of the shock, a grind of the knobby tyres as they clawed over a rock, a moment out of the saddle to increase the speed, a touch of the brake, a controlled slide maintaining speed through corners, but nothing to slow you to a stop.

No burden, but expectation that I put on myself to get a result. That's something I continued to feel but then, right there – at altitude, in the wilderness, on a trail, before a major race, on the national team, ready for a career but still racing as a junior – I was riding for the love of it.

The Hermosa Creek Trail is an experience that I've always wanted to explain. It was an off-road path that led me to where I am now. I still relish the days in Colorado when I was 17, although many other perfect trails and roads have since been ridden.

When you have a really good day mountain biking – when everything is going right – it's close to the feeling of flying. With an uninterrupted path of singletrack it can seem like you're float-ing through a forest. The rush of constant sounds, like the wind past your ears, is amplified by the noise generated by wide tyres on the terrain; it drums out of beat at times to the thud of tree roots, rocks and all else that litters the way. And then come the contributions from the body. The pulse of breath and heart – both rising from surges of adrenaline and effort – add to a soundtrack on this simple machine and you're in nature's playground. You float … drift … sweep. Through turns you delve deeper into the path ahead, diving around the next turn and into the unknown.

He looks out the window. The lines on his face spell it out; the shape of his mouth closely resembles a smile but it's more com-plicated than that. The thrill of his memory takes him away and it's a while before his gaze returns. It takes time and patience to re-engage him.

Cadel is speaking of the Hermosa Creek Trail 14 years later. But it feels like yesterday as he considers what has happened since.

Float … drift … sweep. The path ahead turned such a different direction. It was fun. It still is. Doesn't everyone approaching 32 dream of being 17 again? In half a lifetime, the fundamentals remain but the sensations have changed. Still, memory thrives and emotions become alive.

When I was young I lived too far away from places where organised sports were part of everyday life. There was never any time when I could have been part of a football team or even the 12th man at the cricket. Everywhere I lived was removed from sports that kids of my age got involved with.

In the Northern Territory there was zero. Upper Corindi: zero. I didn't have anyone to play with because there were no kids around, and then it was only when I started playing cricket and soccer when I was seven or eight that I started being able to do organised sport. Back then there wasn't the varied selection of sports that are now on offer. There were the standard options: football in winter, cricket in summer. But because I didn't do either at all when I was young, I didn't have any balls skills or anything like that which people pick up if their dads are footy fans or cricket fans.

The first sport I started training in was swimming. That gave me a base of aerobic fitness. I used to do to swimming laps with my mum before school.

'Cadel was nine or ten when he started swimming with me,' his mother, Helen Cocks, recalls of the training sessions.

I have always swum. When we lived in Bamyili I used the creek, then there was the dam at Upper Corindi and the uni pool when we lived in Armidale.

When we lived in Plenty, the Greensborough pool was about five kilometres away. Cadel had just really got into riding bikes – competing, I mean – and had convinced me to get a new bike. I used to have an old one of my own that had been a prop in a play; it was painted pink; it was given to me by a friend. The new bike was a bit more fancy – but nothing like what I've seen since. We usually used to ride down in the morning before he went to school and before I went to work. Sometimes we'd drive, but usually we rode.

If there is a single point in your life as a parent when you realise your child is bigger and stronger than you, this was it for me. One day we were running late. Cadel said he had to go. We were riding up Diamond Creek Road and he simply took off. He needed to be somewhere else in a hurry, or that was the excuse, and he increased his speed. Gone in a flash; I wouldn't see him again until I arrived home. There was no way I could have kept up with his pace. I knew then that, since we began the routine, he had just been keeping me company on the rides. It wouldn't be long before his bike training became more and more significant and he started going out early, counting up plenty of kilometres and doing efforts up Kinglake Mountain. We stopped swimming together around the same time.

We had a training camp at the Hermosa Creek Trail with the national team before the world championships and it was like living out a dream. At the time I was doing year 12 at high school, the VCE – Victorian Certificate of Education, but finally I had the time and energy to train and prepare properly. No more juggling time between school, the gym and the bike, all at the comprise of a decent nights sleep.

I couldn't wait to finish school. I wasn't against the idea of a good education but it was beginning to become apparent that my career path was coming from sport. Cycling in the form that was already providing me with some earnings had only very recently become an option as a profession. It was an all-new discipline but it was essentially invented in the part of the world where I got my first taste of international competition.

On the trip, I took all my text books with me because I was meant to study in my spare time, but I didn't open them once in the whole six weeks. Instead it was my first taste of really being able to train like a professional. I'd wake up, ride, eat, rest, recover, sleep, train again in the afternoon. And repeat this day after day. We were in the best mountain biking area in the whole world and I was in heaven.

I turned 17 that year and was a first-year junior. I was getting ready for the World Championships and doing a couple of races but it was the whole experience that appealed to me. I was riding near people who I'd only ever seen in magazines – some icons of mountain biking like John Tomac, Ned Overend, Thomas Frischknecht and others. That was cool. I'd read about them months after the events that helped them become off-road pioneers; they were riders who attracted sponsorship from bike companies and made their money by racing their products.

In 1992, when I started reading mountain bike magazines and realising it was possible to actually make a job out of riding a bike, that was what I wanted to do. 'What, you can be a professional at this!? Well, whatever it's going to take – I don't care about the sacrifices – I'm going to do it.' That's when all else took a back seat. School was part of the routine but the first priority was riding.

I'd been to some great places before. I raced the nationals a few times at Thredbo in the Australian alps, but the trip in 1994 was my first time overseas. It was my first time of full-time training. It was the first time I'd slept at altitude. And the riding on the Hermosa Creek Trail still remains as one of my favourite rides of all time.

The first time was incredible. It's a famous singletrack – and it is perfect. You could go for two hours without any distractions: just point your bike and float along over the dirt like you're flying. The ride was around 35 kilometres. It was undulating but the dominant direction was downhill. Starting on a bare outcrop high above a pine forest near Durango you aim your bike along a path less than a metre wide – only enough for one rider to squeeze past if you've got trust in your companions, but really only sufficient room to guide past the rocks and debris littering the track – and like the seemingly endless horizon of a video game that allows you to progress so long as you don't fall victim to the hurdles along the way. You arrive near the tree line after a small creek crossing offering little more than a *splash before a brief uphill section over boulders that line the course and other stones that have split over the years and nestled into the earth in a myriad of shapes – but the tyres and suspension cope.*

Thanks to speed it all skims past without allowing the bike to settle onto it and make it feel like the solid mass that it is. Danger is negated by the speed. You pass the object too quickly to recognise the threat it imposes; a slower pace and you'd think too much about the consequences; in the top gear at the peak of form, you have only the path ahead in your sights.

On the Hermosa Creek Trail, after the fast start and with the river to your right, it's onward. Down. Down. Up. Down, down, down. Down around and up a little. Before another water crossing. Up. Down. Along.

It is the site where Tomac and his ilk contested the first-ever mountain bike World Championships in 1990; a 35-year-old American, Ned Overend, won the title ahead of Frischknecht of Switzerland, the perennial runner-up – and one-time retrospectively awarded winner of the celebrated rainbow colours which had been adopted from the traditional forms of cycling.

I was second in the 1994 World Championships in Vail, Colorado. Miguel Martinez would beat me this time and it wouldn't be the last. He was the Frenchman whose father, Mariano, had won the King of the Mountains crown at the Tour de France in 1978, and would become my nemesis but not my only one in the sport that I'm now practising, which is a complete contrast to the trials on the trails of Vail and beyond.

> *Through the forests of Durango, on my solitary voyage over dirt when education should have been on my mind but the pleasure of the perfect ride interrupted scholarly activity, I would ride like I was flying.*

2

2008: Pissing blood

Determination

There are but a handful of men who can honestly race the season with one primary aim: victory in the Tour de France. Everyone who races a road bike would at one stage entertain the thought; it's the ultimate prize, the yellow jersey – the *maillot jaune* – denoting the rider who wins. The fastest man. He who covers the entire route quicker than anyone else in an elite peloton. While the race is all about stages, you don't have to win one to become the champion. There's luck involved, but consistency is the key.

The order on the results sheets offers a report card and, if you graphed the three weeks of the 2008 Tour, Cadel's peaks – his best performances – would equate to the most important days of the race. It was only in the final stanza that it didn't quite go according to plan. In the final time trial, the one in which his body eventually told him 'enough', he came short. He was a rider ready to seize the moment that he had created for himself.

At the beginning all the circumstances were right. At the start in Brest it was a dream scenario. At the age of 31, Cadel had the best chance to be the best. In the absence of the defending champion, he would wear the number 1 for his fourth start in the race. This was appropriate for the reigning runner-up who was the favourite for the event.

It was the culmination of 15 years of hard work. It was no longer about what the Australian may one day do; now he was prepared to do what had to be done. Ahead lay a course suited to his skills. Behind him was the near miss against a rival who would not be part of the 95th Tour. It was a natural progression that grew from one simple fact: Cadel could ride a bike well.

Cadel got his first mountain bike in 1991 and started racing the next year. In Brest in early July 2008, he was at the centre of the cycling universe. He was content, fit and ready, and keen for the race to begin. Hypothesising on possible outcomes irritates him. There is only one way to know what will happen in a bike race: start it, experience it, watch what unfolds and then you have the answer. The end result tells the story. 'I don't have a crystal ball.' That was his favourite line during the lead-up.

After the race had begun, another one-liner emerged. It had to satisfy the sound-grab hunters: 'So far, so good.'

That was his chorus as the Tour raced east from France's extreme west. In cold, windy and sometimes wet conditions, the peloton aimed towards the Pyrenees. With the number 1 stuck on his back, there was pressure, expectation and attention. And a coil in the normally calm unit that was Cadel at the Grand Départ started to wind up. When pushed for commentary, he maintained his cool and said, 'So far, so good.'

Since Cadel Evans started enjoying success in races at a high level, people suggested he could be the rider – the first Australian rider – who could one day win the Tour de France. He has the ability. One day he might win. By the end of 2008 the question had become, 'Why didn't he win?!'

Going into the Tour I always try to be more prudent, especially when it's a race like that because everyone is watching and everyone has an opinion and everyone has questions. 'Are you going to win this year?' I don't know. I'm going to try, it's all I could say, for that was honestly all there was to tell. I can't make that admission any more simple. One of the things that is beautiful about cycling is the element of surprise. There are so many variables that it's impossible to predict the outcome.

In the lead-up he had excelled; he was the runner-up for a second year in succession in the *Critérium du Dauphiné Libéré* – a traditional test of the legs at the start of June, a one-week race that is centred in the Alps. Was it an omen? Could it be that this was a sign of where he stood in the peloton?

In 2008 I was the favourite because I was the highest ranked rider from the year before who was at the start. I understand that this brings with it added pressure but I was ready, I was fit, healthy, had good support. But nothing is sure in life. There were a lot of people around me – in the team and elsewhere – who were just so sure I was going to win it and I didn't like that at all. It made me uncomfortable. I was just doing my job and wanted as few distractions as possible. It's why they decided that I should have Serge Borlée [a bodyguard] along in 2008, to keep me protected not because of security issues but just because it's impossible to offer time to everyone who wants it during the Tour de France. I am grateful for what Serge did and we became friends during the race; thankfully we got along. It could have been uncomfortable otherwise; he was around all the time. But so was a crew for a documentary that had the working title of 'Yell For Cadel'.

It's a compliment about the faith the team had in me but as well as everything else, I had to agree to regular visits from a film crew making a film that I had no control over and no say in. I was the centrepiece.

Ideally placed to win the race, he would falter. The mantra repetition ended long before the showdown on the penultimate stage. Until the 110 kilometre mark of Stage 9 it had been 'so good'. After that it was just damn hard. He didn't stop pushing himself and after the final surge for the yellow jersey – the moment when his body did surrender – he would arrive so spent that he was pissing blood.

The reasons are varied. But his original diagnosis was correct. He had simply done too much with his body to be able to arrive in Paris completely healthy. The Tour can do that and when it's done honestly and with doses of misfortune – frequent instances that happen regularly in this arena – there are times when it's all just too much.

It began in Stage 9 near Pujos in the Pyrenees. Accidents happen and Cadel was part of one on the verge of a nondescript road on the approach to the Col de Peyresourde which preceded the Col d'Aspin – two components of Desgrange's original plan for the introduction of mountains to the Tour de France almost 100 years earlier.

A stupid incident was caused by an arbitrary character from the Euskaltel–Euskadi team: Gorka Verdugo; his Basque name can be literally and somewhat ominously translated as 'Gorka, the executioner'. It was in Pujos, after ploughing into the 'executioner' that Cadel sustained injuries that would limit his capacity for the remainder of the race.

He would fight for the title all the way; you can be good. But you can only push a body so far.

Chiara Passerini had a special interest in the proceedings of the 2008 Tour de France. An Australian cyclist had charmed her after an introduction from a mutual friend. After he placed eighth in the 2005 Tour de France he proposed. They married six weeks later in Italy. Their dog Molly was there for the ceremony.

Chiara sang in a choir. Cadel rode a bike. And they fell in love. They got to know each other and she got to know cycling. Until then she had only a passing interest. 'If the race came past our house, then I would watch. Maybe. Why not? It's there.'

Chiara, Molly and Manneke, ('Little Man' – Serge's nickname for Cadel) became the three musketeers; one of them might be a dog but they're all for one!

Serge inscribed these names in permanent marker on Cadel's new helmet the evening after the crash. His other helmet had been sacrificed. He arrived in Bagnères-de-Bigorre battered and bruised, his jersey smeared in blood. His only concern was a quick exit so that he could tend to his wounds. Inside the team bus he had refuge from the media but didn't know the full ramifications of the crash yet. He was waiting on a full diagnosis but right then, in the bus, surrounded by hungry journalists and slowed by hordes of spectators, he was obliged to offer something.

It was his shattered helmet he handed to the journalists through the bus window. There was a brief exchange; words were kept to a minimum. What was certain was that the rider's head had made impact with the road. Evans said later that his head was okay. But the consequence of what his mind was telling him turned him pale with fear. Yet to be revealed was the extent to which the road had ripped up other parts of his body. Plenty of skin was missing and deep beneath the obvious wounds were damaged ligaments and bruised muscles. Despite this setback his aim remained; not for a moment did he consider quitting.

Chiara Passerini wasn't watching the Tour on 13 July when it happened. When the executioner brought down her 'Little Man' there were no cameras around at the time of the impact and only a handful of spectators were on the scene.

He would later be quite coherent about the experience, but when it happened he was in a daze. And Chiara would find out.

Chiara Passerini takes up the story:

Everyone had so many expectations on Cadel. He left for France with the heavy weight of being the favourite. Conscious of having done everything naturally possible to be as ready as possible, he had the usual bit of nervousness always present before a Tour de France, but that would soon disappear once the ice was broken with the first stage.

In the meantime, the closer we got to the Tour, the more weight I lost. I'm a generally apprehensive person and this thing was starting to consume me. I wasn't on a diet, I didn't stop eating; nervousness was eating me.

I didn't want Cadel to see me worried; I tried with all of my strength to be like a rock, so I kept everything inside me and always tried to avoid showing him my real feelings. But I'm pretty sure he knew what was going on.

Shortly before Cadel left, I promised myself not to watch the race on television or to visit any stage; I would have risked exploding like a bomb. I could nearly hear the prelude to an explosion resounding in my head and I knew that, sooner or later, I would reach the limit.

My sister Ilaria called. She asked if I was able to go on holiday with her for a week; the idea was to go to Isola d'Elba, a beautiful island in Tuscany, to give my sister a bit of company while looking after her baby daughter Francesca. It was during the second week of the Tour de France – perfect timing.

While I was at Isola D'Elba, my only thought was, of course, Cadel and the race of his life. Cadel and the emotive pressure of his team. Cadel and the media attention. Cadel hating being the centre of attention. Cadel and his uncontrolled spontaneity.

Then there was the crash.

It was about two o'clock in the afternoon. Ilaria, Francesca and

I just got back from the beach in time for the baby's feed, then we planned to watch the finale of the stage. They would have started showing it live at 3.00 pm. The only channel we could watch was Rai Tre and I couldn't stand Auro Bulbarelli and Davide Cassani's live coverage, so we often turned the volume down. I love watching the Swiss Italian Television (RSI) and I like listening to their commentators; they're always well prepared and they talk about interesting subjects and don't enter into mere gossip. Switzerland was too far away, though, so we had to undergo a week of penitence.

At 2.45 pm the phone rings. 'He just crashed.'

Suddenly my blood ran cold. I think a few teardrops fell; I had a flash of what Cadel was going through. I felt a huge sadness for him. Immediately, I didn't think of a possible injury, of his fragile collarbone, of how it could happen. I felt my heart tighten in a grip of pain thinking of his broken dream.

I was reassured: 'Cadel restarted racing immediately, trying to get back to the peloton …' That made me feel better, but the strain I accumulated in the past weeks left me in a whirl for a few minutes.

The live coverage started and the first image they did show was of a bleeding, sore Cadel visiting the medical car. Not the best thing for a quite apprehensive wife.

At the end of that stage, probably only 10 minutes after he crossed the line, I got a call. Shaken and nervous, he only said 'Hello, I'm fine. All okay, I'm fine. I'll call my mum now. I'll call you later.' I didn't say anything, maybe a quick 'Thank you', but I don't remember.

In Stage 9 the mountains loomed – and worst of all, the Tourmalet. It was time for the most proficient climbers to come to the fore – those who chose to put their bodies through torment. The 2115-metre col came *after* the crash.

Chiara Passerini had rules in place that she would break because she could no longer stand by and resist the temptation to follow the exploits of her husband.

Cadel's mother, Helen Cocks, insisted she would remain in Australia. At the start of Stage 10 no one thought they would have reason to celebrate in Paris on the final Sunday.

'I think fear of failure is – whether athletes know it or not – one of the greatest motivators and just trying to get to the finish becomes the subconscious inspiration,' said Cadel, looking back on the race.

Was Stage 9 more important than Stage 10? The crash or the recovery? 'Important? What's important for me is the result at the end of the race. The first thing about doing a good Tour is not losing it by crashing somewhere. I was going well and I was sitting very comfortably playing it conservatively and not showing my cards. The Tour goes over three weeks; you can hold back a bit in the first week and let fly; you can always get an opportunity for that.'

Many conclusions have been drawn about when Cadel lost the 2008 Tour. The majority favour the time trial of the penultimate stage; others suggest the epic day to L'Alpe d'Huez when he was caught off-guard and heavily outnumbered in a classic tactical game between teams. The winner of that stage – the 17th stage of

21 from the 2008 Tour – was the champion of the Tour. Carlos Sastre did exactly what was required of him to achieve the status all riders dream of. He bided his time, remained calm, kept focused on being safe and conserving energy at all but the vital moments of the race, and struck with venom to ensure his victory. Sastre took hold of the yellow jersey and his gains were sufficient for him to retain it all the way to Paris.

Only 53 seconds separated Sastre and Evans in Paris. There are numerous places that contributed to Evans' lost chance to become Australia's first Tour de France champion. They are scattered around the hexagon of France, and are measured in lost seconds here and there – close calls. But in 2008, it was neither the climb to L'Alpe d'Huez or the time trial to Saint-Amand-Montrond; his actual defeat came elsewhere. It happened in Pujos. Stage 9. *Putain!*

Enough had happened leading to that moment when the main rivals of the day were the unseen forces: the wind and demons of the mind that can play havoc. Then there's the body to deal with. The bike is merely a tool but the legs propel it.

The journey somehow conjured a little rhyme:

'Wind, rain, pain and terrain.'

3
Time after time (trial)

Consequences

Each stage of the Tour de France is a crucial one. As Stage 9 – Toulouse to Bagnères-de-Bigorre – illustrated, ambitions can be thwarted with a touch of wheels and a crash. There are so many possibilities during the three weeks when losses can be accrued. Even the strongest riders in the race don't have the luxury of knowing they will survive the distance. Favourites fall and accidents have cost riders the title on numerous occasions in cycling.

In professional cycling ranks, finding the right insurance policy is a costly exercise. 'I pay more now for a year of health cover than what I earned in my first year as a pro,' said Cadel while on his way to a clinic to treat ligament damage at the end of the 2008 season. You repair the damage and get on with the job.

He has broken bones before and spoiled at least one season if not two because of crashes and fractures. His collarbone was particularly susceptible: he broke the same one twice in 2000 and three times between January and September in 2003. But five years later he did have a little luck on his side. Yes, he fell. No, he couldn't have avoided it. But at least he was able to get back on the bike quickly and, with the help of his team-mates, rejoin the peloton.

'I hoped he hadn't broken anything,' said Hendrik Redant, one of Silence–Lotto's *directeurs sportifs*. The Belgian has been in the team car each time Cadel has started the Tour. He has become a friend and confidante – one of the true believers. 'My first concern was his collarbone, and that's what he was thinking as well.' Redant describes what faced them:

> *By the time we arrived at the scene of the accident, Cadel was trying to stay calm but he was becoming overwhelmed; every possible scenario was running through his mind and, in times like that, it's natural to think the worst. There was plenty of blood. His clothes were torn and his helmet had cracked. There was enough evidence to suggest that his Tour was over. But when I saw him on his bike, he was sitting straight and that was the first positive sign that everything could be okay.*

It took five kilometres of chasing before his Silence–Lotto colleagues delivered him back into the bunch. Before catching up with the other riders, he had to weave through the convoy of team cars that follow the race. Hendrik Redant was in the front passenger seat of the tour car, the other directeur sportif, Roberto Damiani, was driving, and the team mechanic Bart Leysen was on the back seat with the window down ready to reach out and attend to any running repairs on the bike. When Cadel came past he barely turned his head to acknowledge his colleagues in the car.

Television cameras were focussed on him during his pursuit of the peloton and live coverage was on. In the Tour, this means that all the images are received in *all* the team cars, which adds a new dimension to tactics. If a rival *directeur sportif* sees that an adversary is suffering it can prompt them to accelerate their teams and cause extra pain. But Cadel had his poker face on. 'It's not Hollywood,' Cadel insists about the drama. 'There's no need to act in the Tour de France. The race creates the story.'

But he was aware of the attention on him and it was beneficial to keep the other teams guessing about his condition. He rode alongside the Silence–Lotto car for a few seconds, barely acknowledging Redant, who also had his window wound down. 'He turned and faced me. There was no smile, no grimace. He nodded his head gently and slowly. "I'll be okay," was all he said.'

Bart had shifted his body so he could reach out of the car and check over the spare bike. Very quietly Cadel uttered a few words while trying to maintain the facial expression of a ventriloquist: 'My collarbone ... it's sore, but don't tell anybody.' He didn't want anyone to know – not even his team mates. He was afraid they would be upset with him.

Nothing was broken. He would survive the three weeks. And all along his team believed in him. They had to: that was what they were there for, and there was every reason for them to maintain their faith. Eleven stages of racing over a span of 13 days led him from Bagnères-de-Bigorre to Saint-Amand-Montrond. And only after his last true bid for the victory in 2008 did he piss into the beaker and collect urine laced with blood. His body was responding to the weeks of torture while the mind played games to combat fatigue and injury to enable his legs to keep turning the pedals. He had been attacked on all fronts; cheats and honest riders got the better of him during the course of the final fortnight. Some of the media needed a story and they created incidents – at some of his weakest and most stressful moments on Tour.

There would be incidents that he would regret, on and off the bike. And for many followers, these transgressions from a rider with an otherwise collected and cool demeanour have coloured what they believe the real Cadel to be. At times he lashed out. The outbursts were caught on cameras, uploaded and replayed hundreds of thousands of times by people who used these snippets to form their opinion of his character. For over half his life he has been, to some degree at least, in public view. Rarely is he anything but diplomatic, conducting himself in an exemplary manner. He enjoys the attention, but only in small doses. But this time it was suffocating.

'The combined time of all the YouTube moments adds up to less than five minutes of my life,' he said, months after the Tour. There's nothing I can do about it. But even when I replay in my mind the moment that's become known as "The Headbutt", I see the things that happened before and after what everyone else has seen.

'I'd just raced over the Lombarde and Bonette-Restefond Passes and been beaten by over two minutes. I was exhausted, crowded and just wanted to get to my team car to escape, to catch my breath, to see the results and figure out what had just happened; if I had in fact lost any hope of winning the Tour, or if Sastre's gains were surmountable. There was a camera crew from Belgium in front of me. If they had stood to one side and asked a question, I could have answered it, but that's not what they did. They walked in front of me and blocked my path. I couldn't move and they didn't even give me the respect that people give to each other when they're just walking down the street. When they stopped to get a better shot, and I wanted to keep riding forward, I used the only available part of me to shoo them away. My hands were on the bars and Serge was by my side and the cameraman didn't move ...' With a shunt of his helmet they were gone. But this is not the real Cadel. It was an instance when the rider trying to win the Tour was under pressure.

There were other incidents he would regret, but Cadel doesn't enjoy looking back. For all his success as a cyclist, he remains unfulfilled. The Big One still eludes him. Of course he's content with his numerous significant victories, and he recognises his prizes – a white jersey as the winner of the ProTour, five yellow jerseys as leader of a Tour de France, boxes full of medals and trophies – these have been accumulated over the years, but there are two that hold pride of place on the mantelpiece in his European home in Stabio, Switzerland, just north of the border with the Lombardia region of Italy. On the shelf above a fireplace in a two-bedroom apartment are two glass items presented to the runner-up in the Tour. They are reminders of how close he came in 2007 and 2008, but they also serve to inspire him in a quest that hasn't yet finished. Cadel explains:

I love riding my bike. I enjoy racing. But television generally bores me. The only time I watch cycling is if I've just finished a big training ride and there's a race being shown and I can't be bothered doing anything else. Even then I don't pay a lot of attention. During the Tour I see some footage but most of the time, if it's a race I've done, I'm only interested in seeing the time trials, then I can look at the positions and techniques of others, and my own, and see how it is, where I might have gained some time by choosing a better line through a turn or by selecting a different gear.

It's interesting to see the form of others, but general classification (GC) riders follow a similar schedule. And it's not ever going to be possible to get a better understanding of rivals by watching footage of them; I prefer to see it from the bike, when I can hear their breathing, see them shifting in the saddle, watch them reaching for a change of gear. Are they standing to dance on the pedals or to just keep them turning over? Are they suffering? Are they better or worse than me? It's easier to get these answers when you're next to them.

It can take only a glimpse of footage for someone who knows cycling to understand if a rider has what it takes to win, especially when it's a time trial. A slight shift in the saddle to get on top of a gear, or a gentle rocking of the hips can illustrate that not all is as good as it could be. Racing the clock requires stability and strength. There's nowhere to hide and observers can ascertain information from clues that don't lie. This can be seen on the bike up against rivals during a road race, but in the solitary discipline of the time trial in which Cadel has won his stage of the Tour de France it's apparent even when you're not right on top of him.

Racing the clock requires stability and strength. There's nowhere to hide and the pictures don't lie.

In Cérilly, when Cadel left the start house, it was obvious to those who knew him what was about to happen. He's too stubborn to concede, too focussed to provide a hint that his body has had enough. But it was obvious to some that this would not be the day in which Cadel would excel. Until he rolled down the ramp and faced that 53-kilometre journey to Saint-Amand-Montrond, Cadel had the ultimate reward in cycling still within reach.

He had built the promise and they had all come to witness what might have been possible. And as his moment of truth arrived, those he cared most about were assembled near the finish for what could have been the crowning moment. From far away they arrived just in time to be there; just in case it happened this time. And with bated breath, they waited to see if he still had it in him.

Helen Cocks arrived in France that morning with two of her son's close friends. As her son prepared for an early-morning reconnaissance of the time trial course, her plane touched down at Charles de Gaulle airport in Paris. While Cadel was familiarising himself with the route, repeating corners to fully comprehend the best possible ways to pinch time back, and taking notes for Redant to use to remind him of the intricate details during competition, his mother and his friends were hiring a car and preparing for the journey south. By the time he was pulling on his skinsuit and sticking the number 1 to his back, after an hour on the stationary trainer to warm the muscles and get his heart rate high, they had arrived at the finish site, received their accreditation from the team and had scouted for a site to watch Cadel race. When he rolled down the ramp, Helen's hands covered her mouth while her daughter-in-law hugged her around the shoulders in silence.

'Cinq. Quatre. Trois. Deux. Un ...'

'Allez!'

'Go Cadel.' Helen let slip. A whisper when others were yelling; his mother and wife had never been so wide-eyed, at once both oblivious to the world around them and entirely aware of all that was going on.

Beside the two was his Silence–Lotto team manager Marc Sergeant. They were huddled inside a broadcast truck fitted out with the equipment that relayed the event to the world via the internet. Typed on the Tour's official site were the words: 'Cadel Starts His Race!' So read the intro to the live coverage.

A sequence of images showed Cadel: in focus, in preparation, in concentration, in contemplation – the same pictures that bounced off satellites and into the rooms of millions of viewers.

Chiara Passerini and Helen Cocks were key players in the evolution of Cadel Evans and have seen enough to know a good time trial from a bad one. But Marc Sergeant, a former cycling professional, saw more in the images than they could. It took just

300 metres for him to know. The Belgian manager of the Silence–Lotto team had no words.

Sergeant is a key man in the team that recruited Cadel in 2005 with hopes of one day 'having a good *classement* rider for the Tour de France'. They got a lot more than good; they got a great rider and adjusted their scope to take aim at more than just a top-10 finish – he had done that every time he started. Now they wanted the yellow jersey. After three years of trying, this was the stage which was to be the most crucial in the fourth attempt.

Sergeant didn't even shake his head. Too intent on the images, and knowing nothing now could be done, he merely widened his eyes and allowed the anxious line of his lips to form the wrong arc. What might have been a smile was sent upside down. He saw enough to know it wasn't to be.

He realised that another year had passed, Cadel had come close, but victory was not going to happen. His hips had a slight tilt.

Cadel is always solid on his time trial bike. When he's on the saddle it's like he's locked into position, legs like pistons but the rest of his body barely moving … but on this day perfect stability was gone. If he was going to win, that was mandatory.

It could be seen as the motorcycle-mounted cameraman revved up to speed in pursuit of Cadel. Within 300 metres of the start there was enough to suggest he wasn't floating on his pedals. There would be pain; that was expected. Everyone remaining in the Tour was coping only because they knew the finish was just over the horizon. They were all hurting, but few knew how much Cadel ached.

The wind is the enemy in the time trial. The demons in the mind can go to hell. The body knows what it must do; it's been done before: let's go to work!

Without compromise Cadel set off in pursuit of the yellow jersey. He slipped into the tuck – falling forward so far that his torso is tilted to a degree that defies ergonomics but he insists that's how it must be.

'Riding slowly on that time trial bike is not an option; it's too painful.'

The only remedy was power. 'If you pedal perfectly, your body is essentially buoyant. You hold yourself away from any pressure points; you are always putting force down and it has the effect of lifting you from the saddle.'

The upper torso is steady. Elbows are locked into position 18 centimetres below his hips. His is an extreme stance, one that can only be achieved with years of Pilates, stretching and exercises 'that are simply too weird to describe' devised by him and his strength and conditioning consultants. Legs hold the bike steady with perfect rhythm. So the theory goes. Aerodynamics push Evans into this but he has adapted and he admits that he relishes that perfect ride. He has had many in his time as a professional cyclist – when it was like he was flying. But the journey from Cérilly to Saint-Amand-Montrond would not be one of them.

Marc Sergeant tried to appear as though he still believed that the gains could be made. In the small room, the only man present who had ridden the Tour tried to put the pieces in the puzzle together to make this quest a reality. Could it still be possible?

Veteran sprinter Robbie McEwen was an early starter in the time trial. 'Just having ridden the course,' he said after he arrived in Saint-Amand-Montrond, 'I think it's great for Cadel.'

The lower-ranked riders in the general classification departed at two-minute intervals early in the day. In the late afternoon when the GC Guys got their turn, three minutes would separate them.

McEwen is a winner, a rider who has amassed 12 stage victories since his Tour debut in 1997, but he's finished in the top 100 of general classification only once. His focus is another prize, the green jersey, for the leading sprint points, which he's won three times – in 2002, 2004 and 2006, as part of the Davitamon/Predictor/Silence–Lotto teams – but he had forsaken personal ambition in 2008 in favour of assisting a compatriot who Robbie knew was capable of winning the *maillot jaune*. And after finishing the time trial course, he gave his appraisal.

'It gives him enough opportunity to take back the time gained by Carlos Sastre,' said McEwen. 'It's 1.7 seconds per kilometre and I think there are sections on the course – long drags – where he'll be able to take chunks of time back. It's a course really suited to a more powerful type of GC rider like Cadel much more than a pure climber like Carlos. If it goes at all like you would normally expect, I think he can take plenty of time.'

The hips told the story early but the times confirmed the facts. At the finish, Evans was seventh. Sastre was twelfth. Position in the stage standings on the day mattered little; position on the bike accounted for a lot more. Carlos lost that round but the title was his. He rocked a lot more than Cadel but he finished only 29 seconds slower and that spelled out an advantage of one minute and five seconds before the parade to Paris.

Cadel had come to win the Tour de France. He was part of the drama and he made the spectacle more exciting by crashing but he didn't want to be the author of thrillers. On the eve of the final time trial of 2007 he had been even closer to the title than in 2008.

He was taking the fight to the others, taking on the best in the world and introducing the sport to people who had never had the experience of watching someone from Australia vying for the title. It was the little warrior from an antipodean cycling nation that attracted the viewers; there are a lot of people who care about the Tour de France because of Cadel Evans.

4

Little things

Distance and difference

Cadel's name means 'battle'; it was chosen, in part, for his father's Welsh heritage. From the moment he first emerged – with a broken nose, three weeks overcooked but still tiny – until he took on rivals in one of sport's biggest stages, he has pushed himself to his limit. But he has always done so with a wealth of support from a host of people who share his passion and appreciate his ability. And he's always had his mother, Helen Cocks, as his number-one fan.

He was due on 26 January 1977 but he wasn't in a hurry to see the world and was born three weeks late. When he did finally emerge, it was not on Australia Day but on 14 February 1977 – Valentine's Day. From the moment he took his first breath he needed to learn how to overcome injuries.

The circumstances of the birth – the surrounds where Helen Cocks and Paul Evans conceived their first and only son – proved that he's a resilient character.

'He was only little when he was born,' Helen remembers of the early hours of that Monday morning. 'He weighed just six pounds but he got to be quite a bruiser as an infant.

'He was not upside down.' No breech presentation. Not Cadel. But he was looking the wrong way; he was a posterior birth.

'When he was induced, in the end – because he was so slow and lazy about coming out – he had cuts on the top of his head where they snipped the amniotic sack. His nose was broken after birth because he was looking up and his face got dragged over all my bony bits.'

According to his mother, the nose was of little concern. It was quickly remedied. 'The doctors just pushed it straight.' Simple solution.

In the town of Katherine in the Northern Territory, he greeted the world. For the next four years, Cadel spent most of the time in the nude; it was hot in Bamyili.

When Helen Cocks reflects on the time she spent there she conjures up a utopia in some descriptions but the harsh reality of what she laments were third-world conditions for some of the community. When Cadel was born, Helen was 19. Two weeks later she turned 20. 'I was young and healthy. It's a good age to have a baby I've decided after all these years. I think I was lucky.

It's really nice to have a relatively small age gap between you and your child. Cadel and I played together. We played like kids and I loved everything about how he was raised. Perhaps that's because I'm not particularly mature.

But she is. Helen had experienced a lot at an early age. Although she describes herself as 'remote', she has a lively presence, and a sweet-toned voice, high in pitch and full of animation, that makes talking with her seem more like song. She drifts in and out of thoughts, savouring moments in her mind – taking the discussion on tangents prompted by delving into the depths of memory or a glimpse of a sun-blemished Polaroid from a time long ago. Some recollections are vague, not so much because she doesn't enjoy reliving them but almost as though she's surprised by considering them in the context of her life these days. It was in the Territory that she grew up. Helen arrived in Bamyili as a wild-child teenager and she left as a mother with real world experiences, some of which invigorated her life; others made her question the basic premise of human nature.

In her community there was kindness and beauty, violence and drudgery, spirited souls surviving extremes, illness and injuries which you could never imagine occurring in a so-called 'developed' nation. It was a lot of things but it wasn't ordinary.

Extremes can make a life exceptional. Even before you consider Cadel as a cyclist, his tale of survival and resilience is significant.

He was raised in Bamyili, a small community in the Northern Territory, Australia. The name has since been changed to Barunga. The birth certificate states 'Katherine' and this is what's listed on his racing licence and where it's often reported that he's from. But Cadel Evans was raised in a remote community 80 kilometres east of Katherine where his father worked for the town council.

The couple met at Eltham High School – they were high school sweethearts. Paul had returned to finish his education after working as an apprentice mechanic for a few years.

I was being a teenager. I was very wicked. I left home when I was

*16 to live with Paul. I was a very bad girl … of course I didn't
think I was, but I must have been. I was rebellious because I really
didn't like the dullness.*

Helen and Paul lived on the outskirts of Melbourne but even
the semi-rural suburban setting didn't appeal to a girl who, as a
woman, admits to having a 'remote' nature. That's also where she
has often found solace – away from it all.

She doesn't classify herself as a hippie but admits it was 'the
1970s' and her aesthetic was typical of the time. Long hair pulled
back in ponytail, a slender body, and a Cheshire grin and a cheeky
glint in her eye. 'I don't know if I'd classify myself like that but I
suppose we were all a bit like hippies then.'

The chance for escape just knocked on the door one day in the
form of a $500 loan from Lee Hunt, Paul's closest friend.

*Lee was living in Katherine. He had been driving the mobile dental
van to the remote communities. He had said, 'Come up from
Melbourne.' So we did.*

*We went up to the Territory. Lee said, 'You'll get a job. Easy!'
But when we got there it was November 1975 and the Whitlam
Government had just been brought down. The senate had blocked
supply, but all of Katherine ran on government money. They weren't
cashing government cheques, and the job that Paul was expecting
to get was as the mechanic working for the works department – a
government job – but they weren't taking on anybody because there
was no money.*

Nobody really knew what was going on. All the government

jobs just dried up.

We were staying at the hostel in Katherine and Paul eventually got a job as a mechanic at a service station. And I cooked part-time at the hostel where we were staying, which was quite odd – I'd never really cooked before.

We were there for two months before Paul got the job as a work supervisor for the new Bamyili town council.

Money had begun to flow again. It was very easy to get work in the Territory. You just had to turn up. And, in those days, it was a very small population and if people were willing to work in re-mote places, then that was great. Not that Bamyili was that remote by Territory standards. Still, it wasn't Eltham. That move was all about getting away from a suburban life and the overhang of con-servative Australia , which I just didn't like.

We moved to Bamyili and made it our home when I was 18, turn-ing 19. We were there for a bit over a year before I got pregnant.

In Bamyili there were three tribal groups: Jawyon, Nkubulon and what Helen knew only as the 'Eva Valley Mob'. Helen explained that around the time Cadel was born there were groups of an-thropologists working on ways to interpret the spoken language and put it into words that could be spelled. So there wasn't a for-mal spelling of the names of any of the tribes. 'Now I think they spell them "Jawoyn",' said Helen, trying to explain the difficulty of interpreting Language, 'but back then I think they spelled it "Djauan".' Helen continues:

Language is really hard to get right because it's phonetic and you just can't get your tongue around the sounds. I couldn't. My best friend, an Aboriginal woman, tried to teach me Language but she spent most of the time just laughing at me. She'd be in hysterics because I said things so wrongly.

It was a very different place to 'down south' with dramatic seasonal shifts that have a powerful influence on the people and their lives. Generally people think of the tropics as having just two seasons: wet and dry. Helen has her own versions of the various phases and hers are based very much on the physical influence of the weather. Her take on Walparr was quite simple – it is 'the Build-up'.

That's the silly season, September–October; people go troppo then. There wouldn't have been a cloud in the sky for months and then gradually, little bits of clouds become these huge masses of white tinged with grey heaped up in the sky. And there are fabulous electrical storms. But the humidity is just awful! It's stifling.

'The Wet', or Wakuringding, begins in November, maybe, and lasts a couple of months, then it gets really wet. Cadel was born in that really wet time, Jiorrk.

Bamyili was extreme in many ways, but it suited Paul. He could do his work, collect his pay, and join friends at the bar to quench one of his many desires, but the taste for beer would eventually send Cadel's mother and father off in another direction. Drinking was part of life in Bamyili. But it would drown more than just the sorrows of men staving off the threat of going troppo.

Alcohol was a problem in Bamyili. Cadel confessed to a disdain for the stuff, especially in his teens when it was – as it is for most generations – an elixir used by his peers for the purpose of inebriation. It can be a nice thing to do but even at a young age he witnessed the effects of the evils of booze and what could happen when it was all about more than quenching a thirst or having a sip for the taste. Paul, too, would ease off the stuff. He admits he still drinks but it's far from what he once did in the tropics.

There is a lot of escape happening in the Territory: 'It is a fabulous place. It's a great joy to have been there. It is so beautiful in the strangest way. It is so unique. And the distance adds to it.' Helen says.

Bamyili is only 80 kilometres from Katherine, but back when Helen and Paul lived there, only 50 kilometres of that journey was done on bitumen – down the Stuart Highway – and then it turned to dirt roads for the final 30 kilometres. The road used to get cut during the wet season and it was impassable a lot of the time for anything but a four-wheel drive; even for them it was tough at times.

When you come in to the township from the highway, you pass over an escarpment or 'jump up'. You can look out on the vast expanse that in the Dry is red-dirt nothingness that goes all the way to the horizon. 'We'd go up there and look down and it was a beautiful sight.'

She can reel you in. Helen explains a place that seems so compelling for its unique beauty and captivating for the freedom that's on offer. But the seasons, the drinking, and the sadness of witnessing the demise of a unique culture while years of failed policy made ruins of people's lives made it a hard place to stay.

Paul's Welsh heritage provided one reason for the name of their son. But it also came from the surname of a Scottish explorer Francis Cadell who, in 1853, first successfully navigated the previously uncharted waters of the Murray River from Goolwa in South Australia all the way to Albury in New South Wales. It was he who was credited with having 'opened the steam navigation and commerce of the River Murray'. He seemed a suitable namesake, but Paul and Helen culled an 'l' and added the name of their mate.

Cadel Lee Evans would become an adventurer, a bike rider and ultimately the personification of the great Aussie battler. He was a blond kid and stood out from the crowd in the Territory.

Paul had a spark of red hair and he wore a long ginger beard during his days in the Territory. He was responsible for introducing Cadel to cycling. 'Cadel's first bike had 16-inch wheels and the handlebars were only about a foot and a half high. He was not game to get on it in the shop or even ride it around in the streets of Katherine where I bought it.'

I had a truck and I used to do a run in and out of town every so often carting freight. I don't know what we were carrying that day but the little bike was chucked up on top of the load and strapped on. Cadel came back in the cab with me and I bought some training wheels the same day and it was only after I put them on that he started to ride it.

At first I set the training wheels so they were level, but it was useless because, as often happens on a dirt road, the two support wheels would get caught on the track and the rear wheel of the bike would just spin.

He soon learned that if he leant one way or the other he'd have the support of at least two wheels at the back, but not all three.

Our garage in Bamyili was not much of a structure; a few timber poles supported an iron roof and my tools lay around the place without a great deal of organisation. On one day when Cadel was almost four, I was in the house and I heard something stirring outside but wasn't sure what it was; I went out and there was Cadel with his little bike with training wheels.

He had been riding it for quite some time and the little arms which fastened the support wheels to the frame had seen plenty of action. They were out of shape and, after so much riding, had bent upwards.

He learnt to ride on all three wheels, but after leaning into corners for a few months the braces had to give way a little. Before long, he found a mid-way position when he was actually balancing on the front and rear wheel alone – the support wheels were superfluous – he didn't really need them. They were actually just a hassle because the terrain out there was different to growing up in the city. There were only dirt roads and the uneven surfaces could play havoc on his rides. The two extra wheels at the back were constantly bending up and although I'd fix them every once in a while, they'd inevitably end up in the same position.

He usually rode with one of the only other children even close to his age, but there was still quite a difference; he was almost four and

Emma Boutell was closer to eight. She had a bigger bike and didn't have training wheels!

Perhaps it was just him thinking, 'I want to be like her – she doesn't need training wheels; why should I?' But something prompted him to take action.

The training wheels were held on with a central axle nut and when I went out to the shed to find out what all the noise was, there he was – working on the bike. He had my biggest shifter spanner which was way too big for the job; you really needed a ring spanner to move the nut at all. But he had the shifter and was trying to adjust it so that he could get a grip of the bolts holding the training wheel arms to the frame. I heard the clunking of the tools and when I got outside I asked what he was up to. He said, 'I want to take these off.'

I told him I'd do it and that the shifter was too big; if he was to do a job, he should use the right tools.

I reached for a 14-mm ring spanner and he stood beside me as I removed the bolts, took the training wheels off and retightened the rear axle. I gave him back the bike. He looked up, got on, put the pedals in the 'go' position, stepped on and took off. He was gone. I wouldn't see him again for hours.

He was never actually taught like most kids were, with hour after hour of an anxious parent holding onto the rear of the saddle and running beside yelling out encouragement. He just rode away.

There'd be times when he'd be gone so long it was dark and we had to go out and look for him. He might not have been riding the whole time. Often he was just exploring the area, looking around for stones in the dirt or whatever it is that entertains the mind of a young boy, but the bike was never far away.

He had the training wheels on for a month or two until that day I found him with a shifter spanner. It only had a back-pedal brake and there was some foam under a wrap on the bars and another on the top tube to save him from breaking his teeth. But that's what started it all. He's still got all his teeth, but I still get anxious when I'm sitting in front of the television now watching what he does. It's not like that first time; he had it all ahead of him and all he could see were the possibilities presented by these two wheels of freedom.

There was great scope for freedom in Bamyili where he discovered many of life's joys. But there was also a lot of misery and suffering. Alcohol was the main culprit for the violence but the attitudes of people outside were a big part of the ugliness. Helen explains:

In the Territory it was extreme. The attitude of the town people to the Aboriginal people from the community was just awful. And Paul and I were part of the community so it was exaggerated for us. My best friend's son died in Katherine hospital; he choked on his vomit. I can't remember why he was there but it wasn't a life-threatening matter. I can't explain how that happened. Who can?

He was just two years old. We went into town to buy him a wreath – his mother and I. The shop people refused to serve us because she was Aboriginal. And they didn't want to have anything to do with me because we were together. It was cruel and horrible.

I was angry, so angry that they finally sold us what we'd come to buy.

Violence was a part of life in Bamyili and the catalyst was usually the daily drinking sessions.

In the hospital waiting for Cadel to come into the world, she witnessed something that has remained with her ever since.

I was walking down the ward to go to the toilet which was at the end of a hall. And I looked at a name that was on the bed in one of the rooms I passed. It was that of a young woman I knew from Bamyili. I recognised the name but couldn't understand why the tag had her name on it. An old woman lay on the bed and I thought, 'Oh, it's just someone else with the same name ...'

And then, walking back to my room I realised: no – it was this young woman. She was maybe 18 – if that old – and her husband, who was really not a nice man, had beaten her up. And she had hidden from him since the attack.

During a scuffle when he was drunk he had broken the butt of a rifle over her head and, because she went bush to get away from him, the wound had filled with maggots. Her arm was broken, her face was pulverised, and she was a shadow of the girl I knew. This 18-year-old girl looked like someone of about 100. She was so brutally beaten.

It's unfair to say that everybody did it, but alcohol was a huge part of the way of life there. It was not only Aboriginal people. Many people drank, and they drank to get drunk – whitefellas and blackfellas.

The supply of alcohol was such a desperate thing. A hotel in Kath-erine used to park a truck filled with beer near the turn-off on the highway, and sell it at hugely inflated prices.

Bamyili had a bar – a shop that opened up with a service area that was once a kitchen. After Paul and I had been up there for about two years, they introduced a can limit. I forget what it was but it meant that people could no longer just drink, drink, drink until they simply fell over. That was good; it made a difference. It eased some of the horrible violence.

And then there were the health and living conditions:

It's hard to explain some of the conditions. It was much closer to third-world than what most Australians would be able to under-stand. There were people with leprosy, with tuberculosis ... there were diseases that you couldn't have imagined were in Australia, but they were. There were living conditions that you would never have believed were possible in an otherwise relatively afflu-ent society.

There were a few houses that Aboriginal people lived in that were connected up to the power grid, but it wasn't many. Most people lived in tin sheds. They were called 'Kingstrands' – and I've never been sure why. It was as basic a dwelling as you could imagine.

They were about five metres by five metres. A square with a veranda all the way around. There were four streets of these and about 10 of these shacks along each side of each street that were little more than lanes of dirt. There was a shared ablutions block for each street – a basic toilet and showers with water pumped up from a spring – but there was no electricity. No hot water. The majority of the population lived there.

All the beds would be outside on the veranda. People would just sleep on these basic excuses for a rudimentary bunk. It wasn't like they had real houses. They definitely had no fridges, because there was no way of powering them. There weren't tables and chairs. Dinner was always eaten as they sat on the ground, generally around a camp fire.

You just have to look at the health statistics. The difference between being born white and being born black is extreme. In health terms it was not a good thing to be black. It was not always a healthy place to live.

As I always swam – no matter what the season – I seemed to have perpetual ear problems. I didn't get tropical ulcers but Paul did, when little cuts would get infected and turn into horrible, great, ugly, festering sores.

But exposure to the Aboriginal culture and the strange beauty and rhythms of the seasons of the remote Top End was a wonderful way to begin a life. Cadel was born towards the end of the Wet – or in the Jawoyn language, Jiorrk – when it is really, really wet. He got to know the four cycles of the dramatic tropical seasons: Bungarung – the windy time or 'Knock Em Downs', then Jungalk – the start of the Dry, Walparr – dry and dusty, Worropini – the build-up and finally Wakuringding and the relief of rain. 'And,' says Helen, 'it just rains and rains and rains.'

Lee Hunt still lives up near Katherine. He has been south to visit. 'I can't comment on how it is there these days,' says Helen. 'I'd love to go back but at the same time I'm happy to have the memories. That was something I did then. It was a life-changing experience and I came away from it with a wonderful son who I know is proud to have been born in that part of Australia.' It was far from ordinary in so many ways, but so too is almost all of the story about Cadel Evans.

Helen now lives in Arthurs Creek, in the rolling foothills to the north-east of Melbourne. She shares a house on 20 acres with Geoff, Wilkie the dog, five horses and a wealth of visiting kangaroos. She rides as often as she can – both the horses and on bikes which have been handed down over the years – and has a love/hate relationship with the Tour de France.

In some parts of the house, you can see trophies with varying amounts of dust gathering. It's not a huge collection – a couple from her son's early years in cycling and a few from her equestrian pursuits – but it says a lot about the two of them. He rides. She rides. He loves it and so does she.

5
Flight response

Survival

There was violence and beauty in the Territory. It was a place of extremes. From the remote location, the lack of infrastructure, the abuse of alcohol, the weather patterns and the combined effects of all these elements, it was an interesting place to grow up.

He was only young when he was there and Cadel's memory of Bamyili is vague. Still, it had an effect on him and what he would become. Like his mother, he is a remote person. He enjoys the company of others but if he had to decide between being amongst a crowd or the option of solitude the latter would always be his preference.

Amidst the drunks and extremes of life in the tropics Helen and Paul established a home and adapted to the surrounds. They were young and adventurous. The move from Victoria liberated Cadel's mother. His father also enjoyed the freedom it offered.

They were lured their by a friend who they had gone to school with. Lee Hunt had played a pivotal role in helping the young couple find a place that, for all its faults, they were happy to live in.

Their wedding was an incidental affair during the time up in the tropics. Pregnant and wanting to reassure Helen's mother who wanted them to formalise their relationship, Paul and Helen drove to Darwin to exchange some vows.

Helen wasn't too keen to expand on the ceremony. It was quaint, without any of the common themes associated with the ritual.

It was in a park. It was just me and Paul, and Lee and Gail Forbutt [one of Cadel's 'Aunties']. Gail gave me my horse Sunshine for my 19th birthday. The fifth person present was the celebrant.

We gave him a slab of beer and said, 'Thanks a lot.' Then we went out for dinner at the flashest restaurant in Darwin at the time. It was called Peppy's, and we had an unbelievable meal. We got married on 30 October, I was almost six months pregnant and the main memory of the day was of the strawberries we had for dessert.

They presented the dessert menu: bombe alaska, chocolate mousse … and I looked at it sadly. One of the big things about living in the Territory then was the desperate longing for fresh fruit. Everything was trained then trucked to the Top End. We used to sit around in circles and fantasise about eating apples.

It has taken me years to be able to walk into a greengrocer and not get openly excited about fresh fruit and vegetables being there.

We were talking about how nice it would be if there were fresh strawberries – the perfect end to a beautiful meal. When the waiter came to take our orders Gail said what we really wanted was strawberries, but what a 'silly notion' that was. The waiter was very pleased for us. We were lucky, he said. They had just taken in an order of strawberries flown in from down south. They were the best strawberries ever. I hate to think how much they would have cost.

Money wasn't flowing in but it didn't have to. Paul still cites one of the reasons for moving to the Territory being because there was work, and plenty of it. But it wasn't as though they were escaping the rat-race to collect fat cheques from the mining boom. They worked an honest day for an honest wage but were clever with their savings.

By the time Cadel was born they were comfortable, but it was a basic upbringing with few luxuries. Remote locations mean you do without a lot of things.

A thin man at that time, Paul Evans would later become a little more rotund – something he blames on a back injury more than anything else. But it's no junk food diet for him in Upper Corindi where he settled after the stint up north. These days he owns a market garden and harvest time comes at various seasons in the year. He married Orada who he met in Thailand in 2003 and established a life that suits his style. 'We hate competition,' he says about his produce. 'If anyone else grows it, we don't bother. We like the rare Asian vegetables that the restaurants can't readily source.'

Cadel makes a point of visiting his father at least once a year. After the 2006 season he returned to Australia with Chiara and her father Aldo and mother Luisa. They hired a campervan and took a journey from Sydney, up the coast to close to the Queensland border and dropped in at Upper Corindi just north of Coffs

Harbour for a few days. A year earlier, at the end of the racing season, Cadel and Chiara caught a train north from Adelaide to Katherine as part of their honeymoon. His Italian wife would get to see the part of the world where he grew up and it would leave a strong impression on the classically trained pianist who, until she met her future husband, had never ventured outside Europe.

As a professional cyclist who is one of the few who can apply himself to the role of GC (general classification) rider, he has little time for distractions. When he does laugh, his dry sense of humour is what prompts the reaction. This is a trait he shares with both his parents but it is Paul who doesn't dance around what he's thinking. While Helen is more diplomatic, Cadel's father jumps straight in and tells it like it is. 'Dad is pretty unique. He has a special personality.' There is a mix of equal parts admiration and frustration for the stubbornness of his father.

We speak relatively often but I suppose it's a bit different now. My life has changed so much now and it happened a lot quicker than what his ever did. At his age, where he lives and what he does, it means that when we do meet he just starts to get to know me again in the three or four days that I'm there, and then I go again. He probably knows more about me from following me in the media and on the internet than from the time we spend together, particularly in the last few years.

He did come and visit me in Europe once. In 1999 he had a holiday for about six months and we went to a few races together, off road and on it, and otherwise he hasn't been back to visit.

On the walls of Paul's home in Upper Corindi are posters and framed jerseys. He has had a lot less to do with Cadel since he and Helen separated in 1982, but he's still very much the proud father of a remarkable son.

Paul has lost the beard now, gained a few kilos, eased off on the drink and become a big fan of Thai food and culture. But he still follows the cycling scene closely from his place that's tucked away in the hinterland at Corindi, a small beachside community near Woolgoolga, roughly midway between Sydney and Brisbane. He admits that a few issues with discs in his spine have saved him from heavy lifting and too much manual labour. He and his wife Orada have a market stand in the Coffs Harbour market. They sell some knives and kitchen cutting implements they source from Orada's uncle who imports them from Thailand and other parts of Asia. At the various harvest times, they sell their exotic Asian vegetables from the garden that Orada diligently tends.

'We mainly grow Asian vegetables,' Paul explained. 'There are about 10 Thai restaurants in town and we supply all of them. There are also about two or three supermarkets that we sell to. That's about all that we can pull out of a little garden like we've got.'

It's lush and green where Cadel's father lives. There have been instances of drought in the time he's lived there but being on the coastal side of the Great Dividing Range has served his patch well. The crops thrive and Paul gloats about his exotic collection of vegetables and is grateful for how he's been able to expand his palate, improve his health and enjoy finding the benefits of another culture.

He laughs at the memory of Orada's early arrival at his property.

Within hours of her first visit she had asked what sort of food he liked. Paul told her he was quite partial to a good satay dish. 'She nodded and went inside to delve around for a few minutes and, as I was stretching my legs after the flight, she re-emerged and started walking down to the garden. "It'll take a while," she called out.'

She took some peanut seed into the garden and proceeded to plant it. 'When the peanuts did grow, they were that yummy that she harvested them and ate them herself, so we still never got satay. So we grew another lot of peanuts, Thai ones … and finally I got some satay chicken.'

Paul and Orada are not idle. They have their seasons to consider, their planning to attend to, their harvest time and their way of life to maintain. And even if one of their few pleasures after all the toil is eating, at least they do so on their terms. Paul can talk without caring for a response for long stretches, and if it's about cycling, Cadel or food, then all the better.

———————————

Both of Cadel's parents are besotted by him. You could not find people more proud. But neither seem too surprised by what he's gone on to achieve. They have lived apart for most of Cadel's life and have very separate lives. Geoff Schmidt and Orada Evans are the perfect complement to Helen and Paul, respectively. The separation was a difficult one, laced with the usual ramifications of knowing that what they once believed would be an ideal life together was not going to be. But they've each since found their own little patch of heaven.

Both places where his parents live suit them perfectly. Paddocks for the horses, room to roam and ride for Cadel's mum. Gardens of exotic vegetables and the regular flood to entertain or isolate for his father.

Both would suit Cadel perfectly but before he considers settling down, he will continue to ride the vagabond life of a professional cyclist – the traveller's life he started as a child. Four years in the tropics in the community of Bamyili, the trip down to Corindi, and a few months living in what was once a horse float, a brief period in a house clad with leftover timber from railway sleepers, then a migration to a sheep farm in the New England Tablelands around Armidale in New South Wales.

It took a long time for Helen and Paul to officially end their relationship, but the pair first separated not too long after arriving in New South Wales. Before Helen could begin her education and Paul had his market garden, they had to face the reality of a marriage that was falling apart for a variety of reasons.

During their time in the Territory the couple had travelled a little. They ventured to Broome for one Christmas when Cadel was three in a Mitsubishi Isuzu truck that they had bought with the intention of putting a horse float on the back. The truck coped with the long trip to the Kimberley along the Great Northern Highway and Helen remembers the holiday fondly.

They had gone west to the coast for this adventure but a few years earlier, during one of their long drives south to Melbourne, the pair were in an optimistic mood. They reached the east coast and hugged the shoreline for the journey down the Pacific Highway aiming for Sydney before turning slightly inland for the run down to the city where their parents lived. After passing through Grafton, they spied a sign that would eventually prompt a significant change to their lives. It advertised parcels of land just a little way inland, just to the west of Red Rock – a sleepy community that was little more than a few houses and a decent-sized camping ground for tourists to pitch a tent or park a caravan. A small shop supplied all the basics for a family in the 1970s to enjoy their holiday time: fishing reels, yabbie traps, as well as all the usual general store offerings.

It was a weekend destination for residents of Coffs Harbour who wanted a change of scenery, or a place where Sydneysiders might spend the summer holidays.

The 530 kilometres from Coffs Harbour to Sydney now includes bypasses and divided sections for much of the drive. But back in 1981 it was a lot longer and far more dangerous. It could take around eight hours on a good day.

'We were driving back up from Melbourne one year and that's when we bought it,' says Helen of their first real estate purchase. 'We drove past this sign. We went to see the land and then decided to buy it. It was $14,000 for 247 acres. It was not enormously expensive.'

It didn't reach the ocean. It lay on the western side of the Pacific Highway just north of Woolgoolga and is now the site of blueberry farms. It's where Orada now picks for Bob Johnson, the man Helen and Paul sold their property to.

We agreed that we would leave the Territory but we didn't just go one day and leave it all behind. It was part of a long-term tactic. We started thinking that it was time to make a move and about two years after we brought the land, we decided it was time to go there and build a house.

Paul's take is roughly the same, but he expands in some places in his laconic way:

We bought the property on one of our annual leaves; just got sick of the Territory. We were there five years. The heat and the flies and being miles from the ocean sort of got to us. Even if we moved to Darwin to be closer to the coast, it wasn't right. You can't swim there; jellyfish sting you and there are crocodiles to consider. It was Australia's last frontier really. Probably still is too.

Bamyili has had a name change. Now they call it Barunga. Things change. You just move on. You get sick of things. Helen was more into doing some more study and stuff like that. It wasn't far from Armidale uni which she later went to …

———————————

Cadel cites his mother as number-one in his inner circle, the five people who have been pivotal in making him what he is. They have enjoyed some of their life's highlights together. She helped him through school; raised him her way, provided and cared for him, nurtured and admired him, cheered and revered this little blond latecomer who bided his time inside but eventually appeared as a lively bundle, small at first but soon chubby and then cheeky. Perpetually naked, he clearly had no restraints upon him in his infancy.

It was Helen and Paul who took Cadel to Corindi. Eventually, she would take him a little further south and a little further west and a little higher up the mountains. The family stayed together in Corindi for a year or so but a time came when Helen decided to leave Paul.

It had been an amazing journey already for a young adventurer, but as she turned 25 it was time to consider the future in the full context. What plagued her most about the relationship was that Paul didn't believe that their child was the most important thing in the world. It's not that he didn't like him – he was besotted by him – but there were other things as well. Helen, at that time, couldn't fathom there being other things with equal importance:

He didn't see it that way. To him Cadel wasn't the most important thing in the world. It didn't make sense to me. It still doesn't. I can't comprehend any parent being that way. Most parents do think that their child is the most important thing in the world. He didn't.

He had his life, and he was happy when the world was revolving around him. I'm not suggesting that all we did had to be for Cadel, but as a parent your energies – everything you do – is for your child. Their growth and development is of prime importance. Not their happiness in the short-term sense. That, everyone hopes, is what you achieve with a healthy active life and understanding of the connections and realising a happy relationship. But the important thing for a parent is about ensuring happiness in the long-term and that means giving them the tools to make them strong so they can build the life they want, so they can be happy.

That doesn't mean being rich and famous and having heaps of stuff. It means being able to face up to the stuff that happens to you when you live. And heaps of stuff does.

When we got to Corindi, we stayed in the back of the truck. Really it was a horse float but modified to suit a family of three. But it was where the horses had travelled with us from the Territory, for the trip of around 4000 kilometres.

Paul explains about developing the block:

We got the land cleared and built the house over a couple of months. We sold half of the property. Now there are blueberry farms there that are still prospering. That gave us enough money to do what we had planned for the place. It allowed us to lay the foundations that saw us build the house. There was a sawmill nearby and, during the time after the excavation work had been done and while we were sleeping in what had been the horses' quarters, we worked out an arrangement for excess timber.

When the sleeper cutters did their work up in the forests that they were logging up around Glenreagh, Nana Glen and Coramba, it was done in a way that meant there were leftovers. They'd take swing saws into the bush and they'd slice off the rounds of trunk. They would be the length of sleepers used to build the railways. They'd slice up the logs and we had a licence to go in and load our truck up with the rounds of the cuttings from the forest. We'd bring them home and cut timber out of the ones that weren't too badly damaged. Of that, we built the cladding of our home. We built the house and stayed there for a little while. That's what we did.

We planted a vegetable garden, constructed fences and looked to find a place for the horses. I had them stabled down in Bellingen when we first arrived in Corindi. A friend of ours lived there and once we had the fences we needed, we went and collected the horses and put them on our property. Then we finished building the house.

The horses were a priority in Helen's life; they still are. Cadel remembers coming back to Australia after one of his two years with the T-Mobile team. He was exhausted after the long flight. He sank down on the lounge and almost fell asleep. Thinking his mother was making a cup of tea, he called out. 'I'd been gone nine months and we had a lot to catch up on,' he said, 'but she had put her boots on and had gone to the stables to tend to the feeding.'

But Cadel was never neglected by his mother. She loved her horses and adored her son. He grew up under her care and was never left wanting. She didn't have a lot of money but made sure he had the opportunity to pursue his passion for cycling. She would go a few years wearing the same clothes, forfeiting a new wardrobe so that she had the means to pay for the travel that allowed him to race his bike as often as possible.

I stayed in Corindi for about three years, and I decided to finish my studies at university instead of remotely, so we moved: Cadel, Trevor – my partner then and someone Cadel has always kept in touch with – and I, so I could attend the University of New England in Armidale.

When we first got there, we lived halfway between Armidale and Guyra. Then Paul and I sold the rest of the land in Corindi and I had enough money to buy a house. It was when Trevor and I were packing up to move again that Cadel had his accident.

It was terrible. We were still at 'Westbrook' – the sheep station we lived on, along the road to Guyra – and had started packing up for the move to Armidale. Rae and Blossom – the foals – were six months old. They hadn't come up with their mothers for the feed in the morning. Cadel went down to the paddock to get them. He knew the drill. He was going down to call them.

The two foals realised that they were all alone and their mothers, Sunshine from the Territory and Stormy, were 'up there'. They just jumped up in the air. Rae kicked out and Cadel was there.

I didn't see it. But Trevor saw it. I heard him call this terrible, terrible, terrible call and I jumped up and ran out to see him running down the hill.

Cadel was lying on the ground. He was this awful colour. He was not breathing right. There was a rattling in his throat.

I don't know if it was the right or wrong thing to do, but it was the instinctive thing to do: I picked him up and held him.

The horses had run off. It was just one of those things horses do. It's something that happens. Cadel was just getting close like he always did; there was nothing different about this from any other day, but Rae jumped up and kicked out. She got Cadel on the side of the head.

Immediately after, there wasn't much blood. There was just a little cut. It turned out to be a depressed skull fracture. The skull had split and a piece of bone had fallen in and was pressing on his brain. It was clear that there was a problem. Trevor had seen it happen. Cadel was unconscious. His brain was bleeding and his system was collapsing. There were problems sending messages to his body and I think that's where the choking sound came from. His breathing was laborious and awkward.

Trevor got the car and we drove in to the hospital to Armidale. Then he was airlifted. They didn't have the CAT scan equipment so they transferred him quickly.

The assumption was that there would be brain damage – if he lived. Some people die from such injuries. He was unconscious when he was taken by helicopter to Newcastle.

It was 25 February, 11 days after his eighth birthday.

I couldn't go in the helicopter and I had to get to the hospital my own way. By the time I got there, the reality of it all had sunk in. It was all about to start again.

The doctor was a man called Mr Bookalil. He was a neurosurgeon and he had a very funny way. They are funny people.

Cadel was in intensive care and they did the scans. It was a couple of days before they did the operation; they had to cut the skull and go in to lift the bone off the brain. They put a stent in his neck, and drilled a hole in his skull to put a drainage option. What often kills people in this situation is that the damage to the brain causes *it to swell, but there's not sufficient room for expansion; it's got nowhere to go and the effects are fatal.*

They considered all those sorts of things and got to work on saving my son. The stent was to drain the fluid. And then they put him in a coma; that way the body and the brain can cope better. He was put on a ventilator and the machines did as much work as possible to allow his brain to recover. He was like that for seven days and then he started to react a little. His pupils started dilating and that was meant to be a major danger sign, so they rushed him off to do more scans.

There wasn't any sign of brain swelling or any other effects on the CAT scan, so they thought it must have been a reaction to the drugs that were keeping him in the coma. They started withdrawing the medication to see what would happen.

The prognosis we had been given was not good. At best, they told us, he would be paralysed down one side. They just couldn't be sure of what he would be like until he came out of the coma.

It was weird to be told it in such basic terms. But the doctors didn't try to disguise what they thought would be the result of the kick to the head. Often such brain damage would affect many facets of normal life. Not being able to talk, or walk; they wouldn't commit to saying that sort of stuff would happen again.

I was with him the whole time he was in hospital.

It's possible to get bed sores very quickly when you're so immobilised. Your ligaments stretch when you're lying flat, so people who have been in a coma — even for a few days — have all sorts of issues.

Their ankles tend to flop out with the weight of their feet falling to the side. And, to keep me busy instead of just sitting there in a hopeless state, they got me to do things – massage and move his arms and legs to try and keep things working.

I sat there the whole time just crying non-stop. It wasn't a loud howling or anything like that, just tears, but I couldn't do anything about it.

My mother came up from Melbourne to be with us and she was always bringing me cups of tea because I 'needed to have more fluids'. She's so gorgeous. She was wonderful.

They used to come and have to suck the phlegm out of his lungs. Mum used to hate it. She'd always be there for me but when the doctors did this, she made sure she snuck out of the room. She couldn't understand me. 'How can you stay there?'

'But it's him who is doing it. It's Cadel's body that is doing that. So it's good. His body is doing something and when I know that, I'm happy!'

I didn't like it, but it was a positive sign; I knew he was living. But it is horrible. Seeing the rise and fall of the chest and the noise and the beeping of the monitors and, all along, the knowledge in the back of your mind of the doctors' doubts.

There was a terrible time when the power went off and it was a moment of sheer panic. It was frightening. He was in the intensive care unit and there always had to be a nurse in the room. And because I didn't think about it, I didn't realise that there always needed to be someone there, and I found it amusing when one of the nurses would need something at some point, and she would stand at the door, almost daring to venture into the rest of the ward but being wary not to leave the room, and she'd stand in the door shouting out for what she needed.

I asked, 'Why didn't you go out and get it?'

'Because I can't leave the room.'

When Cadel finally came to, it was a very weird experience. He was always trying to climb out of the bed. He had a wild look in his eyes and he would describe a journey about going 'through the doors and along the passage and up the stairs and turn right ...' and he would go over the sequence in amazing clarity over and over again.

He was insistent. He never wavered. And all the while he was trying to get out of his bed. It was constant. It lasted all night but the true mania of it started to slow down after a while, but he kept telling the story of what needed to be done.

'We've got to go through the doors and along the corridor and up the stairs ...' It was really bizarre. It was not until ages later, when I went to the school and I realised that what he had been describing was going from the playground to his classroom. Heavens knows why he was considering this, but it was like he was fretting about being late for school.

What goes through your mind when you're out cold, put in a coma and have had damage to the brain!

That sequence of words was repeated but he never actually said, 'Hi mum ...'?

Not that I remember. No. It was a very traumatic time. I was locked in that headspace and there was nothing outside of it. I just couldn't bear to think of anything. I didn't even try to imagine what might have been. I couldn't cope with considering the worst. I must be chronically optimistic but nor was I thinking of the future either. I was just there, doing what I could, tickling the soles of his feet, talking to him, not allowing his ankles to twist and doing the small things that a mother can do. I was very much in a little space and there was nothing beyond that to distract me. For me I couldn't imagine what it would be like. There was no future for me without my boy. I never wanted to take my mind there.

When he did start to move, though, it seemed a lot more like the Cadel I knew than the one that the doctors had been telling me would wake.

After his recovery, he had to wear a helmet for a few months. It was an old, early-generation white cycling helmet. Half his head was shaved and there was a massive scar which was hideous to look at. It was all stitched up with blue cotton; it was puckered and awful.

His balance was very poor, but because of the massage and stuff that I'd been doing when he was in a coma, and from the physios, after he woke he was in reasonably good condition, all things considered. We were only in the hospital for a week after he came to.

They just wanted him to stay long enough to monitor his condition. A hospital is not a place anyone wants to be, and they did what was possible to get us out of there as quickly as possible. And we went back to Armidale.

There wasn't all of the issues that can affect some people who have been in a coma for some time. He just had to recover his strength. His balance was bad for quite a long time. He was wobbly, and even walking was a little awkward for quite some time. For a long time he would have intermittent but very severe headaches. He had this palsy down the side of his face. Half of his face had no expression – he couldn't move the muscles – but apart from those things – and the dramatic look of the actual wound – he didn't seem too badly affected.

He didn't go back to school for quite some time, but the helmet wasn't necessary all the time; it was for protection in case he did fall. He didn't need to sleep with it on.

We'd go and have these sessions with the neuropsychologist. He was from a musical family. He could relate to that aspect of people so he'd ask Cadel to sing. My son can do quite a lot of things well but he cannot sing!

After about six months, the doctor said there was no longer a need for Cadel to see him any more. He looked at me after one of the visits, nodded his head to suggest it was all okay. From where we had been, it was so much more than 'okay'!

That was the worst time of my entire life! It was terrible.

6
MTB: Off the road

Emerging success

It was on one of his work trips to Katherine that Paul bought Cadel his first bike – a small yellow BMX with knobby tyres and training wheels. It was on this that he learned the concept of ped-alling.

Cadel still credits his upbringing in Bamyili – and the freedom of living in a place where he didn't have the concerns of traffic to restrict his adventures – as a key factor in making him a bike rider – not a racer yet, for there's a big difference. It was in the Territory that he got to explore. He could tear along the dirt roads and through the bush with 'Woofy' the dog, visit the waterhole, explore new places and, eventually, when the sun began to set, he would come home. It wasn't as though he went too far, for he was just a child. But it was the start of something:

> Starting riding at two or three gave me a base. I wasn't training for anything – it wasn't like I was riding to get better. I just did it because there wasn't anything else to keep me entertained.

As a four-year-old he tried to remove training wheels with a too-large shifting spanner to set off on a two-wheeled path.

Being kicked in the head by a horse as an eight-year-old slowed his progress and he wore a helmet long before it became mandatory on Australian roads. He enjoyed his BMX, and got a larger one while living near Armidale. By the time his mother returned to Victoria he was confident of his riding skills and wanted to try the new concept of mountain biking:

I'm not sure when it was but I can tell you it was not December or February – because it wasn't around Christmas or my birthday – but I asked Mum if I could have a new bike. She told me, 'Ask your father.' And so I called him up and said, 'Dad, can I have a new bike?' He asked me how much it would be, and I said 'About $500.' I never held any hope but he just said, 'Yep. Righto. I'll send you down the money.' 'I couldn't believe my luck; never did I think he'd agree. But he did.'

That would be the last time he paid the full price for a bike. After that he started to race. And after he started to race, he started to win. And then the knock-on effect followed until he found himself lining up for the Tour de France as the favourite for the title.

Together with his cousin, Jarrah, and Jarrah's cousin Matt, he ventured out on the roads and trails near Plenty in Melbourne's outer suburbs. Cadel and Jarrah were around the same age, both could ride pretty well and they created the little competitions that most kids on bikes do. Race you to the next sign! See who's fastest down this hill? I'll time you for a lap around the block. And so on. It's part of every story involving a successful cyclist. Jarrah and Matt were his riding buddies and at the start of the mountain biking boom – around 1990, the same year that the first official world championships were organised – they decided to enter a local competition.

Cadel's success was not immediate. He lost his first race, but won the next. Then he just kept on winning. Before any formal testing, his 'engine' propelled him around the mountain bike tracks in Victoria faster than anyone else. He progressed through the local competitions and raced enough to realise that he was pretty good. It all stemmed from enjoyment. It was fun; it was close to flying. And so he kept on riding, kept on winning, and eventually lined up for his first national championship.

Helen recalls what ultimately proved to be the first step along a long path to a prosperous career:

> I remember his first race. It was at a place called Blue Lake near where we used to live in Plenty. Jarrah – my brother's son who is six months older – and Cadel used to muck around on their bikes on the property. They'd explore the area together and enjoyed the freedom that riding offered. Jarrah is a stuntman now. But when the boys were young, he was a good downhiller.

This was the early 1990s and suspension was only a concept in mountain biking then; there was little variation in the equipment used in what would become the main categories of the rapidly growing sport: hill climbs, downhill, cross-country; it was the rider's skills that were tested.

One of the pioneers of mountain bike racing was John Tomac.

He was unique; he was one of a rare breed who could win medals in both the cross-country and downhill disciplines at the world championship level. He was a rider most impressionable kids admired – an original. By the time Cadel and Jarrah went to Blue Lake 'Johnny-T' was a legend of his sport. Never mind all the other things he did to enliven the scene by simply being an über-cool, all-American good guy; he also dominated races. He had all the ingredients: charisma, strength, endurance, speed, skill … and he was marketable. At the age of 16 in 1984 he was a national BMX champion. Five years later he won the unofficial MTB world championship, taking the cross-country title in Francorchamps, Belgium. In 1990 he was part of the famous 7-Eleven road cycling team – the first squad from the US to break into the Eurocentric cycling scene. In 1991 that squad morphed into Motorola, and Tomac was part of the roster. But he was a mountain biker who dabbled in road racing. Many have since swapped fat knobby tyres for skinny slick ones, but Tomac was the first. He was a natural born winner on the mountain bike circuit. In the second official World Championships he was first in the cross-country and second in the downhill. He was Mr Versatile. He earned a good living and he inspired riders around the world, and Cadel was one of them.

Cadel rode to Blue Lake on the bike his father bought him. Signed on, raced, got beaten. Rode home and told his mum how much he enjoyed it.

There wasn't much of an infrastructure for races and the true format of how this sport in its infancy should be run was still being figured out. The cross-country circuits were five or six kilometres long and the number of laps varied depending on age or what category the contestants were part of: novices might do two laps, 'experts' four and the 'elite' – or seniors – would do six. But these events were being modelled on what had been done in Colorado or California or other epicentres of this developing sport. The examples of racing came from magazines that were printed months before they arrived in Australia. Reports would filter through about events in Durango or Santa Barbara and administrators could only hazard a guess at how they were staged. The terrain near Plenty provided a good starting point and the efforts of some local enthusiasts helped establish the scene on the outskirts of Melbourne. Helen recalls the early years:

> *In America it had been a sport for a few years, but here it was still in its infancy. There wasn't much of an infrastructure for races but there was this wonderful man called Kim Banks who had organised a lot of the bike races. And he made a lot of opportunities for kids who were interested in racing. He organised the second race that Cadel competed in which was up at Kinglake. It was a really, really hot day. Cadel and Jarrah had ridden up there to compete.*

That's how it was then. There was hardly any traffic and he had become so accustomed to exploring the region on his bike, so riding to a race was nothing out of the ordinary. 'Cadel would just say, "I want to race in this event …" and that's what he'd do.'

Off he would go and hours later, he'd return. Of this second instance Helen fondly remembers the arrival of the weary racer:

> *Trevor and I were sitting on the lawn in the late afternoon and Cadel came home.*
>
> *'How did you go? What was it like?'*
>
> *'I won.'*
>
> *He showed me this little medal and after that he really just kept on improving. The only race he didn't win after that was in Thredbo in the sub-junior national championships in 1992. He came second to a boy called Hugh Morgan who was a year older than he was. Hugh was big and strong compared to the other kids at that early age. As the other kids got older, he lost his physical edge.*

The next year Cadel was still a sub-junior and, this time, he didn't get beaten by a bigger guy. He won cross-country races and he won them often. He won the National Series. He was earnest and impressionable. He explains that because he enjoyed riding his bike, he did rides or circuits that happened to span roughly the same time that a typical event that he competed in did; it was purely a coincidence that it was the perfect training regime.

He honed his skill and went from good to better, and would later be a world-beater. But before then he made acquaintances along the way that were pivotal in his development as a cyclist and an ambassador for his sport.

Damian Grundy had been involved in the bicycle industry since leaving school in 1980. He began racing late in his life, starting out at 21, and he enjoyed some success but it wasn't the results that kept him involved; he just loved the sport and found it addictive in every sense. In the mid-1970s, when Grundy was still in school, he started tinkering with bikes. Together with a few mates he came up with a bastardised version of an off-road bike that would actually predate even the early years of the mountain bike movement in the US:

We had built these three-speed bikes with Sturmey Archer gears and converted them into six-speeds by putting two cogs on the hub. We'd ride these bikes off road. This was around 1974 and lasted for a few years – way before there was any such thing as a mountain bike. We had endless fun riding on dirt tracks back then.

Back then, when the movement was just starting, there were plenty of chances for cross-over inventions. Gary Fisher and other Americans would officially lay claim to creating the mountain bike but the mother of invention in this case was having fun. If you had a bike and had a trail, then surely you could modify your existing machine to suit the circumstances better. Grundy would become a pioneer in the sport, for it would later be he who wrote coaching programs for a young rider named Cadel. But before that, a movement had just begun. He recalls:

I loved riding and I loved racing but mountain biking – when I first became aware of it – didn't interest me too much because I was happy road riding. I was also happy riding in the bush.

Then I went to a mountain bike race in Melbourne late in 1988. I had what is actually not an uncommon experience for road riders: I had a horrendous time. I had no pacing strategy so I just went flat-out from the start, lasted a lap and collapsed on the side of the track and swore that I'd never go back to a mountain bike race ever again. About six months later, I relented.

> *For whatever reason, it then just clicked with me. I won every*
> *race I entered in 1989; I don't think I got beaten the whole year in*
> *Victoria, and then I went to the national championships and ran*
> *second in the cross-country after being beaten in a sprint. I went*
> *to a couple of world championships. I was still working in a bike*
> *shop.*

It's a long way from Bamyili to Plenty, but a lot further from Plenty to Durango, and it was Damian who got Cadel there. The pair lived and worked close to each other when they met but their relationship as rider and coach would see them traverse the globe in pursuit of the rainbow jersey of the world champion.

'I met Cadel because of where I worked,' says Grundy, but it wasn't as memorable as the first time he saw the young rider race. 'I'd spend some time at Eltham Cycle Works and he came in like any other 14-year-old would.'

Cadel was, is and always will be pedantic about his equipment. It's a trait shared by many cyclists – amateur and professional. And even before he realised that this sport could provide him with not just an income but a good one as part of a prosperous career, Cadel wanted the best products, but Helen's income could never cover the costs of such exotica. He would ride to Eltham and saunter around the shop looking at equipment that was way beyond his budget. 'He was just a kid,' says Damian, 'and my wife Rachel really knew him before I did because she was at the shop more than I was. 'I was only part-time at the place where Cadel came to look at bikes.'

Later it was what he did on the bike that caught Grundy's attention and prompted him to seek out the kid who was pushing a heavy bike around the Australian Alps and taking on the best riders in the country.

We were at a national mountain bike championship in Thredbo in 1993 and it was not a very nice day; we were inside but we could see the cross-country course and Rachel pointed out a kid who was racing and said, 'Oh, that's the boy who comes into the shop in Eltham.' She told me he was a regular visitor to the shop. Apparently he came in all the time and she asked if he raced. He told her that he'd tried it a couple of times but not often and the nationals were due to be his first big test.

In Thredbo, through our window, it seemed he was doing fairly well. We knew who was leading the race – Hugh Morgan, who was one of Martin Whiteley's protégés at the time – and Rachel told me that it seemed The Kid was coming about second or third. I thought that was pretty good and I was interested in meeting him so I went down for the final few laps, saw the end of the race and he finished second. I introduced myself: 'Hi, I'm Damian. My wife told me you come into the shop in Eltham.'

I congratulated him and told him that if he needed any help with his cycling – with training or stuff like that – just come in. I wasn't really coaching anybody at that stage. I'd had a little bit of involvement with one or two other athletes but I was not racing too seriously myself. I finished about 15th at that year's nationals, I wasn't riding well.

He liked the idea and said that he'd be in touch. Sure enough, he visited the shop again shortly afterwards and that's when our relationship really began.

Before long Damian would find himself on a list that would be carried in Cadel's mind for many years to come: the key people in his career.

I was 32 and, as an older athlete, you consider how you've done things. Throughout my riding days, I'd never had anyone coach me. I was aware that this was a hindrance so I thought if I could help out a kid with some advice and guidance, then that might help them avoid some of the mistakes I'd made.

Damian Grundy wasn't alone in noticing the talents of this off-road virtuoso who lugged a heavy bike up hills and over trails with panache. He had stamina and power and, weighing under 60 kilograms, he possessed elements of what made a good cyclist. Unlike Tomac – and many before and since – Cadel never raced a BMX. This was a common path that many riders at the time took to discover the joys of racing bikes. They were small and cheap and it opened up cycling to an entirely new crowd. If you consider the stars of Cadel's generation, there are many who first competed as part of the new-wave of cycling, BMX – Bicycle Moto-Cross – an odd acronym for a sport that would make its debut at Olympic level 12 years after mountain biking, even though it was an established sport almost 10 years beforehand.

BMX was for the sprinters anyway. The typical track was

around 400 metres long and was for the anaerobic type of athlete: short bursts of speed combined with strength and skill provided the winning formula. Mountain biking, and cross-country in particular, was for the aerobic riders. To succeed on courses like the ones used in Thredbo or Durango or the myriad other ski stations that began adopting mountain biking as an option for attracting people to the slopes when there was no snow, you needed a good cardiovascular system.

Early in Cadel's career, he had acquired a number of nicknames. None of them were needed, for his name was relatively uncommon and he would pass through his racing days using his first name alone. The Madonna principle, if you like. But he had been dubbed by some as 'The Lung'. Later, when he was starting to take on the world's best while still just a junior, there was a brief stint when he was labelled 'Lance', for he shared some of the characteristics of a brash American five years his senior who had made the jump from triathlon to road cycling and had won the World Championship in his first season as a professional. But really, Cadel is just that: Cadel.

In his first attempt at the national championship, Cadel had sufficient talent to attract the attention of one of the administrators of cycling who had been involved with mountain bike racing (MTB) since its inception. Martin Whiteley was a key player in lobbying the International Olympic Committee (IOC) for MTB's inclusion in the Olympics. He was the CEO of cycling's governing body, the Australian Cycling Federation (later Cycling Australia), at the time that the first off-road championships were being contested. His passion was – and still is – mountain bike racing. Eventually Martin left Cycling Australia to focus his energy on developing the facet of the sport that he enjoyed most at an international level with the UCI (Union Cycliste Internationale). He has watched the evolution of mountain biking and Cadel remains, in his eyes, one of the key contributors in making it mainstream. He too would make Cadel's 'List of Five'. But before that happened Whiteley had never heard his name before.

In 1993 – when Cadel won the cross-country national championship and dominated the season-long Australian MBA series as a sub-junior – Australian Cycling Federation's focus was primarily the established disciplines of track and road. MTB was so young that Martin's role was as the race caller in Thredbo. Whiteley recounts his first encounter with the teenager:

At the time, I was running the Australian national mountain bike series. It was the hill climb which was early in the program of events; it was in the middle of the week, before we got into the cross-country races.

I'd been coaching another junior rider at that time and was doing the commentary. Standing at the top, the first thing you saw in that event is when the competitors labour in to the finish area. There was this gangly little kid who I'd never seen before; he was so far out in front of everybody else. I had to check the program and see what his number was.

I didn't even quite know how to say the word 'Cadel'. I'd never seen it before. I didn't know if it was 'Kay-del', or something else.

He remembers this detail more than I do; he tells me often of being called to the finish line and what I was saying. He reminds me every once in a while, saying, 'That was the first time I heard your voice ... when you were calling the hill climb.'

I was asking Damian Grundy – as I knew it was him who encouraged him to attend the event – 'How do you pronounce that name?'

Then we saw him do well in the cross-country later that weekend and it was clear straight away that he was a special talent.

Martin Whitely and Damian Grundy were to find pride of place on Cadel Evans' list of influential people because they helped him make the jump from an enthusiast to a professional. He loved to ride his bike and they helped him achieve the goals that he set himself when he began to practise what would later become his trade. And the relationships were born because of one thing: they saw a young man ride a bike like he was born to do so.

7
Finding true mountains – The importance of being Cadel

The rise of talent

As early as his second year of racing, extra challenges were needed for a rider who was so far ahead of his peers that he risked riding off into the distance and onward to boredom. Martin Whiteley was the first to suggest a remedy to this potential hazard:

> I made a decision with the AMBA executive to move him from the junior division to the elite because, in those days, he was so dominant that he was starting to believe that it was all too easy. My concern was that if he wasn't being challenged he wouldn't continue to be interested, he would stop developing and just go through the motions of appearing at races and win. That can be fun for a while but it also hinders young riders because they start believing they can ease off on the training.

Cycling is too hard to be complacent. There's a long history of Australians excelling at the junior world championship level. Some have gone on to long, prosperous careers in the professional ranks. But others have simply faded from the scene because of all the usual temptations of life: relationships, cars, booze, drugs.

Cadel had a few steady relationships, but it was some time before he found the woman of his dreams, Chiara.

One of his weaknesses is cars: his mood lights up if he gets to discuss the intricacies of one model over another. With the money he's earned racing his bikes, he's invested in some toys to quell his passion – a 1966 Mustang coupé sits idle for most of the year in Australia, and a Lotus Elise was a reward after his first second place in the Tour de France. But his 'regular' car is a Mini which he got after trading in an Audi TT that he had bought before meeting Chiara.

On the alcohol front, he's developed a taste for fine wines and loves a cold beer to quench a thirst but if you're chasing a scandal prompted by excessive consumption, then turn your attention elsewhere. Nothing to see here.

When it comes to drugs and those who use them to cheat … Cadel is philosophical:

There will always be people in any walk of life who are prepared to be dishonest. Step on a train with a ticket and do the right thing, pay for the fare and find a seat, but take a look around and chances are someone will be taking a chance to get a free ride. It's a trait of human nature, it seems, to try and cheat the system. There will always be people who are going to bend the rules or go beyond the limit of the rules. I don't think there is anything in the world that people don't cheat at, whether it is paying taxes or getting into politics or getting approval to build a dodgy house. There are people who cheat and bend the rules or fiddle the books.

But knowing that doesn't mean you are able to deal with it. Some get exasperated and surrender. What about Cadel? How does he cope with being beaten by fuelled-up fools?

At least the people who criticise me for not attacking them during a race or not winning may think about swallowing their words. Or at least they might realise that if I come second to someone it doesn't mean that I'm not trying as hard as I can.

When he started racing, doping was not on his mind. He didn't need to consider it – he was winning anyway. And the advantage he had on his rivals was such that, if anything, he needed to take something that was detrimental to his system to give others any hope of challenging him. As a sub-junior in the 1993 national championships, in a race that took him just 53 minutes to complete, he won by over five and a half minutes. The promoter of the race in Thredbo, Colin Battersby, recalls:

He started out fast, but he did negative splits for each lap – he was faster each time around. He was so fast it was silly. It was amazing to witness. The conditions were terrible. It was cold and no one wanted to be out there watching a sub-junior race, but Cadel attracted people to the event because of his panache.

Martin Whiteley adds his account of that period:

He was always lapping the entire junior field. That provided a bit of an incentive to him – to see if he could lap every other rider in the race – but it wasn't too great for everyone else. He called and asked what he should do. I thought it was best to move him up to elite, and that meant racing guys like Rob Eva and Scott Stewart at the time. Cadel has never been a very big guy but back then he was tiny, and I just wasn't sure if it was the right decision, because you can often push people too far, and then they get into the situation where they can get demoralised. It was a bit of a gamble just on our own national scene, but it turned out to be the right thing to do.

We put him in with the big boys even though he was a first-year junior, just to see how well he'd do. At the first national champion- ships that he rode as an elite, he had just got his driver's license but it was his learner's permit. He made a bet with me. 'If I win the national title in this category, can I get to drive your Porsche?' His mum was there and I said, 'Okay, fair enough, that sounds like a good deal. You took a gamble moving up, I'll take a gamble with my car ...'

He got second; John Gregory won. And afterward Cadel came up and said, 'Oh well, I just missed out.' And I said, 'Yeah, a bet is a bet.'

And so I thought, that's it: my car is safe. He got a medal and everyone was pretty happy. But then his mum came over with the L plates and said, 'I think you'll be needing these.' And sure enough, he came back from having a shower after the race and said, 'Let's go.' And he got to drive my car. He didn't win the title and I'm still uncertain of how he managed to manipulate it so he could drive my car with his L-plates, but I was happy to have given him an award for such a great performance. It's something that bonded us as friends. We weren't just an official and a rider; we got along well.

The World Championships were in late September and, on the last day of July 1994, Cadel lined up for Australia's first MTB World Cup event to be contested in Cairns. Cadel, Martin and Damian decided that it was a good opportunity for Cadel to test his legs in the senior ranks. He was just out of the sub-juniors and due to race in the upcoming World Championships as a junior but in the tropics of far north Queensland, aged 17 and six months, he rode in the elite group and took on the world's best cross-country riders.

He had a sponsorship from Apollo, an Australian bicycle company that had a history with road cycling but were also committed to supporting the off-road scene. Part of the deal was that Cadel received a race bike and one to train on. With a blue aluminium frame, Apollo 'Team' had front suspension – forks made by RockShox that offered around 30 mm of travel. It was a huge advancement at the time and Cadel had every reason to believe he'd hit the big time. He was racing against the reigning world champion – three-time winner Henrik Djernis of Denmark – and the World Cup leader and future gold medallist in the first MTB Olympic race, Dutchman Bart Brentjens.

The starting order was dictated by position in the World Cup rankings and, as a junior, Cadel had no points, so he was seeded well down the field of 75. It was a five-lap race over a circuit of nine kilometres. After exiting the tropical forest that came after the main climb of the technical circuit, the leader was Brentjens, but just ten seconds behind – as part of a group of eight including Djernis – was Cadel.

Before the race Cadel believed a top 20 finish might be possible. But after an hour of racing he was in second position. Only Brentjens was ahead of him.

The winning time was two hours 38 minutes and 52 seconds; this was almost an hour longer than what Cadel had grown accustomed to racing in the younger grades. He fought hard to maintain his position in the race but started to fade towards the end. By the final pass of what had been dubbed 'Cloudy's Climb', a rise so steep that even the best riders opted to push their bikes rather than ride, Cadel could barely walk. Cramp was stinging his legs, blood seeped from a wound on his left shin, but he reached the finish with barely a speck of dust on his face. Others were coated in dirt. Sweat mixed with sand and grit from the trail was smeared over Brentjens as he threw his victory salute. Then came the wait for minor places. Two riders from the dominant Diamondback team finished second and third – Ralph Berner and Pavel Elsnic, respectively. Fourth was taken by the two-time runner-up in the World Cups of mountain biking's formative years, Mike Kloser of Germany. And then came Cadel. He raised both hands, tendered a salute of sorts, but exhaustion had consumed him. He nearly collapsed at the finish but he had eclipsed everyone's expectations. Even Cadel himself was surprised by the result.

When it came time to present the medals, Whiteley had spoken to the organisers and they agreed that the ride by Cadel was worthy of official recognition. The podium was extended beyond the traditional gold, silver and bronze positions and both Kloser and Cadel Evans joined the medallists for the award ceremony.

From that day forth five riders have stood on the podium at the World Cup races.

The example of Cadel and Apollo in 1994 was exceptional. His success gave the brand credibility and, for all the investments the company director Phillip Watts has made in cycling before or since, he will never gain the same level of exposure that he earned during the brief sponsorship with Cadel at the start of his career.

Mountain biking came alive in Australia in 1992, the same year Cadel first contested the national championships. A dominant rider in the senior ranks was Rob Eva. He was the last of a generation of riders who not only competed in both the cross-country and downhill events, but won them. This was the time when the Thredbo resort hosted the championships, the Australian Mountain Biking Association (AMBA) was growing from an upstart federation of enthusiasts to a promoter of professional events with some good sponsors like Reebok that were keen to tap into the exciting developing sport. Eva explains:

There was some pretty good money on the line. I could take home seven grand after a good weekend of racing, so there was some income to be earned, but it evolved quickly from there.

Having John Tomac out for the nationals in 1992, and former downhill world champion Greg Herbold the next year, really cemented the sport in Australia.

Mountain biking was new. There were roadies coming over, there were people who were getting into it and they wanted to ride. You could go to these races and experience it all from the outset. It was a sport being born.

The nationals between 1993 and 1994 were very close. There were only a few months between them because it changed from a winter series to a summer one and it went quickly from the crescendo of the national series to the World Cup in Cairns, and it just exploded in Australia. That was definitely something that was great to be part of.

And Cadel was at the centre of it all. He was a teenager but he was taking on the best in the country before his experiment in Cairns when he beat some of the finest riders of the generation. But he did so on relatively rudimentary equipment. Eva admits that he wasn't the best rider in the country – that was a title he bestowed on a former road cyclist, Scott Stewart, who had competed in the Seoul Olympics in the team time trial (an event that was scrapped after the 1992 Games to make way for mountain biking, which would make its debut in Atlanta). Damian Grundy was also one of the experienced hands at the cross-country races, but even he admits that his main legacy will be that he was 'the coach of Cadel Evans', rather than a rider who won a few early national titles.

They raced at a time when the skill of the rider was as important as a strong cardiovascular makeup. By the mid-1990s, the downhill would become so equipment-orientated that a bike that wasn't up to standard could cost a better rider a world title. But Cadel was never a downhiller. He was a rider who could climb, who could endure hour after hour of pain and reach the finish a lap ahead of his peers in a five-lap event.

'I was fortunate enough to have one of the early incarnations of the GT RTS frames, which was a state-of-the-art downhill bike at the time,' said Eva of the 1993 championships in Thredbo. He continues:

> It had 40 mm of travel from the suspension, front and rear. It was one of the first real dual suspension frames, but it's impossible to compare that with what's on offer now.
>
> Some guys might go down to a setup with about 150 mm suspension but the norm would be around 220 mm of travel. And this is useable travel; it provides a very significant difference to the rider. It has high-speed and low-speed compression and the rebound can be adjusted to suit the terrain. There are a lot of other features like travel adjustment on-the-run and a lot of other suspension or braking or shifting developments that make a big difference.
>
> In 1994, Cadel rode aluminium Apollo that probably had Shimano XT on it and he would have had a Manitou fork with a maximum of about 40 mm of travel. It weighed about 12 kilograms. At the time it was decent equipment, but compared with today's technology they were heavy. The pedals were clipless but with this early generation off-road style of cleat that was designed to be used in all sort of conditions – mud, dust, you name it – but they were heavy. The tyres were heavy. They were built more for strength than for weight, that's for sure.

Martin Whiteley cannot help but praise the input of Cadel Evans and what he achieved on the mountain bike circuit:

> I was very excited to take him overseas because I knew we had

Cadel with his mother, Helen Cocks at Mataranka hot springs, NT, 1977.

Cadel in the garden at Bamyili, Northern Territory, 1978. Bananas were to become a key part of his racing diet.

Cadel with his father, Paul Evans at Bamyili, NT, 1980.

Cadel with Rae and Sunshine, Armidale, NSW, 1984. A few months later Rae would put Cadel in hospital with a depressed skull fracture.

After the surgery, Armidale 1985.

Cadel riding his first BMX bike at Westbrook near Armidale NSW, 1984.

At Blue Lake, Plenty, Victoria where Cadel entered his first mountain bike race in 1993.

Racing in the Apollo colours, Cadel's first sponsor, at Thredbo, NSW, 1994.

Competing in the 1994 Cairns World Cup elite men's race. This was the first time Australia hosted an international mountain bike event and Cadel's first exposure to international competition. He was still a junior rider.

Cadel being assisted by Martin Whitely (left) and Damien Grundy (right) after finishing the 1994 Cairns World Cup race. He finished fifth, the youngest rider in the race. (© *Sport the library*)

The presentation ceremony for the 1994 World Cup in Cairns. In recognition of Cadel's achievement in coming fifth, all five placegetters were included on the podium. This started a tradition that continues today. (© *Sport the library*)

Cadel with Rob Woods (left) and Paul Rowney (right) in 1996. Cadel was a lot younger and smaller than many of his fellow competitors. (© *Sport the library*)

At 19, Cadel was the youngest rider in the field when he represented Australia at his first Olympics in Atlanta, 1996.

Cadel's first Australian Cycling Federation 'Cyclist of the Year' award for Mountain Biker of the Year, 1997. (© *Sport the library*)

The World Cup race trophy in mountain biking, 1999. (© *Sport the library*)

Winning the 1998 Canmore World Cup race wearing the number 1 plate as leader of the series, and the unique red and blue quartered jersey; the red represents leader of the under-23 category, and the blue represents leader of the elite men's category.

(© *Sport the library*)

On the second place step at the under-23 World Championship, Chatea-d'Oex, 1997.

(© *Sport the library*)

Tackling the downhill in
the 1998 Canmore World
Cup race. (© *Sport the library*)

Cadel riding in the 2000
Sydney Olympics.
(© *Sport the library*)

someone special on the national team and I needed to see how he rated against the rest of the world. At that time, his part of the scene was dominated by another little kid called Miguel Martinez. The worlds in 1994 in Vail was the first time we got to see Cadel race against his peers at the time.

The reason was all about timing. The rider's first true test came at a pivotal moment for the sport. And the one-time CEO of the Australian Cycling Federation was weak at the knees. That was a really proud moment:

Even though we'd been to world championships for four events already for mountain biking, and I'd taken a team abroad each time, this was the first time that we had a real chance at a medal, especially in cross-country.

The sport had really evolved by 1994. The Europeans had really gotten into it. So when we went to Vail and I was standing on the commentary podium with Peter Graves, the voice of mountain biking, and Chris Payne, who was running the sport for the International Cycling Union (UCI) at the time, we could see things were going well. At the end of the first lap, Cadel was right up there and they were saying to me, 'Hey, who is this kid?' And I was just so proud to see him right up there and chasing for a medal.

That began a very long period in Cadel's mountain bike career of racing Miguel Martinez. They were each other's nemesis and they were so amazing in the under-23 category that they were numbered one and two in the world even though they were not yet officially seniors. That hasn't happened since in our sport. There was a very exciting period when Cadel and Miguel were showing everyone what they were capable of in the future.

That whole period from 1993 to 1999, was exciting. We got to see him win his first World Cup, which was in 1997 in Wellington. I was the technical delegate there and I remember, as soon as he crossed the line, he jumped off his bike and jumped up on me like a monkey. He was so excited. It was the first World Cup win by an Australian and to be there was a great experience.

From then on, he went on to win many World Cup races but that one, quite ironically, he was battling with Dario Cioni for the win.

This was the same Dario who would much later be a friend and team mate racing in Europe with Cadel.

He won his World Cup titles – and I think they're more a sign of how much work you put in and how diverse you are as a rider, to win over a series. It doesn't mean you win every single race, but you're consistent. And Cadel was always terribly consistent, which is important in stage racing and any of those sports where you're required to perform over a period of time – and not just pop one on the day.

Cadel was ready to fight as he'd always done, and I think that's why he's continued to thrive in road cycling. He's always challenged. And when I see him on the bike in the Tour and you see the tenacity in his face, that's really who Cadel is: he's there for results more than the money and the fame. He's really in there to achieve his own set agenda, to prove that he can do what he believes is possible.

That's why I have always had absolute confidence in everything he's done on a bike. I've always believed in him because I know that he was believing in himself. And – outside his close circle of friends – he doesn't care how people view him. It's not relevant.

He's not driven by fame, otherwise he'd be seeking the media every day. I don't think he's driven by money. He doesn't live a flash lifestyle. He's not buying a Ferrari or living in Monte Carlo. He's driven by enjoying life – and he knows how to do that – especially with his wife and his close friends. And he knows how to get the most out of his body. That's what he seeks all the time: How can I improve on what I already know and I've already done? He's constantly seeking improvement and I think his results are a by-product of that particular asset: his desire to improve.

Everyone who has been involved with Cadel The Professional Cyclist has a similar story. Damian Grundy could see him evolve. The success came early and relatively easily but that didn't mean he ever felt satisfied, for there was always another objective that would be set. He is grateful for the support he receives and generous with his appreciation. He can accept 100 per cent but anything less is just not worthwhile. He can't cope with ordinary.

It was Whiteley who helped negotiate subsequent deals with sponsors, and Cadel's successful result in Cairns effectively ended his agreement with Apollo. After that he was courted by some of the biggest investors in the sport. Bike sponsors were joined by companies from outside the sport wishing to capitalise on the images of extremes, of a cult pastime which became an Olympic discipline. Teams were created and solid infrastructure put in place to support a band of riders who competed in what were essentially solitary styles of racing. Downhill and cross-country riders alike required more support from their mechanics than do other cycling competitors. The mountain bike scene provided a setting that absolutely suited Cadel's characteristics. By 1996 he was part of the factory-backed Diamondback squad from the US that included some of the sports biggest stars. And it was with this backing that he first began earning money from cycling.

Cadel often says, when he wants to take a breather or still his mind: 'deep blue ocean', and it somehow takes him some place else. Perhaps more important than the proverbial deep blue ocean is to remember the wonderful Hermosa Creek Trail. It was glorious, close to flying, an experience to savour.

8
The AIS years

Nurturing the talent

On the mountain bike, my focus was to stay smooth. It's good for your equipment and to minimise fatigue. I always look for the smoothest path. Obviously, I know where I want to go: in a downhill, it's to the bottom of the descent, that's the objective, and in mountain biking it can't always be about the fastest way. You want the smoothest as well, so that you can maintain control. When you've got tree roots and rocks and holes everywhere on the course, it's not always like on a race track or on the open road when it's all about taking the best line and exiting apex carrying as much speed as traction allows, to make the cornering experience as rapid as possible. There are so many other elements to consider.

Nicolas Vouilloz, one of the smoothest downhillers of the 1990s generation – a Frenchman with a zen attitude and a long resumé of victories, and now a regular winner in the European rally championships – was adamant about his policy of riding. 'As long as my front wheel is on the ground, I don't care what happens.' That was a theme from the early days of downhill mountain bike *racing. In the time that he was really good – and when I first started – front suspension technology was just beginning to emerge. You have to ride in a different style now with fully functioning suspension so that you use it to your advantage. The bikes from the 1990s share few elements of those used even five years later. And I'm a bit of a luddite when it comes to the beauty of off-road cycling.*

I always liked using just front suspension or even no suspension at all. You go slower, and it's harder, but it tests your skill more. You could say I'm a purist in that sense, at least that is the way I like to think it.

It's the same reason that I like a simple Lotus or an old Mustang for a car, because there's no electronic aid – it's just up to you. Unless you ride well, you don't go fast, whereas with a full suspension bike, it's a different story. Okay, to ride against someone who is really good, you will still have to push your limits, but half of the work is already done for you.

The same applies for people who like film cameras. You really have to work it well. Yes, digital does make the process easier but it destroys the art a little bit.

Cadel enjoys cycling in its pure form. He was a rider who could use even rudimentary equipment but still make his bike seem like an instrument. At speed it would sing through the forests of Durango, over the mud flats at the base of Thredbo's mountains or through the dust of Cairns in Walparr, the dry and dusty season. He had a knack of making terrain filled with obstacles seem like a flat stretch of road. You can't beat veteran professional bike riders who have spent their lives perfecting their method unless something comes naturally. He would perfect his method in the mornings and evenings before and after school while living in Plenty.

It was on the Hermosa Creek Trail during his six-week stint in Colorado before the World Championships in 1994 that he would first realise that riding could seem like flying, but before that he savoured the sensation for what it was. He was liberated by the bike. It allowed him to explore. It gave him a passion and sent him on a path to a career that seemed to be his destiny.

It is possible to turn a passion into a profession. From the start of his riding days, Cadel set himself up on a path that would steer him to a job that he loved. His mother insists there was no way this could be avoided:

> *Going to university was never really an option for him. I'm sure he would have liked to study and he would have enjoyed it, but before he could begin to consider what he wanted to do in the future, cycling found him. Everything happened so early that it was so clear that it was what he wanted to do and it was what he could be successful at, and so the decision was made.*
>
> *He does have intellectual curiosity, but when he was 14 or 15, when people generally start considering what the future may hold, his whole life was about being the best mountain biker in the world.*

In his yearbook from Eltham High School, each of the year 12 students appeared with a small photo and a brief caption in which their ambitions and hopes were stated. Cadel's was one for that phase of his life: 'To be the mountain bike world champion.' He missed out on that objective but his influence on the sport he opted out of eight years later is a significant one. John Tomac and Thomas Frischknecht were the originals at the time when the sport was in its infancy. They graced the covers of magazines and inspired a new generation of off-road riders. Amongst them was a young man born in the tropics, raised on the north coast of New South Wales before moving to the high country near Armidale and eventually receiving the last of his formal education at the school where his father and mother met. After a few races, he was on a trajectory that he couldn't avoid. 'People often wonder if his career was planned,' says his mother, and continues:

Of course we didn't plan it. It never seemed like there was any question about it. How do you decide if somebody is going to take on something like racing a bike as a career? It wasn't a decision, for that would imply that there were options. It was so blatantly obvious that it was what he was going to do; it was what he could do.

He loved riding his bike and still does. The boy inspired by the 'originals' became a teenager who rode to the top of the off-road scene and beyond.

Cadel sort of did high school as well. 'For how much energy I put into it, I did okay,' he says of the experience which served as little more than a distraction to his real calling, riding a bike.

It was pretty good. I wasn't really academically accomplished. I could do the things I needed to get by but I had my shortcomings. In maths I was fine until we got to algebra. In science I was fine until we got to chemical equations. And then everything else … I was not great but pretty good.

In the VCE, I did maths, English, photography – except for in the last year. I did physical education; I wanted to do computer studies but they didn't have it at my school. And languages are another story! I got into a lot of trouble in French in the first year at high school and my mum was like, 'I don't blame you for disliking that teacher. I couldn't stand her when I went to that school, either!' And I remember replying, 'No, I never want to go to France. What the hell do I need to learn French for …?'

My first home was in a French-speaking village in Switzerland where no one spoke English. I look back and realise there are so many things you'd change if you knew what lay on the road ahead. As a teenager, listening to your parents is very, very important, although at that age, it is the least important thing in your life.

I also did media studies; my second preference in life was to work in film and television production. I have since spent so many hours on the other side of the camera. I chose what lay on the road ahead. I chose my subjects around what would be the best to allow me to go training as often as possible. There was a topic called outdoor education; we even had to go mountain biking in that class – perfect!

I went to Eltham High School, a public school. I did half of year seven in Armidale and then we moved and I did the rest of high school at the same place.

The teachers were a little lenient with me. There was one who used to run in the morning and see me out training. Even if it was pouring rain or dark in the early hours of the day, we'd see each other before school and, as he could appreciate, if I was late to school it was not because I was sneaking a cigarette with friends or something; it was because I was rushing back from my time on the bike. I was working for something. I had a cause, as opposed to most teenagers who seem to go out of their way to make life difficult for everyone around them. I liked riding the bike and I never had a separation between work and fun.

I wasn't doing structured training – intervals or anything – but I was learning about it as I went along. I talked to people and listened to advice, I searched the library for books about training and nutrition, I did what I could in the time frame I had and with the riding options that existed in my part of the world.

I had my loops – circuits in my area that I used to ride. I'd like to go back now and do them again and see what time I do. It was all in the Plenty area. One loop took me an hour and 20 minutes; another was an hour and five minutes. There was a ride from home to the top of Kinglake that took an hour and nine minutes. It was always a case of, 'Okay, how quickly can I get there?' Before I knew it – before I'd even realised it was a good structure for what was to come – I was doing one-hour intervals. Once I got there, I had to get back as well, so that was the fun, and difficult part, after the real test to see if I could beat the time.

Back then, my goal was to perform at the national level of mountain bike racing so that I could be accepted into the AIS [Australian Institute of Sport] program. I knew that if I could do that, then I could race overseas, get some exposure and then get onto a pro team. That was my plan. If I was able to get into the first 20 in the World Cups regularly, at 17 and 18 years of age, then the teams could see that I was a rider with a fair bit of potential. That was essentially how I could get a contract.

I wanted to go to the AIS but I wasn't selected immediately. I trained as much as I could while I was at school. In year 12 I had Tuesday afternoons when there was a free period which would be the time for my long ride during the week. It was the one day I could do a five-hour ride. Saturdays and Sundays I usually raced so I couldn't do much actual training.

It wasn't until I started going to the AIS that I was doing the strength and high cadence work that I'd started almost by proxy. When I was at the AIS, I was there in a group with the whole day to focus on the ride and make sure it's done properly. Before that it was all about fitting it into my school schedule. The move to the AIS was in 1995 when the mountain bike program started up.

This is the time when digressions often occur for young, gifted athletes. They have other responsibilities and other urges, but Cadel has always loved riding his bike. How did he cope with the issues of peer pressure or the temptation of cars and girls?

It was weird. It was only when I got to the AIS that I hung out with a group of guys who would go out at night and I thought, 'Oh yeah, I'll come along …' but because I never had a habit of going out, it was all rather new to me and still now I don't really like going out too much. It's just a habit and lifestyle thing that you get used to.

For reasons I learned about in my youth, alcoholism was always something that scared me, but then my appreciation of wine is about the only thing that prompted me to drink a little … and sometimes a little too much. It was more of a European mentality that comes from living in Europe. That's when I started drinking: it was out of an appreciation of the combination of good wine and food more than any desire to fit in with a peer group or anything else.

My mother shares a similar opinion but I think her enthusiasm for good food and wine stems from me living in Europe and adopting Italian culture. Now a big family lunch is a part of my life, thanks to my wife.

His timing was perfect. He became good at a sport that was beginning to flourish. He met people who appreciated his talents and could help nurture them. Had he been born just a few years earlier and he might not ever have found the form of cycling that suited his talents so perfectly.

The Australian Institute of Sport (AIS) had been established after what was considered a substandard Olympics by a sports-loving nation. Only four events were won by Australians at the 1984 Olympics. One came from cycling, the elegant team pursuit over 4000 metres contested on the velodrome by four riders who swapped turns of pace as they sped around the concrete banking of the Los Angeles track. Four years later, in Seoul, a different Aussie quartet finished with the bronze medal in a Games which the Eastern Bloc nations didn't boycott. Ahead of them were the Russian and East German teams.

The seeds of the AIS were sown between those two Olympiads,

and the hunt for coaching talent had begun. By 1990 the man responsible for guiding East Germany to three cycling gold medals during the Olympics in Korea had been lured to Australia. Heiko Salzwedel was a young coach from Cottbus. After the fall of the Berlin Wall in 1989 he hoped to escape the confines of the East German system and take his knowledge and experience elsewhere. After a brief tenure as an assistant track cycling coach for the Australian Cycling Federation he was offered a position with the national team. It took considerable negotiation and a fair dose of political wrangling, but Heiko would become the head coach of the national road cycling team. It was a position he cherished. He moved to Canberra with his wife and son, established a base in the Australian capital and set about giving some direction to what had been a relatively neglected component of cycle sport. Until his arrival, track events were given a higher priority over those contested on the road.

Significantly, this also coincided with the time when the Special Broadcasting Service (SBS) claimed the rights to show the Tour de France on television in Australia. Up until 1991, coverage of the three-week event was condensed into a few 15-minute segments and shown as part of Channel Nine's Wide World of Sports program on a Saturday afternoon. Interest was scant on these distant shores because no one had been given the opportunity to see the event unfold. And so, at the time, the only decent coverage of cycling happened only once every four years and, unless the Aussies were winning Olympic medals (which they didn't do in Seoul), cycling on television was almost unheard of.

Initially, SBS opted to show a half-hour highlight package each evening of the Tour de France stage that had been contested the day before. But this was enough to lure people in, and Cadel was one of them.

When I got to see the Tour de France on television, I thought, 'Oh, it would be so cool to ride this race!' Doesn't everyone consider it? If you ride a bike long enough it becomes a dream, or at least the notion is entertained. 'Imagine being in the Tour de France ...' but I had only just started racing a few mountain bike events and it was just a thought thousands of kids have.

Because of the highlights packages, the Tour de France started to generate interest in Australia. Of course road cycling existed before that. There is a rich history of the sport in Australia but the prime years had been left behind. Sir Hubert Opperman and Russell Mockridge are celebrated names in Australian cycling culture, but their times had long since past. With this ground-swell of interest stimulated by the SBS programs, Salzwedel had the right position and sufficient energy not just to help re-ignite interest in road racing but also to make domestic riders realise they could become a force in it.

The former East German had had strict ideas on training but was also very open to new methodologies. He was one of the first to adopt power meters – devices that measured what a rider was capable of and displayed it in wattage. He conducted talent identification camps and was keen to test riders outside a pure race environment inside the precise environment of a laboratory.

Along with his staff, he would conduct tests to measure various physiological aspects of the riders who were interested in road cycling.

At the AIS they did all manner of testing. Some things were completely experimental and, ultimately, not extremely useful. Other methods are still current today. And of all the thousands of riders who passed through the halls of the Institute since those early years, none have ever returned the sort of data that a young Cadel Evans produced during his early screening sessions.

Road cycling, Cadel admitted, was useful because it was good for training. But he wanted to be a mountain biker. And although he had admiration for the likes of Miguel Indurain, at that time winner of five consecutive editions of the Tour de France, he was still most inspired by John Tomac, Ned Overend, Thomas Frischknecht, Bart Brentjens ... the masters of the off-road scene. He was useful as a road rider, but he didn't care; he wanted to be a professional mountain biker.

John Gregory beat him in the cross-country race of the 1994 national championships, the one he should have raced in as a first-year junior. Instead he opted to take on the seniors and see how he fared. Damian Grundy recalls the David-and-Goliath confrontation:

> *It was quite a scene. You had a 17-year-old kid racing a 28-year-old seasoned competitor. John was a full-time professional bike rider in everything but contract. But Cadel was remarkably special, he really was. He's an extraordinarily determined, gifted, focussed rider and it was no longer a case of him being a 'kid with potential';*

he was clearly a rider with a future that was due to start immediately.

At that time we were discussing various elements that would be key in his career. The AIS had just announced a mountain bike program and I had applied and been successful in getting the job as coach. The reason for this new position was that mountain biking would be part of the Olympics for the first time in Atlanta and I can remember the discussions with Cadel about that. In terms of the goal setting and the planning, the potential to go to Atlanta was considered as a bonus – that he might even get onto the team, let alone go there and do anything in terms of performance.

He went. He raced. And he finished ninth. He was in the top 10 and was the youngest in the race.

By then, Damian had stopped being 'one of the MTB pioneers'. He still rode a little but he was no longer racing and although people knew his name, he was known quite simply as: 'Cadel's coach'. He laughs at the thought of that time, although the pair of them took their collaboration very seriously.

Sometimes I wonder if Blind Freddy could have done that job. Cadel is exceptional! Physiologically he's the equivalent of an eight-foot tall basketballer. He's exceptionally gifted genetically and sometimes, on reflection, I wonder if anyone could have taken him to success in racing.

On the other hand, I didn't wreck him, and I know some athletes who have been destroyed before they got anywhere, even before they arrived in the senior ranks, because of overload or pushy coaches. There are any number of reasons but Cadel, and his athletic performances were managed pretty well. He did exceptionally well and continues to do so while riding into his thirties.

Cadel himself doesn't like to consider the numbers too much. He admits that his VO2 max tests were relevant because they proved that he could sustain a long effort at a high power without sustaining too much damage to his muscles from lactic acid. This is what you want from an endurance athlete; it is the best yardstick to use when judging the potential of riders. But the methods vary and the result isn't fair, according to Cadel and many sport scientists, because the parameters used to attain the number can be different. Nonetheless, his optimum has consistently been in the high 80s.

'I'm becoming experienced. I'd say compared to most professional riders I'm motivated and passionate all the time. And in natural ability, yeah, I have what I have, which Dave Martin seems to say is pretty good.' Cadel commented at the time.

Cadel knows that he ranks highly amongst athletes who have been tested at the AIS. From all the sports that are part of the national institute's program – and the list is both varied and long, essentially comprising most of the Olympic disciplines as well as cricket and other sports – he is still rated as 'let's say, one of the best ever tested'.

Dr David Martin, AIS Senior Sports Physiologist, was there from the start. He has been an integral member of an efficient team. The AIS has developed cyclists for every discipline – track, road, MTB, BMX – and there have been remarkable results. The standing of Australian riders in the world league is now rated higher than ever. As we approach the road racing World Championships in Melbourne in 2010, the nation is ranked third in the world. Only Spain and Italy are ahead of Australia. Just prior to the mountain bike worlds being contested in Canberra in 2009, Australia was ranked second in the downhill discipline and ninth in the cross-country. Cadel has been ranked the world's number-one rider both on the road and off it. He has won two cross country mountain bike World Cup series but also the 2007 ProTour crown – the last time that a title in this series included the triple of the Grand Tours (and in which Cadel finished second in France, and fourth in Spain) as well as the World Championships (in which he finished fifth).

Consistency is his key, both in performance and physiology. Take his hematocrit levels (oxygen-carrying capacity of the blood), for example. Hematocrit levels are measured by the blood test that identifies the percentage of the red oxygen carrying blood cells. 'I'm always between 42 and 44,' he says of his hematocrit levels.

I can't say what my next one will be but I know it will be within that range, as it has been for the past 16 years.

It prompts the obvious question: does it vary much during the season? When people are caught with high values, they opt to nominate all sorts of excuses. They say that they're dehydrated or overworked ... so the question arises whether his values alter very much depending on his workload. His comment about his time with Silence–Lotto gives some perspective:

Hopefully you don't get that tired. Normally, if you've got fatigue, you'll know it because you are drained. That's where you notice it first. But obviously, if one of your blood values is going down, it's caused by either fatigue or illness. So our internal testing is one of the things that we do to stay on top of that.

From the early years, he's been subjected to testing. It's part of the drill. It happened on him as much – if not more – than most others in the AIS. First of all, because he was an amazing genetic specimen; and it was good to compare his levels with those of others. But it also happened because he won a lot of races. Throughout it all, his hematocrit remained within the usual parameters.

He became a chart reference during a special time at the AIS, in the lead-up to the Sydney Olympics, when funding and resources had been provided to establish a testing protocol to catch EPO cheats. Before the 2000 Games it was not possible to test for this drug that enriches the supply of oxygen to muscles through the blood. During the study a group of recreational cyclists agreed to be part of a controlled experiment by the AIS's scientists. They answered an advertisement and signed a contract stating that they were not competitive athletes but healthy enthusiasts. One half of the group was injected with a placebo, the other half with EPO. Their blood would be monitored regularly and it helped detect differences in the parameters of the cells, not just the quantity of red blood cells.

They were not AIS athletes. The injections were never done on the facility's campus. None of the AIS doctors had, as AIS

Cycling Physiologist David Martin insists, 'any ability to get their hands on this EPO trial'.

The idea wasn't just to try and find out which of the test subjects had taken EPO; that was known, controlled, strictly monitored and the identities of those in the placebo group and the EPO group were kept confidential. The aim was to monitor the effects of what the drug did to the blood. David Martin explains:

We started to look at the results of accelerating the red blood cell making rate to very high levels. If you start making red blood cells extremely fast, the normal haematological parameters start changing. Instead of looking at the actual EPO itself, you could start looking at the effects of the EPO.

There were no surprises when the EPO group began posting impressive results in the trial. 'They had a higher oxygen uptake, they had a higher hematocrit and they produced a better performance … We knew it was going to work but we were all a bit surprised at just how well it worked,' concluded Dave Martin. 'I had spent six years working with really talented athletes' – and he singled out Cadel Evans as the most exceptional – 'and you see the improvements over that time and they're stunning. But you could replicate those gains in some people with just a four-week course of EPO!'

'If you want to talk about hematocrit,' said Damian Grundy, 'the numbers tell a story. Man, if the guy took drugs and went to 49 or over, and managed it like these other people had been doing, he would be untouchable! And yet he hasn't done that. He's fought to the best of his natural ability, and look how good the guy is.'

He had such ability that, even after only a few meetings with Cadel, Salzwedel was convinced that he'd found a rider with the capabilities of not just performing well at the highest level, but excelling. Salzwedel's appraisal of Cadel is telling:

He was very fragile and single-minded. But in his approach he was very professional. Later on, a long time after I left Australia – when I was working for T-Mobile in my capacity in charge of that team's development program – they asked me about Cadel Evans. They wanted to know if I thought he would fit into the T-Mobile program, and I had some long conversations for some time with the management about him.

There is no doubt about his physical abilities. He always had an exceptional power-to-weight ratio which already made him, even as a mountain bike specialist, one of the best possible chances for a Tour de France overall win. And I'm talking about a time that was 10 years before he made his debut in that race!

People who understood cycling recognised his traits. He is physiologically gifted but, through his own admission, it's not just the ability to be good at something that matters, you've also got to want it and to work for it, and that's what Cadel says he has always done. Salzwedel agrees.

He is gifted. But his strength comes from him having a combination of both an amazing physical capacity and the desire to use it to the maximum of his ability. If you're gifted, it's one thing, but it's also about what you're going to do with this gift. He is a very hard worker. And it is one reason it was a good thing to have the road cyclists and mountain bikers in one group and spending a lot of time together. The different view of both groups stimulated each other. And hard work was always one of my principles. It was always one of the key points I tried to pass on to riders; there's never a clever formula where you can win a race with less training. It was always important to work. That was also one of the points that Cadel really picked up.

Heiko Salzwedel needs little prompting to talk about cycling. He has been passionate about it all his life and from the early days in the Eastern Bloc system, to Australia and several other countries since, he might be described as being a coaching mercenary, but that would only be done by people who didn't know him well. His impact on the sport in Australia should never be underestimated. He, too, has his critics and the politics at the time of his departure were scandalous at worst, unnecessary at best. He would achieve his early objectives and improve the standard of road cyclists from Australia rapidly. At the Barcelona Olympics, only the second time that a women's road race had been contested at the Games, Australian Kathy Watt claimed the gold medal.

In the men's road race Australian Darren Smith, who had been a BMX racer, finished tenth. That was his final national representation. He was killed later that year in a traffic accident on the Gold Coast Highway. He was fast, gracious, young and formidable. A close mate of his vowed to follow the lead and improve upon what 'Smithy' achieved before his death at the age of 20 years and two months.

Robbie McEwen had raced with Darren Smith in BMX days

and later joined him in the 'new pursuit of road cycling'. McEwen missed the Barcelona Olympics but would later join Heiko's team. McEwen raced with Salzwedel's Australian National Road Team until signing on with Rabobank for the 1996 season. He made his Tour debut the following year and at the very end of his third start in the race – on the Champs-Élysées on the last day of the 1999 Tour – he won his first stage. It would be his last appearance for Rabobank in the Tour. He joined Farm Frites for 2000, which became Domo–Farm Frites in 2001, but he was omitted from the Tour line-up, so he moved on and signed up with what became Lotto–Adecco in 2002. Then he won the Australian national championship, four stages of the Tour Down Under, the overall title of his first race in Europe (Étoile de Bessèges), two stages of the Giro d'Italia (Tour of Italy), and two stages of the Tour de France (including the final one on the Champs-Élysées) as well as the green jersey as winner of the points classification. He became one of the Lotto team's finest investments and went on to win another nine stages of the Tour and two more green jerseys (in 2004 and again in 2006) while with the team. He was a co-leader of the team until Cadel Evans demonstrated that he could possibly win the title, and then Robbie became a *domestique* for his younger compatriot.

Robbie is just one of 'Salzwedel's originals'. There are other Australians who have excelled on the international scene since being part of the AIS system. It was Salzwedel who fought hard to increase the level of road cycling at a time when SBS was broadcasting the Tour, inspiring and educating Australians about the beauty of a race that had captivated European sports fans for years. And slowly interest increased. It's uncertain if it has yet reached its zenith but the signs are that it continues to grow in popularity each year, with significant spurts each July.

More Australians ride bikes for recreation than to race, but still, the level of participation on all levels – and across all disciplines – continues to grow. Heiko, Robbie and Cadel can take some credit for this explosion of interest. Each played their own part in the evolution of cycling in this part of the world. And the influence of the cycling facility of the AIS program in Canberra was pivotal in allowing each of them to progress and achieve what they did.

After Salzwedel left Australia in 1998, he worked briefly for British Cycling before moving to Denmark to take care of the national track cycling team up until the 2008 Olympics in Beijing. He then returned to the heavily-funded British squad and, once again, began following the quadrennial cycle of preparing riders for another Olympiad. All the while he maintained contact with the Aussie riders with whom he had established a special bond. Cadel was one of them, but the wandering German was never really close to the mountain biker who he helped in his formative years. The two have many common threads yet there is a distance between the pair despite a successful partnership during the AIS years.

By the time Heiko had departed, Cadel was already living in Europe and starting to consider a change of disciplines, but first he had a few MTB World Cups to win, and an Olympics in

Sydney to consider. He would end up at Saeco on a part-time basis – riding in road races between his commitments on the mountain bike circuit. All along he maintained close contact with Grundy and Salzwedel's successors, always undergoing regular tests as one of the AIS's original guinea pigs. And each time any blood was withdrawn, he showed the same readings as the time before. He was not, as a future *directeur sportif* laughingly suggested, lost.

His blood was pure. His intentions were good. And his approach was honest.

Cadel met Heiko because the AIS had decided to merge a newly created MTB program, created in response to cross-country having been accepted into the Olympics, with the road cycling corp that had come of age after Salzwedel's arrival. Initially this concept, which was first considered at the start of 1994, didn't impress Salzwedel:

> *When we started having to incorporate mountain biking into our program, I was not very keen on the idea. I didn't want the mountain bike riders mixed together with my very, very serious road cyclists.*

He laughs aloud at the memory. He had progressive, contemporary ideas when it came to coaching, but he was from the Eastern Bloc. He had traditional views. He admits it himself; he was from the 'old school':

> *I was led to believe that the mountain bikers were a bunch of partygoers, that they were a group of guys who loved life but they didn't*

really like to put a real effort into the sport. But it was made an Olympic discipline in 1996 and that changed the whole sport.

Serious cycling was done in a velodrome. Real cycling was done on the road. Salzwedel had coached endurance athletes in both disciplines. He had been to the Olympics. His riders won medals and he didn't originally want any off-road impostors coming in to spoil his grand plan. But then he had an awakening.

It didn't take long for my opinion to change. I think it was a very good thing to have the mountain bike program in Canberra. When I first went to the Australian Mountain Bike Championships in the Snowy Mountains I saw something special unfold. It was something that prompted me to start rethinking my road cycling program, actually. After a road cycling competition, 90 per cent of people went home miserable because they didn't make the top-10 places, whereas in the mountain bike scene 90 per cent of the participants went home after having had a great weekend in a very competitive environment.

You could ride a bike, race it even, and have a lot of fun. It was a revelation. Until then, sport was only about achieving very specific targets: Olympic medals paid his bills. He had always needed to prove that his methods were working. And the only way to do so convincingly was to return to base after every four-year cycle with a haul he and his athletes could be proud of.

The mountain bikers were having fun. They were impressive athletes. And now there was serious potential to win medals, so 'from that point of view, after my first hesitation was over, I was really thrilled to have the mountain bike program in Canberra, especially to have Cadel Evans in that group.'

Damian Grundy's transformation would soon become complete. After his meeting with Salzwedel he stopped riding competitively and was put in charge of the MTB program and the one-time pioneer teamed up well with the former East German track cycling coach. 'I can only speak in compliments when it comes to Damian Grundy. What he did back in the old days was quite tremendous.'

The coaches were pivotal in establishing an environment that promoted co-operation between the diverse groups of cyclists and encouraged cross-training. 'There were many good things about having the mountain bike and road cycling programs together, but one aspect was that it opened up the opportunities for Cadel,' says Salzwedel. 'It exposed him to other forms of the sport and opened his mind towards road cycling. When I first met him he was all about one thing: mountain bike, mountain bike ... mountain biking! There was nothing else as far as he was concerned. He had no relationship with road cycling.' But this would soon change.

Cadel and the other early-generation AIS mountain bike athletes, including John Gregory, Paul Rowney and Mary Grigson, were encouraged by Heiko Salzwedel and Damian Grundy to race road events. It was a strategy that had benefits in developing their strength as well as giving them some diversity. And, again, Cadel became a standout performer. In a happy coincidence – another example of the good timing of the young athlete's progression

– he demonstrated that he wasn't just a good off-road rider, he was an extraordinary cyclist. Salzwedel takes up the story:

I had always tried to encourage my riders to try out all that was available to them. I put road cyclists on mountain bikes, especially during the preparation period because I noticed that the mountain bikers had a big advantage over the road cyclists when it came to power-to-weight ratio, when it comes to really getting into strength and endurance training. So I did a lot of that sort of work with the road riders on mountain bikes. And also vice-versa, the mountain bikers did a lot of training with the road cyclists on the road. It was beneficial in both ways. I also encouraged the mountain bikers to do some road races as well.

Suddenly an opportunity to test Cadel's form came up. He was still a junior rider in those days but we still found that he was one of the biggest talents that mountain biking had to offer so we included him in the AIS mountain bike program from the very beginning. Somehow he also qualified for the road cycling junior World Championships which were to be held in San Marino in 1995.

During the season I made a point of maintaining contact with Cadel. I had been on the phone to him and was talking to him about a couple of things. Purely from a motivational perspective, I was offering him a few suggestions on events that might suit him and I asked, 'Do you want to try out Robbie McEwen's time trial bike?'

Cadel was always really very specific with his equipment. He was a freak about his products, but immediately, when he heard 'Robbie McEwen's time trial bike', he said, 'Yes! I want to try that!'

I said, 'Okay.'

The next day I pulled the wheels off the bike and threw it in my car and I drove over from where I was staying in Koblenz, Germany to where the national team was based during a bout of racing and training in Italy.

It was one week before the junior World Championships.

He had never been on a time trial bike before in his life. But he hopped on and immediately said, 'Yes! I love this bike. I want to ride it at the World Championships!'

For a proper road cyclist, this is unheard of. You don't just jump on a time trial bike – one that was used by someone else – and, just a week before the World Championships, declare: 'This is great. I'll give it a try.' But Cadel did exactly that.

He looked really good on that bike. We made a few small adjustments, raised the saddle a little and so on, and he had a reasonable position instantly. Even then he had great flexibility and he was able to find a good stance.

He had no idea how to ride a time trial, let me remind you of that! I had a chat with him before the race and told him, 'Cadel, it's not like mountain biking where you really jump out of the blocks full-on. You've got to settle in, find your threshold level, go a little above that if you can and then power your way through. But do not start too hard.'

'Okay. Okay,' he told me.

But he's a racer. Cadel cannot resist. He loves to compete. He stood on the starting line and went out of the blocks like a rocket! He had the fastest five kilometres by far. He was well ahead of everyone. He had overpaced himself a little bit but then faded towards the finish. Still, he managed to finish third. It was a great result for Cadel, but physically, I'm absolutely certain that he could have won the World Championship that year.

But the thought had never occurred to him until a few days before the race. To have seen what I did was impressive. He had an amazing ability.

He had no concept of what was involved in a time trial but he had a determination. He could really squeeze the best out of himself. He was so motivated. He could really hurt himself. It was one of the things that I noticed about him even in training. It was confirmed every time I watched him in competition.

9
The pink years

Fulfilling the promise

He was the most consistent cross-country mountain bike professional of the season in 1998 and 1999. Cadel had been enlisted
by Cannondale and it was on this team that he truly built his
world-beating reputation. It was in the Volvo–Cannondale team
that he won his World Cup titles. It was with this squad – sponsored by a car company and a US bike manufacturer – that he set
his sights on the Sydney Olympics. It was as part of this roster
that he captured the imagination of fans around the world. And it
was here that he found contentment … for a few years at least.

The influence Cadel exerted even at the start of his career
because he could ride a bike well was impressive. His primary goal
was to win races. But by chasing the rainbow jersey, by competing,
by being an ambassador for the sport, he acquired a following.
Mike Cotty now works for Cannondale. He rides. He races. He is
passionate about many things but above all, he cannot get enough
of the bike.

'He's the reason I do what I do.'

Mike has never met Cadel. But he explains the influence that the Australian has had on his life:

As an easily influenced teenager, with dreams of being a pro, it didn't take long before one team – and one rider in particular – would influence my life more than I could ever have imagined. The world-conquering Volvo–Cannondale Mountain Bike Team was the pinnacle of mountain bike racing. 'Übercool' just doesn't come close to describing what it was like. This squad were far beyond that. I remember gazing at pictures of the fat-tubed Cannondale hardtails with HeadShok Fatty forks, glossy blue paintwork and yellow decals for hours. Just thinking about it now makes my heart beat a little faster as I smile with nostalgia. The team truck was a veritable work of art. The outside was emblazoned with sponsors, rider's names and country flags. I longed to get a glimpse inside, to see what it was like, but maybe not knowing kept the mystique and my dream alive for longer.

It wasn't until 1998 when Round 5 of the Grundig World Cup came to Newnham Park, Plymouth, UK that I got a chance to witness top-level racing first hand.

I was nervous with excitement on the drive to the venue and wanted to visit the Volvo–Cannondale team immediately but instead decided to unpack my bike and ride a couple of laps of the course. For every pedal stroke my mind was consumed with thoughts and dreams. I then visited all of the other teams in turn and finally, when I felt ready, rolled over to The Truck. I stood in awe. It was even cleaner in real life. Bikes was immaculately lined up outside, energy bars and bottles on a table under the awning. Turbo trainers were set up with spare bikes ready for duty. The door slowly opened, with each rider revealed one by one to the fans with autograph books and t-shirts ready to be signed.

Juarez, Sauser, Sydor, Giove, Chausson, Gracia. The number of iconic riders in the team is long. But for me there was only one rider – a rider I felt I could relate to more than any of the others.

Maybe it was because he was English speaking and just a couple of years older than I was. Maybe it was because he had the fight to rip the heart out of the dominant Sunn–Chipie team from France. Maybe it was simply because I liked the way he rode a bike. Head down, arms bent, in the red from the moment the gun went. He couldn't hide the pain; there was no poker face; it was guts, grit and determination all the way. I could see how much he wanted it in his eyes and shared the jubilation when he won.

'I loved those years. I'll always love those years,' Cotty declares. Cadel was part of a team he loved and good results were common in races, but after a few years cracks were beginning to emerge. The connection with Cannondale helped him form a relationship with Saeco – an elite-level Italian road cycling team that was also sponsored by the US bicycle manufacturer, and after the Olympics he reached an accord: when time permitted, he could mix in some professional road racing to his program. The focus for 2001 was to be the cross-country events at the World Cup. But his motivation for the off-road scene was beginning to wane. He didn't win a race in the series but finished on the podium a couple of times. In the meantime, there were several victories in his adopted discipline of road racing.

He won the Traverse Lausanne in Switzerland beating, among others, Lance Armstrong. But before that he'd claimed a mountain stage of the Tour of Austria at Kitzbüheler Horn as well as winning the general classification (GC) and the GC of the inaugural Brixia Tour in Italy.

Cadel has what he calls his EMC theory on the three key elements that are required from professionals. It could apply to most vocations but he relates it to what he knows: cycling teams. It needn't matter if it's road cycling or mountain biking, the principles apply equally:

The three major elements are: experience, motivation/passion and capability; if you're looking for a rider or a soigneur *(a rider's masseur and personal support person) or a mechanic it's the same consideration.*

Having more or less of one aspect can directly affect the others. And he looks for the right mix:

Passion can make up for the other two; someone who is passionate but doesn't have great capability will do their maximum to get the right result. Conversely, there can be someone who has a great deal of talent but if they don't want to use it – if they don't train or they don't put the research into it and they just go through the motions – then the best result is never achieved.

And while motivation – or passion – can subside, if it was there in the first place then that means that they would have also acquired some degree of capability along the way. Even if they're losing interest, they have the experience to do the job anyway. What you need to find is the highest mix of the three.

For the sake of explanation, let's say we're looking for a mechanic. A young guy applies. His experience is okay. And, in time, capability will grow but only if he has motivation, so that's important. Whereas, say there's another mechanic who is old and experienced. Capability is high because he's been doing it for so long but maybe his motivation is low. Who is going to do a better job?

He likes his EMC theory. He graphs some of the people he knows in a variety of roles and offers an appraisal. Dario Cioni and Charlie Wegelius rank very highly when the discussion of the perfect *domestique* is considered. They will turn themselves inside out to do their job. They are both motivated and have experience. When it comes to himself, he recognises his strengths – capability is high, experience continues to grow as it does for everyone, and motivation is also high. 'It does change. It unfortunately cannot be constant.'

If you have twice won the MTB World Cup and there are teams lobbying to have you on their roster for an entirely new challenge … there's a chance to work on that EMC formula again. Experience is low. Motivation is high. Capacity is there!

In 2001, it was time for a change.

The blue Cannondale with suspension on the front and fat tyres was swapped for a rigid red frame and skinny tyres. Once he'd decided it was time to change, he wanted to do so immediately. He had done mountain biking and loved it for eight years, but another cycle of his life was about to begin. His first taste of success was off the road but it was on the road that he would take his capacity to a higher level.

———————

'I remember one season before the 2000 Olympics when I thought he was growing up,' says Damian Grundy about the realisation that the boy was becoming a man. 'There was a change in the athlete/coach relationship and it got to a point where I thought, "Cadel, you know what you're doing and what needs to be done. In the pre-season, what we could do is just give you some respon-sibility." He was keen to continue the discussion. I told him I'd set the volume: this week you have to do x kilometres, and next week you need to do y, and the week after, z. And he knew enough of what we'd done to be able to manage each week on his own, and I was going to let it fit in with his schedule.

He lasted about four days before he called in a panic. 'Damian, I just can't do this. You have to tell me what I've got to do each day. I can't do it like this!'

He was quite agitated. He needed the prescription: he needed to know what he was doing each day. And he would fit his schedule around that. With other athletes that I've coached there are always excuses about why they can't do something asked of them because they're busy with something else. Everyone else that I've coached would try to get out of some part of the routine, but this was never an issue with Cadel. I don't ever recall a conversation of that kind with him. We would discuss his schedule for his team and often these have very little to do with training; it's more about media, meeting sponsors, and schmoozing – there's often little time to actually ride the bike.

He would get the schedules from the team and explain what was on when, and I would set the training appropriately. And he would do it.

Over eight years of coaching prescriptions for Cadel every day, there would have been less than five occasions when he would have rung me to say, 'Look, I'm really tired and I don't know if I'm going to get done with what you're asking.'

I can also recall him once calling me after a training session and saying, 'Hey, I went out today and it just wasn't happening so I came home.'

Never did I say 'That was terrible.' It's common sense. And the approach that we developed very early was that the training plan is the training plan and we were not going to change it. It is structured to generate the right adaptation and responses, and if you're always changing it and the sequences become majorly disrupted, then the training plan is worthless.

His approach, his capacity, was first-class even at the end of his mountain biking days, but he was ready for a change of scene. With his victories in Lausanne and Austria, he had earned a reputation as a rider with a lot of promise. Exactly how far he could go, he wasn't sure, but the challenge provided fresh motivation.

Another test for the new road cyclist was adapting to the different culture of road cycling. A move away from his isolated nature needed to be nurtured if he was going to make it work in this team sport.

Cadel ended the 2001 season with a second place in the Japan Cup behind the winner of that year's Giro d'Italia, Gilberto Simoni. By then his defection from the MTB scene was almost complete. He had signed a contract to race for the Mapei team for 2002 and was being primed as a *domestique* for the Giro d'Italia.

Mapei had a formidable line-up in 2002 that included the rider who would go on to win three World Cup titles on the road, the Olympic road race at the Olympics in Athens and two world championships, Paolo Bettini. Others on the line-up were Stefano Garzelli, Fabian Cancellara, Paolo Fornaciari, the reigning world champion Óscar Freire, Miguel Martinez, an earlier mountain biking competitor, compatriot and gold medallist in the madison from the Sydney 2000 Olympics (the only cycling victory for the host nation in Sydney) Scott McGrory, Classics legend Andrea Tafi and other future team-mates, Charlie Wegelius and Dario Cioni.

This was where he was expected to add a dose of experience to his formidable other strengths. He just didn't expect that he would find himself propelled so quickly into the status of leader.

The Giro d'Italia began in Groningen, the capital city of a province of the same name in the north of the Netherlands. It was a distant start for the Italian Grand Tour. Clad in the Mapei colours, Cadel finished 16th in the prologue, the best result of the team. The leader of the squad was the 2000 champion, Stefano

Garzelli, who finished 22nd on Day 1 – three seconds behind his Australian colleague. In the first stage, from Groningen to Münster in Germany, the Italian sprinting showman Mario Cipollini beat two Aussies – Graeme Brown and Robbie McEwen – to take the win. And then came Garzelli's chance to shine. After the 209-kilometre race from Cologne in Germany to Liège in Belgium, the leader of Mapei claimed the stage victory and took over the lead of the general classification. He was in pole position already and the three-week event was only three days old. But his reign wouldn't last; 29 nanograms of probenecid was found in his urine. It's a product that very nearly cost Pedro Delgado his 1988 Tour de France title. Although it doesn't enhance a rider's performance it is considered a masking agent for steroids. It was not on the list of banned products when Delgado was found with it in his system, but by 2002 it was officially an illegal substance.

Garzelli was labelled positive and promptly evicted from the race before the sixth stage. Even before his eviction a number of riders had been tossed off the race for EPO use but they were relatively minor players. But when the mighty Mapei team was implicated, including the rider in the *maglia rosa* denoting the leader of the race, it rocked the sport. The race continued. The Mapei team remained on the start list. But it had lost direction.

'When Garzelli had to go home, Andrea Noè and I were in a position where both of us were in contention to be the team captain,' explained Cadel at the time. The Italian had experience. He had finished fourth and sixth, respectively, in the two previous editions. The Australian was making his debut in a three-week race, as a first-year professional or 'neo pro', so a selection policy of sorts was drafted.

'It was sensible to race for him,' said Cadel about Andrea. 'With me, the team just wanted to see how I'd go. Maybe I would improve when we got to the mountains. Perhaps I'd have a good time trial. It was a hard decision to make.

'With road racing,' Cadel observed in January 2002, 'it's all about individuals within a group. It's a real team mentality where you're really putting yourself on the line to help someone else. Doing what you want is great, but I'd been in a situation like that for eight years.'

The decision was made to make the two equal leaders up until the 14th stage, a 30-kilometre time trial. And whoever was ranked best in that test would earn the status as protected rider. Just one day before the designated deciding race against the clock, Cadel had finished second in a mountain stage that had been won by the Mexican climbing specialist Julio Perez Cuapio (a member of the team that had two EPO positives before the Groningen start). The Australian was ranked fifth overall after 13 stages. The Italian was 16th. Already it was becoming clear who the most capable rider was, and it had nothing to do with experience.

Then came Mapei's deciding stage. Tyler Hamilton won. Sergei Gontchar was second. Cadel Evans was third, and Andrea Noè was 13th. On GC, Cadel was ranked second, 48 seconds behind Jens Heppner of the Deutsche Telekom team. Cipollini would win a sprint the next day and there would be no change to GC after Stage 15. But then came the epic journey taking in the 2239-metre high Passo Pordoi and the 1875 metre Passo di Campolongo before a fast descent to the finish. Cadel finished seventh but Heppner collapsed and the pink jersey was presented to an Australian for the first time in history.

At the particular moment I got the jersey, it was a bit surreal. There was so much going on that it was all a little confusing. 'Where am I going? Oh, I'm going to the podium? You want me to stand up there … ? Oh look what I've got! I don't have to wear my Mapei jersey; I've got another one!'

—————

Before he expected to, Cadel was experienced. He would feel what it's like to be the centre of the cycling universe. He would wear the *maglia rosa* in the third week of the Giro d'Italia. He would be the leader of the Mapei team. He would never forget that day … for that's just how long his reign lasted. One of the more spectacular collapses of a rider poised to win a major title occurred on the final major climb of the 2002 Giro. The Passo Coe will forever be part of Cadel's history. At the base of the climb, he appeared to be riding within his limits. The 222-kilometre 17th stage has some fearsome climbs. With five major passes on the itinerary, it was to be the deciding day of that year's race.

After almost seven hours of racing, Evans appeared as though he would survive the stage. He had marked his rivals to perfection for 210 kilometres. He responded to surges, matched accelerations, and led with panache.

Midway up the final ascent, he was still in a position to end the day in pink. If he could do that it was highly likely that the Mapei's leader by default would be the winner of the 85th Giro d'Italia. But …

After seven hours of racing in the mountains it was starting to hurt. Noè was upping the pace – pushing harder and harder to stop any attacks – and I left a bit of a gap. I wouldn't say I was feeling really tired, I was just talking on the radio and lost a little bit of concentration. Hamilton saw the gap and he went on the attack. Then, all of a sudden, bang! My lights went out.

When Hamilton attacked, I had to make another surge and that was the very last drop of fuel. I was completely empty.

In the final seven kilometres of Stage 17 of the 2002 Giro d'Italia, Cadel lost 17 minutes and 11 seconds. He would finish the stage riding on auto-pilot. Barely able to turn the pedals, he was weaving up the road. He later admitted to seeing virtually nothing of the climb. His mind was blank. His legs were turning, but he had none of the usual sensations. 'I was *completely* empty.'

It was a phenomenal display. It was outstanding. It was a revolution for cycling in an era when riders seemed to have limitless supplies of energy. He was human.

He virtually stopped pedalling because he had reached his limit. And when that happens, there's nothing that can be done but hope you survive and have enough pain tolerance to reach the end.

Cadel looks back over what he can remember of the ride over the Passo Coe in 2002:

I can recall what happened that day, but there are missing elements. I know it was a long day. And I remember the attacks. And I was aware that I was losing the lead of the race. My mind took control of my body. I had nothing left in the legs but as a cyclist, you just keep going until the finish. I kept reminding myself that I had to get to the finish.

It was painful for him to do and upsetting to watch yet it was oddly compelling to see a man who had reached his limit continue to ride. In a daze he pushed on. It seemed like the finish would never come.

Men who had been dropped on the climbs preceding the final one would pass him and gain time. Riders who had thought that the Australian had effectively won the title would ride alongside him, checking that he was okay and then, politely, continue on ahead.

The stage was won by Pavel Tonkov, and the *maglia rosa* want to Paolo Savoldelli. And Cadel would finish 41st, supported by Noè and his old mate from the mountain biking days, Dario Cioni. When he eventually reached the finish line, he continued to pedal. His *soigneur* chased after him. And Cioni tried to put a jacket over his friend but Cadel just kept on riding. By then his mind was dominating his body: ride, it told him. Ride! And that's all he knew. It wasn't until he'd gone a few hundred metres uphill beyond the finish line that someone was finally able to convince him that it was all over. He had reached the end. He could stop.

———————

The road cycling world received an important introduction to Cadel by witnessing what unfolded on the Passo Coe. People got to see an honest performance. It was spectacular, but it was a collapse. There have been few such examples of an overall leader faltering to such an extent after coming so close to victory. One of the key members of the Australian's team was Dario Cioni. He is an Italian who was born in Reading, England and was a rival during the mountain bike days, but he had longer dalliances with road racing thanks to his involvement with a Mapei-sponsored MTB team. He rode for Mapei as a *stagiaire* – an apprentice – in 1996 when he was just 21 years old. He then raced a few years with the Mapei–Kona off-road team in 1997 and joined the Mapei–Quickstep road squad in 2000. Cadel came to join him in 2002. The pair would later ride two seasons together at Predictor–Lotto in 2007 and Silence–Lotto in 2008. They remain close friends. Cioni was there on that day on the Passo Coe.

Dario Cioni spoke about the day of the collapse on Passo Coe, in Stage 17 of the Giro d'Italia 2002:

> *I was to ride to the second-to-final climb and then Noè was the last man left to help Cadel. Basically my job was to ride tempo over the fourth of the five passes that day. Two of them were over 2000 metres high and the others were also very hard. I needed to get to the base of Passo Bordala. It was quite steep and then there was a difficult descent, a flat section and then we started the Passo Coe. It was to Folgaria and then up to the top.*
>
> *It was up to me to ride as hard as possible and maybe, if I had the legs, to the last climb. Then there was still Noè and Cadel himself to*

do the job. There was a breakaway and the second-to-last climb was quite steep, so I just rode tempo to be sure it was fast enough to stop the others from attacking – or, if they did, I was to go fast enough to ensure they wouldn't get too far ahead.

Eventually Tonkov attacked but, coming up to the main break, we made it to the top and he just floated a little bit in front of us. He never got that much time anyway.

We knew it would be difficult. It was the stage that would decide the Giro. Cadel had the pink jersey and we had a lot of confidence in him. It had been a very hard and strange Giro d'Italia because of several reasons. When we started out, we were meant to be riding for Garzelli, and then there was that strange positive case that ruined our original plans and Cadel came out good. He eventually took the pink jersey, to everyone's surprise. Most of the team thought that the Giro was over when Garzelli went away. But Cadel had some good rides in the Dolomites and Passo Coe would be the deciding climb.

At the beginning, Cadel's position was to be a key man in the mountains for Garzelli. He was never there specifically to be a leader; it was his first Grand Tour. He had a really difficult season up until then anyway. He had started the season at the Tour Down Under, and he was very good in the races he did in France, Italy and Spain. The team had faith in him and he started a lot of events. In the early season he was solid and posted some impressive results.

We had started the Giro with a clear leader and Cadel was to be one of the key men for Garzelli in the mountains, but then he proved that he could be even better. But I don't think anyone expected that he could get into the pink jersey.

When the collapse happened I wasn't sure what had happened. It was a strange sequence and it was presented to me in such a way that it's still quite curious when I consider it. At the moment his lights went out I wasn't with him. I had done my job. I caught up to him one and a half kilometres from the end.

Before that I pulled at the front of the peloton for about 30 kilometres on my own, setting up a good tempo. Of course, when I did my job it's not that I just stayed there and tried to follow the leaders. When I've done what the team tells me to do, I've given everything. That's what a domestique *is supposed to do. It was not for me to have anything left. My race would stop at the base of the last climb, if I was good. But I had to give all of what I had by then to limit the risk of an assault from his rivals. When I'm done, I take it as easy as possible. I go into energy savings mode. That is how I've been taught: to ride, do your job and then save energy for the days that follow. I started the last climb leading the front group and then when I said, 'Okay, I'm finished,' Noè started to ride. And I took it as easy as possible. I put the chain on the biggest cog on my cluster and I switched to survival mode. I wasn't even looking at the groups going by or considering the riders who were going past me.*

I could hear on the radio that Dario Frigo had cracked before Cadel did. And then I thought it was good; he was the last real threat to GC. Then I heard that Hamilton had attacked and I heard them tell Cadel on the radio, 'Okay, go tempo. And keep them in sight …' and then the distance was growing and the radio signal was no longer too clear. I thought, 'Okay, he's losing a bit of time but he's got a bit of time to play with …' The rider we were most afraid of was Frigo anyway, so he had a time cushion and there was still a time trial to come. Cadel was good in that. He could retrieve any lost ground. I was still content. Sure, he's losing time but it's not a big deal. I continued to ride as easy as possible.

Eventually it started to seem a little strange. I got near the top to where there were some big crowds, and with about two kilometres to go I saw a car – the team car – ahead of me. I thought, 'Huh, that's strange. It must have a breakdown.' I really thought it was a mechanical issue with the team car. I thought that's why it was stopped.

I was still riding up slowly and then, at one point, I thought I saw pink. No. It's not possible. It must be a spectator. And then, as I got closer and closer I realised it was Cadel. He had Noè near him. Then I started to understand what had happened. In no time, I had caught up with him. And he looked terrible. There was nothing we could do but ride with him; support him; talk to him; encourage him to reach the finish. He had the leader's jersey. He was our team captain, and it was difficult for him.

I stayed there with him and tried to get him to the finish. I remember quite clearly telling him, 'Come on, Cadel, you're almost there. Great job. Anyway …'

The day after he told me, 'I know you were speaking to me but I could not hear what you were saying.' He was so blanked out that he couldn't connect any more. He had really collapsed. He was going very, very slow.

It was not as though I thought he would fall. No. It wasn't quite that bad, but I could understand that he was in discomfort.

Sometimes I've felt like that. I've seen riders where you know that they're going to be in big trouble to make the time limit. I had a similar experience on L'Alpe d'Huez and it's not nice. It is a pain to talk about such moments when you just cannot find the energy to turn the pedals, when the gradient is pushing you backwards and you struggle. People who ride understand how it can feel. It is cramp. It is the limit. The end. No sensation comes to your legs and the world looks blank ahead of you.

He was not a failure. His season had not been managed so that he was in perfect form just for the Giro.

I think what he did anyway was amazing. Just to be able to ride, not as the leader, and then continue to improve so much that he went up the rankings until he was the best man in the race. The team was just thinking, 'Okay, we'll take him to the Giro and see what he can do.' It was an experiment. No one really believed he could do what he did. But he really made it. Him taking pink was a great achievement and it proved that he was really going to do something in the future.

In Italy it was a big surprise. It's not often that a newcomer to the road scene can lead the Giro d'Italia.

He had been a World Cup winner in the mountain bikes so it's not that it could be said that he was a nobody, but it was a surprise that someone from an entirely different background could make such an amazing impression in his first full season as a road cycling professional. It's not often that a rider with such little experience can do something like that. It's not that he got the pink jersey by getting in a break and gaining minutes on the other favourites. He had fought for it as a leader.

Once you have finished the race it is easy to say, 'Maybe we made a mistake here or there,' but that's the race situation. When you are inside the peloton, you don't have a clear vision of all the circumstances. That is what you get with hindsight. When you sit down and analyse the stages, you can calculate where losses happened, but by then there's nothing you can do about it. That was the case in 2002 and it is the same for what happened in 2007 and 2008 at the Tour de France. He thought he could win but he is human. He has grace and there is strength — both in character and in a very physical reality — and it's amazing to have been part of that ride.

It must be kept in mind that, in the race, you're going through the act and you try to close gaps or follow attacks but you've got to be able to ride within yourself. It's no help to consider things afterwards.

From one perspective it's a shame that he was second in the Tour twice, especially when it was so close each time; with one minute less in two Tours, he would have been the champion!

Still, it's difficult to say that he lost here or there. He might have lost some time during one stage but he could have gained time elsewhere. A tour is a tour. It's not a single day event. A lot of things must go well all the way from start to finish and it's not just in the race that things matter. It's what happens beforehand, and after the stages, and in the evenings, and with the staff, and with the team-mates and managers and the media and everything else that's part of the package. It's complicated.

10

Behind every great man ...

Emotional fulfilment

'I don't think Cadel trusts a lot of people. It's not like he is suspicious or paranoid, but it takes time and effort to earn a place in his heart.' Hendrik Redant has become a close friend. Like anyone who has a close association with another person, there are times when the two have conflicting opinions or they vent their frustration about certain things that affect what they do. They don't spend a lot of time together but when they do see each other, it's for a reason or during an important time. The rider needs to have trust in their *directeur sportif.* Without trust, the relationship is worth nothing. Cadel and Hendrik have become friends. The Belgian is 15 years older. He was a professional cyclist. He has been through a separation with a long-term partner during the time that he has known Cadel, and it cost him dearly. The lovely house he proudly owned was lost in the settlement and Redant admits that he had to start all over again. But he's happy.

Hendrik shares several traits with Cadel. Honesty is one of them. Through sincerity they have been able to bond. That's not to say that the two act like a happy couple, but it's difficult to be annoyed by the former rider who has always been the man calling the shots during the years in which Cadel has contested the Tour de France.

I know he trusts me. I don't try to mislead him. His goal is our goal and that's why he can have confidence that I won't fuck with him.

The relationship between a rider and a *directeur* is a curious one. There are some showmen in the peloton – on and off the bike – who like to make a race seem as though it's born from a Hollywood script. There are some riders who like to attract attention. They recognise that it can help them to make a name for themselves and for those who are capable of managing it to suit their agenda; such an approach has its rewards.

There are also some *directeurs* who like to milk publicity when the opportunity presents itself. There are sponsors to satisfy and if exposure translates to satisfaction, then some will chase coverage by putting on a performance that offers nothing to the rider they're supporting, but it makes for good television or provides an anecdote that can be relayed and exaggerated, told and perpetuated for years to come. But between Hendrik and Cadel, it's just the facts.

I will never lie to him for the sake of the show. He doesn't respond to that. 'Come on! You're 15 seconds down. Come on, go faster!' It doesn't help. No one needs those distractions in a time trial. Maybe he will go faster for 15 seconds longer and he just gets in the red and he blows himself up.

Exchanges between the team car and the riders in the peloton offer a little mystique. It is one aspect of the sport that varies significantly between one squad and the next. And Hendrik's honest approach suits Cadel perfectly. The show goes on but there's no sign of any showman.

I give information. Sometimes I give some encouragement. If rivals are being dropped, I'll tell them but I won't get emotional about it. I will say it as it is: 'Kirchen has been dropped. That's good guys. We can take the yellow jersey ... ' But I'm not going to sing about it.

'I won't ever say: 'Oh! Come on Cadel – you can do it. This one is for your wife and for your mother and for your dog! They will love you more if you win!' It's bullshit. I just want him to know what he has to do and he can respond to that.

Chiara and Helen and Molly will love Cadel if he wins or loses. Cycling is a part of his life. It consumes him. But there is a lot more to the man than just being able to ride a bike well. Although there are many people who have been attracted to him or intrigued by what he does, the person who matters most to him didn't care about cycling at all before he came into her life.

Chiara Passerini married Cadel Evans on 8 September 2005, less than two months after he proposed on the Champs-Élysées. She never expected to be a cyclist's wife but knows that she won't be one forever. For the moment, part of her routine includes considering elements of his day and making sure that she has the time to do things in a partnership that is centred on his goals. 'There is only so long that a person can race a bike for a job,' she says.

We have talked about the future and there will come a time when

I will expect that his world will revolve around me. I've seen him experience a lot of emotions because of how seriously he takes cycling, but I don't let it get to me. Okay, if he's nervous, so am I. But I can remove myself from it. I enjoy the good, get annoyed at the bad but also realise that it's only for a limited time.

The couple are uncertain about what the future will hold once cycling stops being the central theme of daily life. Chiara has accepted that, until he retires, bike racing and all that goes along with it will consume her life.

She helps with filling in his athlete's whereabouts forms, and knows the best ways to wash a pair of knicks covered in the salt of sweat or sprays of mud. Chiara is there to help Cadel in every aspect of his job. He has a team that caters to some of his needs and accepts some of his quirks, but they don't love him like she does. It's impossible for any organisation to be everything that his wife is.

It can seem suffocating, but she can remove herself from it and recharge. There's no need for her to watch every minute of the races he does when they're broadcast. At times it may happen that way, but if he's away racing or training then she takes the chance to return to what she knew before he happened to her life.

I had never met any sports people before Cadel. He was the only one.

She sings in a choir. She plays the piano. She is a typical Italian girl who happens to have long (natural) blonde hair, the voice of an angel and the patience of a saint. When she explains how their first encounter came about it doesn't sound as though it would have formed the basis of what has become a strong, enduring relationship. It never seemed likely, this partnership between Aldo and Luisa Passerini's little girl and a wandering Australian bike rider.

'Pietro!' It's a name that sings. And she says it in such a way that you feel the need to exclaim it. Chiara has a lovely intonation. When she speaks her second language, it's a beautiful sound. She applies the phonetic principles of Italian to her English and it emerges like a tune.

It was her father's friend, Pietro Scampini who decided it was time to arrange a rendezvous between the two and, as Chiara would say, 'it change-ed my life'. If the letters are there to be read, then enunciate them – that's her habit. (In spoken English, it's 'changed'. By Chiara's method, it's 'change. ed.')

Her Italian accent was much stronger a few years ago, but unfortunately it's dying off as her vocabulary improves. In English, she speaks with accented emphasis. In Italian, particularly when she's around friends and/or family, she ... well, she tends to yell. Nothing in her native tongue ever sounds subtle. And so, when Chiara says 'Pietro!' – the name of the man who introduced her to her future husband – there is a lovely familiarity. Hear it in her tone, see it on her face as she calls the word and, once it's escaped her mouth, a grin results. 'Ah, Pietro!'

She didn't need the introduction. She didn't want a relationship. She was happy continuing her musical and cultural studies. So how did it come to be that Chiara met Cadel?

I was sort of obliged to. I had been introduced by a mutual friend who is a friend of my family and he got to know Cadel. He lives not far away from my parents' house in Gallarate.

My dad helped Pietro with some of his sculptures. Pietro! He's a sculptor. He's known me since I was born. He's a fan of any sorts of sport. He's a fan of many things and, somehow, he seems to know everybody. He knew Cadel because he knew people at Mapei when Cadel used to race for them.

It was the end of 2002. It had been Cadel's first full season as a road cyclist and throughout the year, Cadel had stayed at Pietro's home during his frequent trips from the village where he lived near Neuchâtel, in the French part of Switzerland, down to the Mapei centre in Castellanza in the north of Italy. Pietro and his wife Lorenza became Cadel's 'Italian family'.

Cadel needed just somewhere to stay overnight. It happened to be that Pietro had the room.

They became friends and Pietro thought about me; to introduce Cadel to me. He started saying things like, 'Oh Aldo, you know, there's this friend of mine … and you have to meet him.'

And to Cadel it was something similar, but there was more to it. Pietro suggested that Cadel would enjoy talking to my father but he would also remind him of other motives: 'He has a daughter and, oh – she's a nice girl!'

Pietro started bringing Cadel to see my dad at his house. And, because I used to live with them, the plan was that we'd probably meet. I wasn't there the first time but I was the second time.

Actually, my mum saw Cadel the first time and she told me, 'Oh, Pietro came here with this guy ... he's an Australian. He's a cyclist ...'

And I was asking what he was like, 'Oh, an Australian!? And why? And, ah, how come he came here ... ?'

'Oh, he's a cyclist. He's not interested in women, his mind is on the job.'

That's what she told me, laughs Chiara six years later. 'Oh. My poor mum. She had no idea.'

Why would she need this introduction?

I was doing my music studies. I had my routine. I wasn't much into sport. I used to follow skiing a little bit and that's it. Not much more. I was happy with my life. I didn't have a boyfriend; I wasn't interested.

She didn't know much about cycling but that would soon change. There's a perception that all Italians are besotted by the sport, but even after Chiara heard the name of this boy Pietro was trying to introduce her to, it didn't make a difference:

It's not that true that everybody knows about cycling in Italy. In Italy people are mad about football. It is huge. And then there are other sports like Formula One ... and then maybe cycling is the next most popular. Okay, people know about the Giro, a little bit about the Tour, but the Italians are generally focussed on Italian cyclists. I was supposed to know about cycling but I didn't.

I used to go and watch Tre Valli Varesine, the race that is held close to Varese. And that's it. One day, when I was very young, I saw a stage of the Giro when it passed by Gallarate, but we just stood outside the house and saw it go by. That's all I'd ever done with cycling before.

I had no knowledge of cycling as a sport. My dad knew a little bit but nobody in my family knew who Cadel was. There were comments that went around the table: 'Oh, a mountain biker.' 'Oh yeah, I can ride a mountain bike.' 'He's now racing on the road ...' 'Maybe he did the Giro this year.' But that's all I knew.

He wasn't as well known as he is today. Even if he was really a big star in cycling, I would not have heard of him. Okay, I knew of Cipollini and I'd heard of Bettini but that was it. I didn't even know Armstrong. Okay, I knew that there was this race – the Tour de France but ...'

She pauses in the retelling, realising that it all seems so odd. After a moment of silence, she begins again ... 'Can you imagine? Now. Look. I'm surrounded by it.'

Cycling can and does consume people. It is able to force its way into relationships even if one part of a pair has little or no interest in the sport. Like any pastime, if one person has a passion for it, then it affects those around them. Considering the circumstances, however, Chiara is relatively unaffected.

When her husband had crashed in Stage 9 of the Tour de France, which he was supposed to win, she was on the beach. Three weeks is a long time.

These days, Helen Cocks rearranges her schedule in July so that she is able to tune in to European time, and watches the race unfold on the television as she sits up late at night on the other side of the world. She loves riding, but horses are her passion. Bikes happen to be what her son races for a living, so she has an interest by default. The rider's mother takes holidays, sleeps on a strange schedule and adjusts her life so that she can see as much of the race as she can endure, but it's not possible to watch all of it.

The same rule applies to Chiara. When it's a crucial stage, she knows to pay attention. She jumps with anxiety whenever she hears commentators talk of a crash. But she doesn't let the race dominate her days. What would that help? 'Cadel is just a simple guy. He doesn't need attention,' Chiara says now, but the two enjoy being able to talk about things other than cycling.

I like what he does but I'm not crazy about everything that comes from it.

The Tour de France has become the focus of their lives but it doesn't mean it will be that way forever. Through his job and because of his heritage she has seen a lot of the world, but for her to actually attend a race is a rarity. In five years of the Tour, the final stage is the only one that she's been to each time. There have been other visits: the stage to Morzine in 2006, the time trial around Angoulême in 2007, the time when the Tour visited Italy in 2008, and the penultimate stage to Saint-Amand-Montrond that same year, and the day to Verbier in 2009. Molly has also made the journey and, Chiara jokes, 'Cadel's usually happier to see his dog than his wife'. But it's not true.

Chiara has a charm that puts people at ease. If there's one element of Cadel's life since meeting her that all the people he knows agree on, it's that she has an ability to lift his spirits – as well as those of everyone else involved.

To see the two together is to appreciate how a curious mix of personalities can combine to make a happy unit. They argue like most couples can but generally they are happy when they are together. They finish each other's sentences, order food in a restaurant for one another without consultation because they know what the other likes or dislikes. They grumble about the same things, cheer similar circumstances and always chime together when their dog does anything – good or bad: 'Mm-ooh-leee! Oh, Molly …'

Their life is complex because of all the demands. It is complicated thanks to the interest generated by what he does as a professional cyclist. But they cope by keeping things simple. There's a synergy that is easy to admire, even if it's difficult to understand. It is a high-maintenance lifestyle and she grounds him. She's still the happy-go-lucky girl who can light up a room when she enters it. And he's still racing his bike with intent and determination. But now they do these things as part of a package. Oh, Pietro!

Before it was all about me. Doing my music, seeing my friends. Doing what I want. I'd been in the same house for 25 years in Gallarate. It was just simple. It was a little bit less international than what I know now. I was happy before and I'm happy now. But it's just different.

Pietro came to my parents' house for a second time with Cadel and, this time, I was there. He started straight away at it: 'Oh, why don't you two go out together?'

I didn't say anything but my parents also chimed in.

'Oh go! Take him out with your friends, Chiara.'

'Oh, okay. Let's go then ...'

I don't know what Cadel thought, but I did not want to go any-where just with him. It's not that I wasn't interested in him – I wasn't interested in anyone. I didn't want to lead him on, so I called my best friend, Alessandro Scandroglio; I call him Sca.

'Sca, can you please come along with me because I'm going out with this guy ...'

He agreed. And we went. I picked Cadel up from Pietro's with Sca. We went out and started talking; we were having fun but it was getting late. Suddenly Sca just said, 'I'm tired. I'm going home. Can you please take Cadel home?'

'Ah. Okay. Ah ...' And then everything started.

She blushes when remembering the first encounter and admits that, by the end of the evening, they shared their first kiss. But it took her by surprise:

I was still not too interested in him but I felt attracted by him. Not because of who he was or what he had done; that didn't matter to me. We didn't talk about cycling, but he listened when Sca and I talked about the choir because we had done that together since we were teenagers. I could tell that I liked Cadel as a person. He was interesting. I'd never spent much time with someone who is not

Italian. He held me captivated.

As soon as it started, it could have ended.

The day after our dinner he left Italy and returned to Australia. We met and then he was gone for three months. And the thing that shocked me a bit was that, the day after we met, I was on the train going to Milan and he called to say, 'I can stay a bit longer ...'

Now that I know him, I can't imagine what was going through his mind, because he's not the sort of guy who would change his routine for very much at all.

I didn't want him to stay in Europe just because of me. I didn't know anything about him, so I said, 'Just go back home and we'll see ...'

I thought I'd see if he calls back again or if he replies to emails. We exchanged two or three emails every day and we sent each other messages and we really hooked up by the communication. We've stayed in touch ever since. I felt that he was very close even though he was on the other side of the world. When he came back, we started our relationship.

In the time Chiara has known him, a lot has happened. He's become more difficult to talk to. He's more protective of himself. She has become a big element in his life because he trusts her; he can be honest with someone who he cares about.

There are four other pivotal people that Cadel nominates as making him the way he is: Helen Cocks, Damian Grundy, Martin

Whiteley and Roberto Damiani, but they are scattered around the world and they can't always be there in the dark times. Chiara is the person to do that, with her vivacious ways and the shining light of her personality.

She talks about the 2003 and 2004 racing seasons:

In the first years of our story there were some lost years for him. It was a happy time for us but he was very discontented with what was happening in his career; it was the T-Mobile years. He didn't like that environment. He had injuries. He was really unhappy. People were not interested in him as a cyclist so he only had me at that time.

I didn't care about if he was going well on the bike or bad ... it didn't factor into our relationship. I remember in 2004 he got third in a stage of the Tour of Murcia and I was beside myself with joy. 'Oh Cadel! You're great.'

'What do you mean? I only got third in a stage ...'

But I wasn't used to it. I didn't understand what results were important and which ones were just part of the expectation. He was a star for me because of that third place. I had a look on the internet, saw the result and I was so pleased for him.

He didn't say it, but he insinuated that it was okay but that he really would have preferred to win. For me it was just fantastic.

What happened afterwards with the Tour de France – even in the first year when he got eighth – was amazing for me to see. I was learning about the sport and I could appreciate his result a lot more. Especially because our relationship started just when it was confirmed that the team he was with was not at all right for the way he is. He had two years of bad luck and strange management. But then you see how things can change. Suddenly everybody was interested in him. But we don't know what the future holds.

Is he happy now? Does success on the bike bring joy to someone who believes that victory in the Tour de France is what he's capable of, yet he's not yet achieved that objective? 'I think it brings relief and satisfaction,' is Chiara's answer. 'But I don't know if it brings happiness. She explains further:

He hates attention, and pressure makes things worse for him. I think he was happier in 2007 than in 2008 because the first time he was second in the Tour, his goal was to be on the podium. He did that. And so he had reason to feel some satisfaction. For me, it was incredible and I enjoyed that year a great deal. But the next time around he didn't achieve his goal, which was to improve on his place from the previous year.

When you start to get some fame, you get all sorts of publicity: good and bad. This is part of the game but there is no manual – no instruction – on how to handle that sort of attention.

After one July it was like he had the world in his hands. He was voted as the most popular sportsman in a big poll in Australia, he got to carry the Melbourne Cup onto the track at Flemington; he was invited to functions and given a real welcome when he came home. But the next year there was another goal for him and more expectation from those who had just started to discover who this 'Cadel Evans' was. It's not that he needs attention because pressure is not good for him. But everybody expected him to win and he didn't. That's life. He always wins to me, so it doesn't matter to me.

At the age of 14 he realised he was good at something. At 15 he was winning everything. At 16 he was going to represent his country. At 17 he was preparing for the Olympics. At 18 he was being paid to do what he loved. At 19 he started getting paid even more. At 20 he was travelling the world, learning languages, meeting helpful advisors and sycophants alike. But it was what happened when he was at the end of his first year as a road cyclist when he was 25 that is one of the most important events of all: he met his future wife.

It's revealing to take a glimpse of his diary for 7 September 2005:

Since the Tour of Germany, I started really preparing for the wedding and then got back on the bike in the last couple of weeks. I only really had a couple of days off, but since then I've done some really good training to get ready for racing in the Tour of Poland.

My best man, Simon Skerry, arrived in Europe on Monday night and on Tuesday he was out for a 170-kilometre ride. He was, however, on the scooter. For a non-cyclist, I reckon that's a pretty good effort even if he had the advantage of a motor.

Right now I've got other things on my mind. I'm getting married tomorrow so I won't be going training today.

From Australia, there are eight guests for the wedding. I'll have another reception when I get home. There are 80 guests in total attending the wedding ceremony. We're getting married in Gallarate, Chiara's hometown. I'm really looking forward to the day. It'll be a simple wedding and the after party with my friends is something we're both excited about and really looking forward to. The reception will be in a traditional, old Italian farmhouse, 'Cascina dei Brut', which has been converted into a restaurant.

The best part about the wedding is that my Australian friends have arrived in Europe. My mum and Gran (or Super-Nonna, as she's known in Italy) arrived a few days ago. On the other side of the family, the Italians are very excited but nervous at the same time.

Me, I've never been married before so I don't know what to expect.

Poor Chiara will be a newlywed bride and I'll be flying out to the Tour of Poland. I leave on Sunday, so we'll only get three nights together as husband and wife before I go away for racing. But November awaits and that's when we'll have our real honeymoon. The plan is to holiday somewhere between Thailand and Australia.

———————

Cadel has settled well into the Italian way of life. It helps that he loves the place where he's based during the season and happily leaves his home in Barwon Heads, Australia. Of course, he adores the time he gets to spend in Australia but when it's time for racing to commence in February, he's happy enough to return to Europe. Aldo and Luisa take care of Molly when Cadel and Chiara head south for a summertime Christmas.

The off-season lasts just four weeks. Officially there are about three months without competition – November, December and January – but he's back on the bike and training after only a brief hiatus. In a typical season he will ride close to 40,000 kilometres – much of it in racing, plenty of it behind a car or scooter piloted by Chiara (or other friends recruited when required), but also plenty of it in isolation. For most cyclists, the hours alone with little more than pre-set tasks from the trainer and the long road ahead, this is the perfect time to think. The option for contemplation can make the actual work seem less laborious. This is the time when he ponders his allotment, considers what concerns him, plans his holidays or thinks about the various elements of a life that has become quite complex.

When the opportunity to escape does come, Cadel doesn't always take the simple solution. He has ended a season on a deck chair overlooking the ocean from a tropical island off the Queensland coast, but he and Chiara have also opted for more complicated holidays. In 2006 they hired a campervan and drove up the coast from Sydney to introduce Aldo and Luisa to his father, Paul, in Upper Corindi. They ventured all over the northern parts of New South Wales, and covered significant territory, but never left that state. It was the first time Chiara's parents had been out of Europe; just to get to Australia provided Luisa with a first: until then, she had never been on a plane before.

Chiara is more adventurous. She has found a partner who appreciates similar things to her. They love the funghi season in Italy, and they cheer Paul's wife Orada when she presents a spicy Thai concoction for dinner. The thought of having children is there but they're in no rush while he's still spending half the year living out of suitcases as he travels from one race to a training camp to another race.

That simple creation – two wheels, a frame, a chain and a set of pedals – has changed his life and hers. The distances Cadel travels on and with the bike extend to the off season. There is the annual journey across the world back to Australia for the summer and a brief opportunity for quiet happy moments with his wife and away from the bike.

Not that Cadel and Chiara opt to relax. Even when he's not obliged to travel, he continues to wander. Just as they undertook a complicated journey after the hectic 2008 racing season to visit their Tibetan foster child's school in Nepal, their honeymoon was a journey across the vast country of Cadel's past.

But let us hear from Chiara about their honeymoon:

In September 2005, after we got married, we decided to do our honeymoon after the cycling season. As we do every year, we planned to go to Australia at the end of October, so we started to consider what to do and where to go to celebrate our wedding. Cadel's idea was to show me the places where he came from; I was still quite new to Australia; this would be the first year that I would spend three months there. There were still many things to learn about this great, unknown country.

Cadel came up with the idea of taking the train from Melbourne to Adelaide and then from Adelaide to Darwin, stopping in Alice Springs and Katherine.

After having dinner in Melbourne at Cadel's favourite restaurant in town, Syracuse, we went to the train station and started our short, delayed but adventurous honeymoon.

We travelled overnight to Adelaide and spent the next morning waiting for the Ghan, the famous train that travels from south to north of Australia. We had plenty of time but were in holiday mode and somehow we very nearly missed out scheduled departure time.

For a European, Australia is such a different place – a wide country with so much space and it's hard for an Italian to conjure what it really is without getting to see such vast nothingness like in the centre of his country. With the trip, Cadel wanted to show me another side of Australia, as well as going back to his roots himself. It was a journey of discovery for us both.

Cadel first did a trip when he was about two years old but it was in a car when the only air conditioning came from winding down the window and hoping that the dust didn't choke you. But he was too young to remember what it was like. We were both amazed at how a desert can be so interesting to watch. We could sit for hours on the train, always looking out the window and never getting bored. A few weeks before we did our trip, there was some good rain on the desert, so there was some vegetation as well.

Alice Springs was the first stop. We stayed there two days; we wanted to go to visit Uluru and have a look around in the area, but we had someone waiting for us in Alice, Helen's long-time friend Ruth. It was nice to meet her; even nicer for Cadel to see a friend of his mother's after all these years. The day after, we went on a day trip – we decided to go for the adventure one – so we spent hours on a bus trip to Uluru.

Back on the Ghan, next stop: Katherine. Cadel's godfather still lived there with his family. When we arrived, Lee Hunt came to meet us; as with Ruth, it was nice to see him and to talk about all sorts of things about Katherine and Cadel's time up there when he was very young. Our time in Katherine was very limited – we had to get back on the train in the afternoon – so Lee took us for a boat trip on the Katherine Gorge.

We continued with our train trip until Darwin, where we spent a few hours before our flight to Brisbane. Our 'official' honeymoon finished up there in Darwin, but in reality we continued to travel more and to get back to Cadel's origins. He was keen to show me the other places where he'd lived and, most important, I still had to meet his father. So, after train and plane, it was time to rent a car. We spent a few days in Noosa, and then we travelled south towards Upper Corindi. It was quite fun, the idea to meet his father, especially after we got married. Cadel described many times where he lives, how he lives, Orada, the bush around the house. I always had to use my imagination to work out the places Cadel came from. So finally I could dive into his past.

After meeting Paul Evans, we went to meet someone else who had a significant role in Cadel's life, Trevor. We went to Armidale and Uralla (where Trevor still lives), passing by the house where he had the horse accident that left him unconscious for one week when he was a kid. Wow! It was impressive to finally see what you have imagined for a long time. He looked as if he freshly remembered most of the things there. That trip gave me a chance to know and to understand Cadel even more, and for him it was like walking through his evolution as a man, getting back to the origins.

11
Ideals and two Olympics – Under the jersey

What is sport and why

> *Representing Australia has always been an honour and a privilege, and the older and more experienced I get, the more I enjoy it. (Cadel Evans, 2009)*

It is a long road from a small indigenous community in the Top End of Australia to its temperate south. From Australia to Europe it is even longer. You can learn a lot along the way and for Cadel it was not only about training to make himself the best in the world, it was about people, language and cultures. He was young when he left the Territory but he carried with him the influences of his formative experiences.

Things had not started well for Cadel in 2000. A small mishap during a warm-up lap in the first race of the season had resulted in a broken collarbone. Five weeks before the mountain bike race in the Sydney Olympics a hamstring injury hindered both physical and mental strength.

But he had got through all of that, and he was going to race.

Cadel was standing in a queue of athletes lining up to be measured for their Olympic uniforms, and here he was, standing behind one of the track cycling sprinters, Sean Eadie.

Since his Olympic debut at the Atlanta Games in 1996, the mountain biker was leaner and his body shape was that of a man. The adolescent who was recruited by the AIS when he was still a junior weighed between 68 and 69 kilograms when Damian Grundy first started coaching him. The original data sheets from testing at the national sporting institute reflect the statistics of a teenage rider.

He would never have the physique of the cycling sprinter he was standing next to – Sean Eadie, the sprinter who would win the Sprint World Championship, an event in which the final 200 metres are the most crucial, who is a giant compared with Cadel. Eadie weighs in at 98 kilograms and stands 183 centimetres tall. Cadel is 174 centimetres tall. At the Olympics in Sydney he was at the peak of his mountain bike years and weighed around 64 kilograms; he admits that these were his leanest years. His racing weight is now closer to 67 or 68 kilograms, depending on the time of the year. He is still lean, but his muscles have developed and muscles weigh more than fat. The numbers do tell some of the story but the manner in which a body is shaped depends a lot on the discipline they are developed for.

By 2008, when he started as the number-one ranked road cyclist in the world (and defending champion of the UCI's ProTour), he had considerably bulky medial gastrocnemius, the muscle group below the knee and on the inside of the leg, and the same for the lateral group (on the outside of the leg). They grew because of his age but much of the difference in the recruitment of muscles came from very specific and disciplined exercises that he has practised throughout his career as a cyclist. He needed to ensure he was as efficient with the upstroke as he could be.

This is the reason a cyclist wears cleated shoes. If cyclists pedal only by applying force on the downstroke of the pedalling action, the thighs would be the only part of the leg being utilised for power. Having shoes that clip into a binding system makes the calf muscles active and able to pull the pedal back to the top of the arc. Not only is it a natural instinct, it is more efficient.

The reason Cadel's body is a little different now to what it was when he was the number-one mountain biker in the world is that the mountain bike and road disciplines are contrasting. His style as a mountain biker was one that you could notice from a long way off. With elbows at right angles, pinning the front wheel to the ground, he ducked his head and hunched his shoulders when he was on the flats. It was a position he considered the most effective to control the bike, and it clearly worked.

On the World Cup scene in 1996, he was third in the under-23 World Championships in Cairns. In 1997, he won the World Cup races in Wellington, New Zealand and Vail, USA. Chiotti was third in both and Christophe Dupouey and Michael Rasmussen were the runners-up, respectively. Cadel was also second in St Wendell in Germany and Budapest, Hungary. In 1998 when road cycling was wracked by the Festina Affair, Cadel was rocking through the mountain biking races taking three first places – in

Silves, Portugal then Plymouth, Britain and again in Canmore, Canada. He was beating Martinez and was more consistent than any other rider. He won the most races, took the title of World Cup Champion, and was the pin-up boy for his sponsor Cannondale, the US bicycle manufacturer with a proud history of making fine aluminium frames.

Cadel was a major influence in making a name for the brand. A stencilled image of him riding his mountain bike was emblazoned on every MTB bike box from Cannondale for years. He became the face of the company at a time when it was making enormous headway into the road market as well. But the first successes were off-road. And it was Cadel who was spreading the word.

In 1999 he won the World Cup race in El Escoral, Spain – his only victory for the season – but the points for his four runner-ups totalled more than any other rider that year to win a second World Cup title. The one-day World Championship title went to Michael Rasmussen that year.

Then came 2000 and the appeal of the new challenge was growing. But he wouldn't be pushed. 'I have a contract that runs until the Olympics in Sydney – and that is to race mountain bikes,' he said at the end of 1998. 'I'm going to worry about that first. That's enough to focus on for the time being. I'll look at my options after that.' The incessant enquiries about when he was going to give up his job to do another were irritating. He was a mountain biker – he started his career as one, he wanted to be a professional, and he was doing just that – and why would he change?

Stabio is a rather nondescript, almost rural area in southern Switzerland, very close to the Italian border. Outside a small apartment block a Mini Cooper is parked. Cadel and Chiara have a small rented apartment there. You walk up two flights of stairs and inevitably hear the welcoming yappy bark – it's Molly. It's a regular chorus. To the left of the apartments is a small paddock, home to a horse and a small pony; to the right is a vegetable patch. On the other side of the apartment block is a small shady laneway that heads up the hill to where the centre of the town is; at least, it's where the café is that Chiara and Cadel frequent.

Behind the shed where Cadel's car is parked there's a basement. Down a flight of stairs is a grille with a heavy padlock that secures a humble collection of bikes. You hardly notice them amidst the other paraphernalia: shoe cleats – packages of them waiting to be used, and a bucket of discarded ones, an orderly collection of tools on a small work bench, a myriad of tyres hanging up – off-road ones, with their big knobby discarded grips. The off-season was a long time ago; the fun of what once was is now hidden behind the tyres waiting for their day on his thin wheels.

He trains around the area and has to carry his passport as he can cross the border with Italy several times on a single ride, but he's rarely stopped. 'They're used to pro cyclists around here. There are a lot who live nearby and there are a few who I like to ride with when we are home between the races.'

But his serious work is often done alone, or elsewhere. There are hills near Stabio – good solid climbs. But sometimes he needs mountains and the thin air of altitude. That's part of the routine now.

But Livigno is not far away and the 2750-metre Passo Stelvio is a useful stretch of road for a session of serious training. He's done it many times a day during the lead-up to races. He considers it just another requirement for him to achieve his quest. 'Ah, seven hours on the bike in the mountains today …' he sings as he walks down to the shed. 'Perfect weather. No phones. What could be wrong with that?'

In the shed is a bike that has a special crank configuration. It is aluminium but golden coloured. You notice the difference immediately when you see the frame, without wheels, hanging from a hook as you enter the shed. It's on the back wall and it's really a bike of pain devised to perfect pedalling. He doesn't like to talk about it. 'It's something I do,' he says, trying to dismiss any enquiry. 'It's to force me to use my hamstrings as well as my quadriceps.' The idea is this: the pedals have a free wheel, clutched axle assembly and unless you pull the crank arm up, it will not follow the natural flow and the urge of the other crank arm. You can push them down, but first you have to pull back, and up, and forward – or else it just hovers at the bottom of the pedalling arc. 'It took me ages to perfect,' he says of the first rides, 'but now I'll use this bike, especially at the start of the season when I'm reminding my legs of what's about to come.'

The effect can be seen. He has a muscle that bulges out from below his long cycling shorts. It's like a sphere when his leg is arcing up and it prods out just above the rear of the kneecap, below the hamstring. Physiotherapists and biomechanists are always impressed by it.

He's not alone. There are other riders in the pro peloton who have such muscle structures, such as Tony Rominger – a rider who was a runner-up in the Tour and had considerable success including a Giro title (in 1995) and the Vuelta a España (Tour of Spain). He had huge calves. He liked to sit well behind the bottom bracket and his legs were shaped by that practised position.

For Cadel, this little extra emphasis as the thigh dives down behind the knee is just part of the deal. He's swapped disciplines since he first started racing and he looks different as a road cyclist. When questioned, he explains, but will not elaborate on what his measurement actually is because different tests by different practitioners use different methods, and they vary:

Body fat is not an accurate enough measure to compare one measure to another. I can do two tests at the Mapei training centre and one says four per cent [fat] the next six or seven per cent [fat]. Basically, I hang at the lower end of the leanest scale, particularly when I was a mountain biker. That's when I had to be super-lean to be at the top level. I spent five years at the top and I was very hungry. That is something that is quite draining mentally as well.

Cadel's professionalism has naturally spilled over into what he does to ensure his fitness is achieved in the right manner for his discipline. In the gym his focus is on strength, but not necessarily for the purpose of bulking up.

Most of the exercises I do are specific to my sport. It's not like I can say, 'I bench this weight and I squat this'. I do squats but they are leg squats with dumbbells. I train so that I don't compensate to one side

– to my stronger side. I concentrate on being of equal strength.

To be a cyclist, you have to be careful about strength and balances. Obviously if you've got a stronger leg, you're going to favour that leg and that affects your hips, your back and all sorts of injuries can result from that.

Most of my strength work is based not only around increasing strength, but also as an injury deterrent or focussing on maintaining a balance in strength.

The AIS had one of its crowning moments in 2000 – the Olympics were in Australia. Sport would unite a nation, bring people together and make them cheer. For a fortnight there would be festivities and fun. Spring arrived right on cue and the weather seemed like something out of a tourist brochure – blue skies, cool nights, warm days. With Heiko Salzwedel as the head coach of road and mountain bike disciplines, there were other riders who stood a chance of delivering medals for the host nation in the six cycling events for both men and women in which weather can have an effect – road races, time trials and mountain bike cross-country.

Rain did fall, but the only cycling event affected was the women's road race. This was another event in which Australia had a strong contender. Anna Wilson had finished second in both the time trial and road race at the World Championships less than a year earlier. Like others, she had benefited greatly from the breeding ground of talent that had emerged in Canberra. Alas, in Sydney she would finish with the 'chocolate' medal in both disciplines: fourth!

A star-studded cast assembled for the men's road events: Robbie McEwen was the nominated leader. He could sprint. He had won a stage of the Tour de France a year earlier. He had begun to earn a reputation in the pro peloton and he was being given a chance to show himself at Olympic level. Like Cadel Evans, Robbie had been to Atlanta as well, but for both that was more of a learning experience than anything else.

For Australian cycling, the Sydney Games marked the end of a significant era. Charlie Walsh, the pragmatic track coach with a strong opinion, bold reputation and divisive personality, stood aside from his position and handed over the reins to Shayne Bannan. Shayne, a former cyclist, was also born in the Northern Territory and he would remain at the helm of Cycling Australia's program for at least another decade. He saw the progression of Cadel from teenage mountain bike prodigy to World Cup champion. He assisted the young rider in a variety of ways over the years and supported him when the decision came to swap disciplines. In Sydney, he observed how the whole Australian team performed, and by the next Olympics he ensured that the medal haul was not only significantly better from the three forms of cycling that were contested in Athens in 2004, but that the squad would be the most dominant of the Games.

Since the time that Cadel has been racing, he's competed in three Olympics – 1996, 2000 and 2008 – twice as a mountain biker, once as a road cyclist.

In 1992, Australia earned its first gold medal on the road (with Kathy Watt) but in Atlanta 1996 the team didn't win any cycling events. In 2000, there was plenty of success but the only 'victory' was in the Madison event on the track. The two-man relay event was introduced to the Olympic program that year and six-day specialist Scott McGrory teamed up with former team pursuit world champion Brett Aitken. The pair won the only gold medal for the home team in cycling.

As yet, however, no Australian has been able to get on the podium in the MTB events at the three Olympics that have had the cross-country on the agenda. If it were to be won, it should have been in Sydney with Cadel Evans. But it was Miguel Martinez who lifted his bike aloft as he walked across the line as the champion in 2000. Cadel was seventh.

My first Olympics was when I went to Atlanta as a 19-year-old in 1996. I was too young to take a step back and treat it as 'another race' and I didn't enjoy it at all. Four years later, in Sydney, I was a medal favourite but I didn't have the experience to insulate myself from expectations of the media or the public. My results were very disappointing, but hanging around in the village afterwards was great fun.

Both times he was the best Australian in his event. Years later he would quote former Tour de France race director Jean-Marie Leblanc when searching for a way of describing his feelings about the Olympics and its apparent ideals:

There are so many restrictions to what an athlete is or is not allowed to do at the Olympic Games. The Tour de France has its regulations but at least we are still treated like human beings when we race there; we are subjected to strict doping controls and there are other elements that we must adhere to, but it's still possible to voice your concerns and not be afraid of the ramifications.

At the Olympics you're not even allowed to wear your own socks. You sign a contract that essentially puts a limit on what you're allowed to do as a person. I remember reading my contract with the AOC from the Sydney Olympics and it stipulated that athletes weren't allowed to comment on any facet of life other than sport. We were only allowed to comment on what we were there to compete in; you weren't allowed to talk about anything but your own event.

I like the Tour. I like its philosophy, like what Leblanc said during the first Tour I went to. It was his last tour as sole director of the race and he offered his appraisal on what makes the race beautiful. He said, 'The Tour will always remain; the philosophy of the Tour is sport.' There are other elements that make the event spectacular, but at its foundation is the actual competition. On the last day of the 2005 race, I went to the race director's car and shook Jean-Marie's hand and told him how much I appreciated his summary. The Tour does have its flaws but sport is at the core. At the Olympics, the sports seem to be much further down the agenda.

The Sydney experience was the first time in which he would see how he coped with the extremes of being a favourite for an important event. He did insulate himself when possible but he also enjoyed the attention. Cycling, as he's said, is all about balance. So too is managing the weight of expectation – from himself and the public. Someone who saw how he handled it from up close was Damian Grundy.

I didn't perceive the pressure that Cadel was under, and maybe that was a mistake for me. Certainly the race wasn't what we had hoped for or tried to achieve. How much of that performance was impacted on by what was going on around him? I'm not sure, but he is susceptible to outside influences even when he's trying to isolate himself.

I thought he managed it as well as he could. Going into the Games everybody talked about the pressures that the Australian athletes would be under and so, within the planning, there was a lot of consideration given and contingencies put in place to minimise those impacts as far as it could possibly be.

Damian and Cadel ceased their collaboration once the rider swapped to road cycling. Cadel was going into a new world, an unknown world to Damian. Cadel took on Aldo Sassi, an Italian from the Mapei training centre, as his coach. But there is a long history between them from the early days. Still, his first true coach wonders what the rider's perception of the Sydney experience is.

'I'd be interested to know how he might have felt that it impacted on him,' he said of the way in which he was adopted as the hometown favourite. 'That was a tough day. Standing along the course were 30,000 or so people, and around 25,000 of them were there riding the race with Cadel, for him, wishing him on. You can be weighed down by that or you can be uplifted by that support. It's really important to try and find the way to be uplifted by it.'

It would be eight years before Cadel raced another Olympics. In 2008, the physical and professional transition from mountain biker to road cyclist was well and truly complete. Among the long list of his successes in 2007 he had won the Beijing Olympic Test Event and was an obvious inclusion in the Australian men's road team for the Beijing Olympics.

Before the final Olympic selection was announced Cadel had a program of races to complete, among them the Liège–Bastogne– Liège race at the end of April 2008, known as La Doyenne – the 'old girl'. Of the one-day Classics, it is one of cycling's monuments. It is a race feted in history and suited to the GC Guys.

Perhaps the most memorable moment in its history was when Bernard Hinault won the race in 1980 when there was snow and sleet. It was horribly cold and the Frenchman sped off on his own in pursuit of two escapees when there were still 100 kilometres to go in a race with a total distance of 244 kilometres. The roads were white with snow and snow was falling on the riders. The snow turned to ice and, with 80 kilometres to go, Hinault was in the lead. He never eased off, powering up and down the rollercoaster undulations of the Belgian Ardennes like a man possessed. He finished over nine minutes ahead of the runner-up and achieved a victory that is still celebrated today as one of the most emphatic in modern cycling. But it came at a cost. 'That was one of the hardest days I've ever had,' Hinault said 25 years later. 'The tips of my fingers were numb for months and there are still parts behind my fingernails that have no feeling at all. I froze. But I won.'

They were different days.

Cadel didn't win Liège–Bastogne–Liège. He just got warm on an unseasonably hot day in Belgium and unzipped his shirt. The next day he was on the front page of newspapers around Australia. He had a political view and, without speaking, he put his message out there in the public arena.

Cadel Evans has been able to raise the level of awareness of cycling in a nation that is starting to rediscover the beauty of the simple notion: riding a bike is good. Cycling is fun. He loves to ride and he gains a lot of enjoyment from the fact that a chance exists for him to show Australia what cycling is all about. He has also taken the opportunity to express his beliefs.

With the simple gesture of unzipping a team jersey and exposing an undershirt with a graphic that has been banned by the Chinese government since 1959 – with the words 'Free Tibet' clearly legible – he earned headlines.

Cadel knows the plight of the Tibetan people is a complex one. He doesn't have the answers but he's aware that questions should be asked about the Chinese occupation. And in the year in which the focus of the world was going to be centred on Beijing, the Australian cyclist played a role in encouraging people to become aware of the political situation on the 'Roof of the World'. He explains his views about Tibet:

I've been intrigued by it. I like to learn about places I've not been to and cultures that are different to those that have been part of my life. I'm not a religious person but I'm interested in Buddhism and the principles of that way of thinking.

The Dalai Lama once said, 'Work for the welfare of all. With a pure heart you can carry on any work and your profession becomes a real instrument to help the human community'.

I read about Tibet and try to learn about it. I'm no expert but when I read about the situation – as the Tibetans put it, China's 'invasion' in 1951 – it seems a little bit to me like what happened with the European settlers and the Aborigines in Australia. Cultures nearly get destroyed and I don't think that's right.

The previous year Chiara had given Cadel something very special.

I decided to give Cadel a special gift for his birthday. It took me a while with the researches, but at the end my present for Cadel was the chance to sponsor a Tibetan child studying in a Tibetan school in Kathmandu. Thanks to the Italian association Asia Onlus, I could get in touch with them and organise everything. That's how we got to know another reality that changed a bit our lives. The child we started sponsoring was Tashi, a cute kid whose parents lived too far away and were too poor to pay for Tashi's school.

Cadel explains further:

I can't do much about these situations given the context of my job. I'm paid to race a bike. I can't do much for Aborigines in Australia at this point or the Tibetans in their occupied territory, but I can raise some awareness to something I feel strongly about.

Some people appreciate it and some people think I'm completely wrong. Some people think I should mind my own business. But it's something I feel for and wearing the t-shirt stating 'Free Tibet' got the media to at least talk about the issue.

Fifty-seven years, almost to the day when they had to close down Tibet to foreign media for the riots that broke out there, I wore my undershirt in Liège–Bastogne–Liège. I didn't even expect that it would be seen, because it's not often that you get hot enough to unzip a jersey in that race. It just happened to be around the same time that the media began looking for stories that related to the Olympics in Beijing.

By displaying a political message in an historic cycling race, Cadel gained exposure for the cause, but it was risky for him to do so. He received a warning from the Australian Olympic Committee and was strongly advised to keep opinions such as this to himself. If he wanted to ride his bike at the Olympics, that's fine, but that's all the administrators wanted him to do.

He describes how it was put to him:

We were told not to criticise the organising committee. We weren't allowed to state any opinion on political issues. Nothing.

I'm not trying to say to everyone that China should get out of Tibet or people should spend all their spare money on Tibet to help these people; I just want to make people aware of it and people can then form their own opinion.

As a person, when you go to the Olympics and you sign the Olympic contract, you go there and you're not allowed to talk about anything but your own sport. It's a little bit too much for me, and they're just trying to control things too much.

The IOC also reacted to what Cadel did in Liège–Bastogne–Liège. It revised and then reiterated its regulations for athletes hoping to be part of the Beijing Games' 'One World, One Dream' and declared that athletes were 'free to express their opinions' but 'such conduct must also, of course, comply with the laws of the host state.'

No kind of demonstration or political, religious or racial propaganda is permitted in any Olympic sites, venues or other areas.

'The important thing in the Olympic Games is not winning but taking part.' So said the founder of the IOC, Baron de Coubertin, in 1890. 'The essential thing in life is not conquering but fighting well.'

No problem. Cadel is good at fighting well. He had a week after the Tour de France to overcome the effects of a ruptured anterior cruciate ligament, followed by a hectic round of visits to an orthopaedic surgeon, and physiotherapy and osteopath sessions. At the end of that week he was in Beijing. It was two weeks after the Tour de France and he was lining up for the men's time trial event and a fifth place. Then, a few days later, joining the Australian team for the men's road race.

Before leaving, the Australian Federation wanted to make sure that Cadel didn't say anything about Tibet once he was in China. But if you know Cadel, you would also know that that had never been Cadel's intention. No 'Free Tibet' undershirts, no statements against China, just the pure love for sport and the Olympics.

But according to Cadel, the Beijing Games were not the unifying experience they were intended to be:

For me it's sad that China got the Olympics. Nothing to do with their political ideals. As a participant I saw that they had to fabricate everything to make it look like it was a good event for television.

Every Olympics is made for television. The IOC wouldn't exist if it didn't have the money it earns from the TV rights from the Olympics. But in China, they had to go to the nth degree to make it.

What really pointed that fact out was when Chiara couldn't go and see the race. She couldn't even buy a ticket to get to the venue – well, she could, but they cancelled the train. You couldn't go to the road race as a spectator. And, if you did, they had all these grandstands erected but they were full of Chinese people who were all dressed in the same colour t-shirt, all had the same flags and who all had a big neon screen in front of them telling them to cheer – in both Chinese and English – when the race came by.

As we came by the start/finish area, there was one screen with the time to the escape group and there was another pointed at the crowd to tell them to cheer. I saw it in the race as I was riding along.

Cadel didn't protest in China. He did race. His wife did eventually get to see him compete – but she had to do it in a clandestine way, by sneaking into the media compound in the car of a television network that then allowed her into the commentary position. If anyone asked why she was there, they were to say she was there to do a special commentary. She watched the event unfold. Like everyone else, she could hear the breathing of the peloton as they panted past on the climb, without the interruption that so many other races were affected by – a crowd enjoying the spectacle!

To me, that's the perfect example of the manner in which the Games were conducted. It was what I saw, I spoke my mind about it and I was criticised for making those comments.

At the end of that season, after the Tour of Lombardy, the Olympics, the injuries and the Tour of France and as part of the long annual journey back to Australia, Cadel and Chiara fulfilled one of their own dreams. Chiara tells how they planned the visit:

An idea came to our minds: why don't we go to visit Tashi? Every year, after the Tour of Lombardy, we go back to Australia for about three months. Going from Europe to Australia, the flight is so long that you are obliged to do a stop in some airport. Starting from this fact, we decided to take a longer loop and pass by Nepal; much easier said than done! We didn't seek any help from a travel agent, we just booked the flights (many flights!) and got in touch with the headmistress from the school in Kathmandu, who couldn't believe we were doing the trip to visit them.

It all sounded damn exciting! We dreamt for months to go and see Tashi and then we were on our way to Nepal. And Nepal was so close to Tibet ... A little dream in Cadel's heart.

Tsultrim Sangmo, the headmistress of the Manasarovar Academy, took us for a walk in the surroundings of the school. We've learnt so much about their lives, the kids, what they do, how they live. Nearly all the kids in that school are sponsored by the association Asia Onlus and some of the kids live in the school because they don't have another place to go.

Cadel's secret dream was to go as close as possible to the border with Tibet, but a few things were against us. The main reason was that we didn't know how to get there and what we would have found, especially this last one. And time wasn't helping.

Cadel and Chiara stay in touch with Tashi's school, exchanging photos and news of how things are. Pride of place at the school is a photo of Cadel wearing his yellow jersey at the Tour de France in 2008. And his Free Tibet undershirt.

12

2005: Cadel's Tour debut ...

The level of the playing field

He had been warned that the Tour de France would be bigger than any other race in his career but Cadel Evans wasn't daunted. He turned up knowing he had a lot to learn and finished in the top 10 on general classification. He explains his emotions after the three-week race:

The Tour de France ... what's it really like to be there? How does it feel to finally be at the start? How hard is it? I've been asked one of these questions almost daily since the end of July and I'm still coming to terms with the whole experience. I'll try and sum up my feelings from those three weeks. One thing I now know, however, is that there is always more to learn about this enormous event.

La Grande Boucle – the big lap of France – is one race where everyone is riding well. Each rider has an objective, a mission he hopes to fulfil; whether it's a result for himself or victory for a team-mate, it doesn't matter because everyone is motivated and at the peak of his form. No one goes to the Tour with the hope of gaining some condition.

It's not the same as other races; not even the Giro d'Italia or the Vuelta a España can compare because even these are often used as form finders. At the Tour there aren't riders present because they filled a last-minute position opened up by a sick or injured team-mate. It's a race where everyone is 100 per cent committed to performing.

But there's a lot more to it than racing alone. Outside the peloton everything is on a larger scale than at any other race I've been involved in. There are more journalists and television cameras, enormous crowds, and a seemingly endless line of publicity vehicles. It's a circus and of course everyone involved believes their role is the most important.

Even if you ignore what the actual participants are doing, it's still a constant hubbub of action. There are things to acquire and jobs to do. Photos, stories, video footage and autographs are collected. Roads need to be blocked and then cleared. There are promotions that should yield results for the sponsors. Holidays must be enjoyed and cheering should be loud. It's a bike race but there's much more to it than that. The Tour prompts a lot of fuss and unhealthy levels of stress.

'You won't believe how crazy they are!' was a tip about the spectators that I'd often received from riders who'd done the Tour. And the media! They have a job to do – articles to write, programs to produce, movies to make or photos to take. Everyone needs something: from a throwaway line to use as a quote, to a discarded hat, or even an empty bidon [drink bottle] ... it's all important to those involved.

As a rider all you want to do is get to the finish as fast as you can and then focus on recovering well so you can do it all again the next day. Rest is essential, but there's hardly any time for that. If your name is Lance Armstrong there are demands that must take a lot of energy, but they must be met. I've seen the guy work and he earns his money.

And me, did I have any real expectations or hopes? No. The Tour this year was just a big test. I was in a slightly different position to usual; a debutant but also a team leader. When I met up with the other guys before the start I admit that I was nervous, but Davitamon—Lotto has a relatively calm atmosphere compared to most other big sporting formations.

My anxiety wasn't created by the prospect of my first Tour or the fact that family, friends and fans would be glued to the television to see how I was coping. No, what worried me all related to what had happened during May. On Friday the 13th, I had a stupid crash while training which resulted in my sixth broken collarbone, and it disrupted my preparation for the big goal of the season. I wanted to prove myself but it can be a bit intimidating when your whole season is judged on what you do for three weeks in July.

The opening time trial was similar to others I've ridden. At the Tour, however, there are 10 times more people on the side of the road and you need to be going 20 per cent better than usual just to be competitive. I followed our earliest starter and my good friend Mario Aerts in the team car before I was due to ride. I wanted to get an idea of what the course was like. This turned out to be a good plan. *Any energy you can save during the Tour pays dividends and bonuses later.*

That first day was my introduction to 'Mad Tour Disease', a state of excitement that verges on panic and affects the fans, journalists and everyone else involved. Three weeks later it all seemed so normal. On the Tour everything is larger than life and not only did I grow accustomed to it, I began to enjoy the mayhem.

During the first week the racing was hectic. There was always someone trying to create The Winning Escape. There are many other races within the race. Teams with a sprinter, like ours – Robbie McEwen – want the peloton to be together at the end of the stage. Every team with a GC rider wants its man to be in the first group to avoid incidents and wasted energy.

Since Miguel Indurain's five-year tour domination started in 1991, when the Spaniard made a career out of concentrating solely on the Tour, teams have been forced to specialise, to put all their eggs in one basket – building a team around one general classification rider. Davitamon–Lotto is a little more diverse by modern standards, having a very capable sprinter in Robbie and, hopefully, a reasonable GC rider (me). This was something that had not been done successfully since Team Telekom won both the green and yellow jerseys at the 1997 Tour de France.

My role during the opening stages was only to stay out of trouble and not lose any time or valuable energy. So with Robbie out in front and winning, I could pretty much sit back and enjoy a relatively pressure-free ride to the team time trial and the mountains.

After Rabobank's successful couple of days with Pieter Weening and Michael Rasmussen claiming wins in the mountains of the Vosges region, we arrived in the Alps.

Courchevel was my first real taste of a mountain at the Tour. It was also my first big test and I was fine until Lance started to dance. The group was down to eight when he threw in several surges to thin out the selection even more. The guy is strong! I couldn't follow this pace with eight kilometres still to climb. It was a quick lesson in being outclassed, but I wasn't out of the race. My appraisal of the day? My climbing abilities were around eighth best in the race. Not a bad start, considering my injury-plagued lead-up to the race.

As the Tour progresses a pecking order in the peloton becomes apparent. You don't bother pushing your way in front of the climber or sprinter who consistently finishes in front of you. Neither do you tolerate climbers or sprinters who regularly finish behind you.

The first stage finish at the top of a mountain in 2005 provided Australian fans with a hint of what was yet to come from Cadel Evans. In his Tour debut he knew that he had simply to follow the leaders; an early attack may have made him look foolish. The Davitamon–Lotto GC candidate was there to learn what it takes to race against the world's elite in the month which matters most to them, and what his real capabilities were.

Jan Ullrich, Floyd Landis and Levi Leipheimer all failed to keep up on the early incline of the road to Courchevel but Cadel was steadfast. He joined an elite posse of six riders: Armstrong, Basso, Rasmussen, Mancebo and the great new Spanish hope

Alejandro Valverde. Six kilometres from the summit Evans was dropped, but he was getting his education. 'You think you're goin' okay but just looking at the face of Armstrong tells you another story,' he said. 'While you're gasping for breath, he's takin' a drink or talking on the radio. It's demoralising to see him so composed and within his aerobic limits.'

Valverde lived up to the high expectations of the Spanish media. He won the stage ahead of Armstrong but the yellow jersey would return to the Texan once again. The race had officially begun and almost every other rider shared Cadel's sentiment. How can you challenge a man who is so in control he seems to breathe through his eyes?

'Merci Lance. Au Revoir'

In Paris on the final day of the 2005 Tour de France Lance Armstrong stood on the podium and declared that his career was over. The seven-time champion was thinking of retirement. A lot has unfolded since ...

In the final race of his career, as was meant to be the case in 2005, Lance Armstrong did the same thing he'd done every July since 1999 – dominate the Tour de France. The Texan was always strong enough to respond to his challengers and won an unprecedented seventh title. The 92nd edition of the race marked the end of an era but allegations a month later raised questions about the legitimacy of the champion's Tour achievements.

Lance Armstrong likes to be in control. This is not surprising in a man who has become such a force in cycling that the world now pays close attention to a sport which in some countries was largely ignored until his story and success caught their attention. The Tour is why he's a global phenomenon and his name is firmly entrenched in the history of the race. No rider had been able to win six titles before. Armstrong did, then raised the bar again and the tally to beat seven!

At the age of 34 he was in command throughout the final race of his career. Only two riders, both from the CSC team – first Dave Zabriskie then Jens Voigt – were able to get in the way of an all-yellow trip around France in July 2005. Of course Lance won a stage, but he waited until the end to sign off with a fine display of his time trial style.

In the car that followed sat John Kerry, a candidate at the previous US presidential elections who made the trip to the Tour to witness history. At an informal gathering in the car park of a hotel in Saint-Étienne on the final Friday of the Tour he expressed his admiration of Armstrong:

I admire the guy for so many reasons. Of course there's the cancer story. I've read the book but I'd followed his career before that anyway. He rides with panache and although I did appreciate what the Tour was all about before, he has made it even more interesting.

Senator Kerry sipped champagne from a plastic cup and admitted it was the first time since the election he'd been without bodyguards. He clapped along as Laurent Bezault played on drums from Burkina Faso while other Tour staff sang songs they'd learned in the African nation that also hosts one of the races organised by ASO (Amaury Sport Organisation). This was not an official function. It was a gathering at the end of a long day and an arduous three weeks. But the Tour de France has a way of bringing nationalities together and attracting interest from the millions who gather on the roadside to cheer, or the television audience around the world, or visiting movie stars and politicians.

Armstrong's return from cancer coincided with the first post-Festina Affair race. EPO had been exposed and the peloton was rife with it. All cyclists were now under suspicion because of the 1998 race which very nearly came to a grinding halt after a team car was found to be carrying a cache of doping products. Subsequent police raids revealed that Festina was not the only team implicated, even if the Andorran-registered squad did earn naming rights for the infamous, problem-plagued Tour.

The last man to win before the Armstrong era was Marco Pantani. The Italian didn't cope with the pressure created by his success. He became a recluse and although he returned to the race and even won two more stages, his career was in tatters after having failed a doping control on the eve of what should have been a second Giro d'Italia victory in 1999. He developed an addiction and a little over five years after his Tour triumph, Pantani was found dead in a hotel room.

The Tour lost some of its sparkle at the end of the 1990s. Redemption was required and that's when Armstrong reappeared on the scene. Between the prologue in 1999 and the final day of the 2005 Tour, Lance won seven titles, 22 stages and the hearts of fans everywhere. He set a new standard for racing the Tour with a pragmatic approach, single-minded focus, committed team-mates and guidance from team director and tactician Johan Bruyneel.

Lance was the first winner to finish the three-week race with an average speed higher than 40 km/h. He achieved this in 1999 and again in 2001, 2003 and 2004. His winning time in 2005 lifted the speed to a new record. He rode 3595.5 kilometres in rain and wind, over mountains and onward to Paris at an average of 41.654 km/h! He was spurred on by some of the best athletes in the world but even his nearest rival was four minutes and 40 seconds slower. It was his farewell race and he was still in complete control. Clearly there's a reason why he is known as 'The Boss' of the bunch. Seven titles demand respect.

On the bike Armstrong had the power to control almost every circumstance. His legs would spin the cranks at a rapid rate and while others would follow, they eventually dropped by the wayside because they just weren't able to continue with the effort. There are many places where Lance has stamped his authority on the peloton with a fine display of climbing or time trialling. The names of these towns and ski stations are now recognised. Some have become the title of products that are now part of the Armstrong catalogue. Sestriere. Hautacam. L'Alpe d'Huez. Luz Ardiden ... They are all sites of great conquests. On the last day of his career, Armstrong narrowly escaped crashing into three teammates who had fallen on slippery roads in Châtenay-Malabry just after the first intermediate sprint on the way to Paris. It was yet another example of the luck this man has experienced at the Tour over the years. On the tarmac lay the Best Young Rider, Yaroslav Popovych, but Lance missed riding into him more by chance than anything else.

Armstrong learned a lot between 1999 and 2005, and not all of it relates to how to win the Tour de France. Other riders have been quick to try and imitate his approach but one thing is certain: there will never be another athlete like him. With his victory over cancer he became a role model for millions. Through his conquests at the Tour he has left a lasting legacy in the sport. He believes in miracles and helps others do likewise.

2nd: Ivan Basso

With the Armstrong era over, the obvious question about 2006 was asked many times: who will be the winner? Judging by his performance in 2004 and 2005, Ivan Basso was a clear favourite.

Basso didn't behave like a star in 2005 when he discussed the race:

> *I don't know what I can do. Every day I try but he's [Armstrong] always there.*
>
> *People think we race for second, but why would we do that? I look at him and think he's tired, so I attack. And he just follows. Next year, sure, but ...'*

He stopped. Winning the Tour is one thing, but to do it against Lance was what every man wanted in 2005. Ivan had become a complete rider at CSC. He had been a climber but now the Italian also had a strong time trial. He was a contender who wanted to prove himself.

I'll try again tomorrow. Only one more day in the mountains ... I hope I have a good one.

He did, but this time it was still not quite good enough. Next year, sure. That was the sentiment then. But there wouldn't be another time in the next four years. He would never start in the 2006 Tour. He was there for the presentation but was sent home before the race began. He had been implicated in the *Operaciòn Puerto* scandal, denied it but accepted the team's decision to suspend him. He would later be sacked because of the rumours. Then he signed a contract with the Discovery Channel team to race for the squad that Lance owned but was no longer racing for. But it would eventually all come to a grinding halt. He would be suspended for two years and, in 2009, make a comeback – the same year as Lance Armstrong.

3rd: Jan Ullrich

In 2005, aside from Armstrong, Jan Ullrich was the only active rider to have previously won the Tour de France. The German had always been consistent in July but also had a mandatory bad day every year. With a bit more luck and much better tactics he could have been a far greater star.

When he previously had claimed the runner-up position in 1996, the race was sensational to watch. Back in 2003 he defected from T-Mobile and arrived at the Tour only days after the birth of his child. In 2005 he was back in the magenta team stripe of Team Telekom and was again declared the most serious rival by Lance Armstrong. 'Jan is in excellent shape and he will get better as the Tour goes on,' said the Texan. 'We expect him to be a major threat.'

Again the German was racing at a time when his personal life was in a state of change. He'd separated from his long-term girl-friend Gabbi and begun dating the sister of team-mate Tobias Steinhauser. But he was motivated by the race he won back in 1997 while only a second-year pro. 'We have a very strong team and we want to impress with exciting and attacking cycling.'

While reconnoitring the time trial course on the eve of the first stage he slammed into the rear of the team car he was following. Shattering the window, he suffered abrasions on his neck.

That night he was outside his hotel holding court with all the members of his team except Alexandre Vinokourov. He was cracking jokes and appeared in good spirits. His management had entered a squad that was committed to winning the *maillot jaune*.

Since 1997, Jan had always had one bad day. In 2005 he had more than one. Yes, he improved as the race progressed, but vic-tory had already been achieved by his nemesis. It happened as early as Stage 1 when Armstrong caught Ullrich before the end of the 19-kilometre time trial. A podium place, it seemed, was the best he could hope for and although he tried it was all in vain after the *Grand Départ*.

He too would be singled out as a client of Dr Eufemiano Fuentes, the doctor at the centre of the Operaciòn Puerto blood doping scandal. He threatened a comeback, threatened legal action – and has been in and out of the courts – but has never come back to ride the Tour. Like Basso, he was presented in Strasbourg in 2006 as part of the line-up but he never even got to roll down the prologue start-ramp. He was sent home before the race and has never competed again. The end of Lance's post-cancer career also marked the end of Ullrich's presence in the Tour, but no one would be sure of that for a few years.

8th: Cadel Evans

The longer the race lasts, the more natural talent and experience take over from good fortune. After about 10 days the body gets a real taste of fatigue. Soon everyone – the riders, directors, masseurs, mechanics, race organisers and journalists – are so stuffed that no one knows the difference. Then the third week starts ...

It's the end that really surprises you. It's amazing to experience how the human body adapts to combat fatigue. After the final time trial I remember gibbering away to Robbie about how tired I was. I was just pleased that I could string a sentence together ... or could I? It was hard to tell because I sure didn't get much of a reaction from Robbie. He was still focused on the challenge of winning the final stage, while I was just relieved to be arriving in Paris. I'm pleased I made it and if you want my estimation of how I thought I performed, I'd say that I was around the eighth best in the race ... well, at least that's what the results show.

13
2006: Hope fades

The playing field is not level

The benefit of hindsight allows us to look at the events of the 93rd Tour de France and the man who was crowned champion on 23 July. Floyd Landis – fabulous fable or a failed fight?

Floyd Landis knew he could win the 2006 Tour de France and his quest for the yellow jersey eventually became a reality. But a series of events ensured that the anticipation of exactly who the winner of the 93rd edition would be remained high until the dying days. As he stepped off the podium at the end of Stage 17 in Morzine after receiving a bouquet for his stage victory it was the end of a special day, one that would be talked about for many years to come. The rider couldn't stop grinning. He had just achieved a major coup one day after a mighty collapse.

His tactic on the Col des Saisies was from yesteryear – old-school risk taking that would either pay big dividends or see him slip further down the rankings and into obscurity. He had worn the *maillot jaune* after the first mountain top stage finish but let the prize go two days later, before regaining it again at the summit of L'Alpe d'Huez.

But he lost ten minutes in the mountains at La Toussuire and slipped from first to 11th overall. He recovered by Stage 17, the final day in the mountains, but if he still wanted to win, his only choice was to attack. He couldn't wait until the last of five ascents and hope that he could accelerate with such force that he would make up the eight-minute deficit to Oscar Pereiro's lead. The Spaniard, Pereiro, was given a gift of a half hour advantage in Stage 13; he was in the overall lead and had the tenacity to hold on until Paris.

Until the halfway mark of the final day in the mountains, Pereiro's team was in charge of the peloton. An escape group had gone clear but there were no GC challengers present in the group. Pereiro's Caisse d'Epargne–Illes Balears team had to set a tempo that was fast enough to discourage other riders at the top of the overall standings from stealing time. And that's what they were doing when the green and gold posse from Floyd Landis' Phonak squad moved to the front of the bunch. At the base of the category-one Saisies climb, Phonak was on the move.

Landis' colleagues raced through until there was nothing left in their legs. One by one they fell by the wayside and then the team leader left everyone in his wake.

'I was up front on the approach to the Col des Saisies,' said Cadel Evans who was one of the last riders to lose contact with Landis.

All of a sudden I saw Phonak getting organised and I remember thinking, 'What the hell are they doing?' They rode and rode and rode … it was so fast! And by the time we hit the steeper parts of the climb, Landis was the only one left from his team. He was totally committed. He wanted to ride everyone off his wheel.

It was a phenomenal display, something not seen at the Tour for decades. This was the sort of stuff meant to make the 2006 Tour one to savour – an awe-inspiring attack that was so ambitious it seemed ridiculous. He had 125 kilometres still to race. It was obscenely hot and four climbs were still ahead of him, yet Floyd never looked back. And it was all premeditated.

The Australian Michael Rogers was the last rider capable of matching the pace being pounded out by Landis. On the Col des Saisies he did what he could to follow but, like everyone else before him, he succumbed. 'He was flying,' said Rogers. 'We were motoring up a gradient of 10 per cent and Floyd was doing 38 km/h and still accelerating. Of course I wanted to stay with him but I just couldn't.'

The heat was taking its toll. With the temperature soaring above 40 degrees it was not a day to push beyond your limits. 'I paid for it later,' confessed Rogers. 'I vomited about eight times during the stage. You had to keep drinking and eating but everything I took on board just came back up a few minutes later.'

As everyone suffered, Landis pushed on. At the summit of the 1650 m high Saisies climb he was over three minutes ahead of the peloton. This advantage continued to increase. At the top of the Col des Aravis, Floyd led by four minutes 30 seconds. By the final category-one ascent of the 2006 Tour, the Phonak captain was the virtual leader of the race. He'd swept past most of the early escapees and put over eight and a half minutes between himself and the peloton. This was no ordinary ride!

Evans appraised what was happening behind Phonak's captain and Renaissance man:

We were all stuffed! Caisse d'Epargne was doing the work but they ran out of puff and Pereiro simply ran out of team-mates. That said, the CSC and T-Mobile teams still had numbers but they didn't do anything until they eventually realised, 'We're going to lose the Tour!'

After this became apparent, they rode well. It was really fast. It was a good move to do what they did because Carlos Sastre [CSC] was the best rider in the third week of the Tour.

That may have been the case, but Sastre's captaincy was an improvised arrangement at CSC that year. The Spaniard was originally a support rider for Ivan Basso, but the Italian never got to the start. Basso's exclusion because of *Operaciòn Puerto* wasn't the only factor at work on that day to Morzine when Sastre finished as the second-best rider, five minutes and 42 seconds slower than Landis.

All but three riders finished over seven minutes behind the American in Stage 17. Óscar Pereiro was seventh and still in yellow but he knew his days in the lead of the Tour were now numbered.

'It's clear that Floyd is the strongest rider in the race,' said Pereiro in Morzine. He had a 12-second lead on Sastre, and Landis was at 30 seconds behind, but his humility allowed him to become a fan of the stage winner. 'It's incredible what he did today. I'm happy for him because he just dominated.'

Pereiro summed up the general feeling on the day. Landis was on fire and even the cynics in the *salle de presse* were inspired by what they'd seen in Stage 17. 'The Tour is alive,' declared journalist Jean-François Quénet. 'This is the sort of thing we've been waiting for: a rider with panache taking a chance and winning!'

It wasn't until the final time trial that Pereiro reached his limit. He'd hung on by the skin of his teeth and was beaten by a ride by Landis that was phenomenal. Pereiro finished fourth in the last race against the clock and arrived in Paris with a deficit of less than one minute.

Landis had a wealth of courage, that could not be argued. But was there something else at work on the day he captured everyone's imagination with his aggression on the bike? By the following Thursday a different tone prevailed. Praise quickly turned to scorn when the UCI (Union Cycliste Internationale) prematurely announced that the A-sample of the winner in Morzine failed a routine doping control … and for such a simple product!

Floyd was apparently resorting to a synthetic form of the hormone that's produced primarily in the testes – testosterone. Big balls indeed! Floyd Landis would claim innocence based on flaws in what is a complicated testing protocol.

The basic method employed to find the product is to examine the ratio of testosterone to epitestosterone. To do this a lab performs a gas chromatograph–combustion–isotope ratio mass spectrometry test (GC-C-IRMS). This test became a focal point in the case surrounding his urine sample, which was found to be positive for exogenous testosterone after Stage 17.

Testosterone, whether it be natural or synthetic, contains both C-12 and C-13 carbon atoms in its molecular structure. What the mass spectrometer is trying to measure is the weight (mass) of the carbon atoms in the molecule, which is like a fingerprint for a molecule. Natural testosterone theoretically contains more C-13 carbon atoms than synthetic testosterone, so the two compounds should produce different mass spectra. The difference in C-13 between natural and synthetic testosterone, when determined using GC-C-MS, is as small as 0.01% – an exceedingly small number – and the ability to accurately calculate such a difference requires precisely calibrated laboratory instruments and rigorous statistical methods.

This was happening in an era when the benefits of EPO were being exposed. The drug designed to increase the oxygenation of blood was appearing on a regular basis. The history of blood testing in cycling is a long one. And it's been more sustained than any other sport. Before you even consider the blood passport regimen that is required in modern professional cycling – a world first in the fight against doping in sport – it's worth noting that this was the sport that first started examining blood values in 1997. In part of a new ruling, if a rider's hematocrit was above 50, then they were considered 'not fit to compete' and a mandatory two-week cooling off period was immediately issued. This is how it was and would be until it could be definitively ruled that someone had used EPO. The natural levels of an average healthy man can be in the 40s, and there's nothing too unusual about that. Often it can be in the high 30s. But it is noted in cycling circles that '43' is not a number that's too extreme as an average. There have been riders – including one who won the Tour de France in 1996, and later admitted to using EPO to achieve the title – who have had nicknames based on, effectively, their percentage of red blood cells. It's a second language. If you talked about 'Mr 60' then most people understood who you were talking about.

In the 1999 Tour de France, there had been a favourable tailwind for the 194-kilometre Stage 4. The peloton raced along the flat lands between Laval and Blois and, in a rush controlled by the Saeco team of Mario Cipollini ('Cipo'), the famous Italian dashed over the line first. His average speed, and that of the 174 others who finished in the same bunch, was recorded as 50.353 km/h. A joke circulated the pressroom before the end of the day. 'Oh hey,' they laughed, for it was the post-Festina Affair Tour after several EPO doping scandals, investigations and confessions mainly focussed on the Festina team, but also implicating others. This was after drugs had been too prevalent and too exposed, surely, for any fool to consider the temptation. But Mario Cipollini was the fastest man in the history of the Tour. No other road stage had ever finished at an average of over 50 km/h.

Blame the wind.

So the joke was simple: Why should no one be happy?

Because everyone was over 50!

It's not simple science and because of the many sensational doping revelations testing is ongoing and relentless for cyclists.

Many other sports have much less challenging testing requirements.

Operación Puerto and the Festina affair gave cycling a bad name and many cyclists have acquired asterisks beside their names indicating a bad test, retrospectively stripping them of an award or implicating them in a doping scandal. Often forgotten were the many riders who have, as a result of these revisions of the results, won stages retrospectively, including Cadel Evans, long after the cheats have enjoyed the accolades on the podium.

The doping debacles of 2006 and then again in the 2007 Tour de France acted as catalysts for cycling's governing body, the UCI (Union Cycliste Internationale), to introduce what it called a 'Blood Passport'. In October 2007 the notion of a collection of data of all doping controls undertaken by riders with a professional licence emerged at a summit in Paris. The conference was arranged to find new means to combat the scourge of cheating that had become synonymous with sport. And while doping had been prevalent in bicycle racing for years, it was following the infamous Festina Affair that cycling became the veritable whipping boy; it was as though the performance-enhancing drug culture was the exclusive domain of those who raced on two wheels. According to Eufemiano Fuentes, the doctor at the centre of the scandal, cyclists were not his only clients; many were footballers and tennis players. Of the 200-plus names on the famous dossier the only athletes who suffered any consequences were cyclists.

Landis and his legal team were to claim that a significant margin for error existed using GC-C-MS testing and that not even the

World Anti-Doping Agency WADA has approved of the protocol used by the French lab that issued the positive findings.

On 11 September, Landis' attorney asked the United States Anti-Doping Agency to dismiss the case. It didn't. It found Landis guilty and declared the original tests were valid. Floyd Landis had synthetic testosterone in his system, and that wasn't allowed.

Even before the positive test was announced, however, questions were being asked. Was it physically possible to achieve what Landis did in Stage 17? Of course we'd like to think so; it was displays of force like this that made the 2006 Tour such a thrilling contest. But was it clean? Evans is the same height and weight as Landis. He explains:

> *On the internet, Floyd's power output from that climb had been published. He uses the PowerTap system and the power profile he had for the Col des Saisies was absolutely incredible. If you look at that effort alone – not even taking into account the fact that he continued on alone for another 125 kilometres, it just seems beyond human capacity. I can't remember the power and the exact details of the watts per kilogram, but it was impressive. The ride he did that day was the most incredible athletic performance I've ever seen.*

Landis had a rollercoaster ride around France in July. He experienced spectacular highs and demoralising lows. Hindsight allows us to look at the comments made during the race in a different light. 'There should be an asterisk next to the name of the winner,' said Lance Armstrong on the second rest day. 'But it's unfair to say that this is a tainted Tour.'

When Lance said that, he was referring to the exclusion of riders implicated in *Operaciòn Puerto*, not those who made it such a spectacular race.

These guys train their tails off. They show and beat everybody who starts so they are the winner. It doesn't matter who has retired or who was kicked out, whoever steps on the top of the podium in Paris … they are the winner.

That would ultimately prove not to be the case but at the base of the Parisian podium on 23 July, Landis insisted he was 'proud of the way I raced, even if it was a bit stressful at times'.

When asked about his plans for the future, he could not have known what was about to unfold:

For now I have no intentions of changing teams; I'm very happy here. The best case scenario is that I won't miss any racing. I should be all-right. I've always believed in fighting for what you want.

3rd (then 2nd): Andreas Klöden (T-Mobile)

Leadership by default was a theme of the 2006 Tour de France. The T-Mobile squad lost two riders before the start, Jan Ullrich and Oscar Sevilla, yet still had the power to win three stages, put two men in the top 10 and claim the team classification. But did Andreas Klöden let an opportunity slip?

Once they'd come to terms with Jan Ullrich's dramatic exit, T-Mobile rallied to ensure it had a significant presence in the race they expected to dominate. On Day 4 there was already a reason to celebrate: Matthias Kessler won the stage to Valkenburg, and his team-mate, Australian Michael Rogers, was second in the stage, which was enough to put him into second on general classification, only one second behind his former team-mate Tom Boonen. Rogers commented at the time:

> *We needed something like this. It wasn't a great mood for a few days there, but Kessler only has one speed: full gas! It's that sort of attitude that has helped us recognise that there's still a lot worth racing for. We just didn't know how to go about it ... but now the motivation is back. We all had good form so we're going to capitalise on it.*

By the start of the second week the German T-Mobile team was in charge. Serhiy Honchar was the only rider to finish the 52-kilometre time trial course for Stage 7 at over 50 km/h. The Ukranian obliterated his opposition and repeated his Giro d'Italia coup by claiming the leader's jersey, just five days before he turned 36. He explained:

> *I'm sorry for what happened with Jan at the start but we all prepared 100 per cent for the Tour. I think we are now showing that this is a very competitive team, even if we're not exactly sure of what's yet to come.*

T-Mobile had several leadership options but it quickly became apparent that the tactic was to look after Andreas Klöden. The 31-year-old finished second in 2004 and while he is a fragile character, he has the pedigree to be a champion. All he needed was good support and a hint of luck. Klöden commented on the second rest day:

> *The team has bonded very well. Maybe it was good to have had*

only seven riders at the start. [Matthias] Kessler is riding the Tour of his life; he's both our motor and motivator. Patrik Sinkewitz is also on a roll, so is Mick Rogers … and you can't replace Giuseppe [Guerini] with his vast experience in the Alps. I will try not to give an inch, should Landis or [Denis] Menchov attack. And if the moment is right, I will have a go myself. I haven't lost sight of winning the Tour yet.

This was on the eve of the L'Alpe d'Huez stage. Klöden had been consistent but never dominant and it was clear he should be the protected rider. He'd finished in the top five of 12 stages including four second places – two in close sprints at the end of a day in the mountains and two in time trials – but victory had eluded him.

But errors at crucial times meant Klöden was destined to stand on the third step of the podium. Had T-Mobile cooperated with Phonak's chase on the day of Pereiro's big escape, and had Landis not been given the leeway to gain so much time to Morzine, it all could have been different.

4th (then 3rd): Carlos Sastre (CSC)

Bjarne Riis had a plan to win the 2006 Tour with Italian Ivan Basso, but it promptly fell apart a day before the start when Ivan Basso was implicated in *Operaciòn Puerto*. Carlos Sastre then stepped up and duly delivered the first of his two Grand Tour fourth places for the season.

The boss of the CSC team was sitting on a park bench about two hours after Floyd Landis won Stage 17. Bjarne Riis stared into the distance and appeared to be asking himself what else could be done. Carlos Sastre had a deficit of just 12 seconds in the general classification. According to many, the Spaniard was the strongest man in the race, but the mountains were over. The only place where time could be gained now was in the time trial on the penultimate day.

'He feels good,' said CSC *soigneur* Josep Colomer about Sastre at the site of the finish for Stage 19. 'He has no stress. He said, "I'll do my best, what more can I do?" And that's it. Carlos rode the last part of the course with Bjarne early today and then he went back to the hotel to rest.'

There was no use putting any extra pressure on Carlos. He had worked hard on the climbs to be within striking distance of the overall lead, and although he'd never worn a leader's jersey in his career, hope remained right up until he reached the finish of the 57-kilometre individual test in Montceau-les-Mines. Alas, races against the clock are not his forte: he finished four minutes 42 seconds behind Serhiy Honchar and over three minutes behind Landis. A day that had begun with a slight chance that the American would falter again ended with 19 riders finishing ahead of the Spaniard.

'The time trial is a tough discipline,' said Riis afterwards. 'If you haven't got the legs, you lose a lot of time … Of course it would have been nice to make the podium, but we have to be happy about what we have shown this past week.' Exactly! Why lament an honest fourth place that would later become a third?

5th (then 4th): Cadel Evans (Davitamon–Lotto)

'It's an amazing event,' is how Cadel Evans described his second Tour de France. 'You've got to be there to really appreciate it.' After several years missing out on the opportunity to start, he had achieved two top-10 finishes from two attempts. 'My results have certainly won me a lot of respect …'

In 2006 Cadel Evans would eventually earn the best Australian result in the general classification at the Tour (he would surpass this in the two subsequent years). On the final day of the race in 2006, aged 29, he was fifth. That's the same place Phil Anderson claimed in 1982, when he made his second appearance (and again in 1985). Once Floyd Landis was flicked from the top spot, Cadel moved up a place. When asked how he thought he had finished, he commented after considering the matter, 'It depends,' he said, before the final result was resolved. 'If you look at the results from the French laboratory, I think I'm fourth. If you look at the American legal system I might be fifth.'

At the time, no one was quite sure what would happen, although everyone had an opinion. But what concerned Evans was that he had put in the best performance possible. And he did so clean. After finishing his second Tour, he added in his soft voice:

I'd like to improve still. Going to fourth would be interesting but it's not like I'm holding any hope of that happening. And who cares about retrospective awards? I'm looking forward to next year. All things considered, I'm happy with my Tour. With another year of experience the podium is a realistic target.

You didn't see a lot of Cadel during the coverage, but he was hiding from the wind, not the cameras. He dismissed requests for interviews only because he was focused on a job. 'I don't attack to be on television or to make journalists happy. I do it to win the Tour.'

Cycling is not like motor sport. Although a rider can appear to be in a good position to attack, that doesn't mean the motor can respond.

> *I know what my limit is and I'm fully aware of when I'm going above and beyond it. I don't know if people believe how hard I was going. They'd say, 'Why didn't you just go a bit harder and put in an attack?'*
>
> *I thought, 'Well, I was actually starting to lose vision at that point on the climb …' The fact that I was even at the front at the end of some mountain stages is more than what many riders could do. The Tour's not a short event; it's not a case of, 'I'll just hang on a little bit more …' I'd already been hanging on for 20 days!*

The Australian's name was high on the list of favourites. And with good reason; he's a naturally gifted athlete who relishes tough terrain; the steeper, the better. Or so he thought … until he got to L'Alpe d'Huez. He was in fourth place on general classification. Landis' advantage was just one minute 17 seconds. Then, on the climb that should have suited him, Cadel faltered.

> *L'Alpe d'Huez was my worst day on the Tour. It's a climb I'd normally do well on but it wasn't a stage that suited me. When we hit the final climb it was really, really fast. Phonak rode at an*

incredible speed at the start and about two kilometres up there were three of us left: Landis, Klöden and me ... that was it. Everyone else rode at their own pace.

In hindsight, I think it might have been better if I'd ignored the antics up front and approached the final climb of Stage 15 at my own speed, but I wanted to maximise my chances of winning the Tour. That's why I followed Landis. They say everyone has one bad day. Maybe that was mine.

Evans lost contact with Landis, was caught by other riders and settled into a rhythm with the group containing Pereiro and Michael Rogers. He dropped down the rankings but there was still hope. In the stage that followed, the day to La Toussuire when Landis suffered a dramatic collapse, Cadel finished fourth and moved back into the top five of the general classification. Evans described the day that Michael Rasmussen won and Landis dropped from first to 11th:

Floyd looked like he was playing a bluff. He's cunning, and as we approached the Col de la Croix de Fer, I thought he was either having a really bad day or ... If I had followed him, I would have lost 10 minutes.

'It was what went on before the final climb that mattered,' said Evans about the stage that began with the Col du Galibier and concluded with an 18-kilometre climb that is by no means as tough as L'Alpe d'Huez even though it claimed a major scalp.

What happened after the day to La Toussuire will never be forgotten. And although Floyd's spectacular ride to Morzine was a solo effort, it was set up by a team committed to one cause. Many people believe Cadel is hindered by Davitamon–Lotto's two-tier focus: Cadel's GC result and Robbie McEwen's quest for stage wins. Cadel doesn't agree:

Of all the sprinters, Robbie's the one that needs the least help. He can win without a lead-out train. If he has someone who can get him in the right position in the finale like he had [with Gert Steegmans], then he can finish off the job.

As a GC rider, I'm also able to find my own way pretty well. I don't think there are other GC riders or sprinters who could do what we do. Robbie's done so much on his own and I suppose he learnt to find his own way. Now it's paying off. And I'm happy to make the most of what the other teams do.

And it was only a few injuries that limited the support Cadel could have had. 'If I'd had a healthy Christophe Brandt and Chris Horner, that would've been enough for me,' said Evans, before pointing out the work that's often done before the live coverage begins.

It's not obvious on television – things like Johan Van Summeren riding into the wind for 120 kilometres; all I did was sit behind him all day just to save my legs. That might have been the difference for me finishing where I did in Morzine, or losing five minutes.

Next year Davitamon–Lotto was going to have a stage race specialist calling the shots from the team car at the Tour. The squad had recruited Roberto Damiani, the directeur sportif who provided guidance for Evans when he was a neo pro at Mapei. Another good friend from the early days was Dario Cioni, who had been poached from Liquigas to offer support in the mountains.

Cadel was content with the result but knew more was possible.

We did win three stages, and had a rider in the top five, and we won the green jersey. The only team that was close to that was Rabobank. I wouldn't say we had a bad Tour!

14
2007: Most consistent performer

The two seconds

It's winning that everyone is interested in and it's normally only the victors who are remembered. I'm an athlete and a competitor so it's a win that's the focus.

One evening at the end of 2007, only a few hours after Cadel Evans came sixth in the Giro di Lombardia, the final race in the ProTour series, there was a gala dinner hosted by cycling's governing body, Union Cycliste Internationale. The UCI had a year-long 27-race program that featured all the major events on the calendar: one-day classics and stage races including the three Grand Tours. Called to the podium for the main presentation that night was Cadel Evans. It was a nice prize, one the UCI wanted to present to the best road cyclist in the world, as determined by a complicated points system. The man who acquired more than any other was an Australian, Cadel Evans.

He was part of the Predictor–Lotto team when it claimed first place in a team time trial in the Coppi–Bartali stage race at the end of March. Of the races that made up the ProTour in 2007, Cadel won just once and it was retrospectively awarded. And even though he wore the white jersey for the Giro di Lombardia that year, he never received it in a ceremony, as he inherited the lead from a rider who was absent because the UCI had banned him from representing. Danilo Di Luca had been at the head of the rankings but was unceremoniously withdrawn from the series because he had been involved with a doctor with a dubious reputation, and was part of a saga that became known as 'Oil For Drugs'. So Cadel wore white because Danilo Di Luca was gone – evicted while in the lead from the series that was the reason for the gala affair on the shores of Lake Como in October 2007.

The winner of the Giro d'Italia that year had led the ProTour. But he was out of the equation and, years later, gone for a longer time after testing positive to EPO–CERA (in 2009, after finishing second to Denis Menchov in a nail-biting finale of the centenary edition of the Giro).

At the ceremony to conclude the series, during the speeches, Cadel was introduced and, as he strode up to the dais, the commentator explained that he was a rider who 'never won a race in the series'. Of course, in his acceptance response, the winner reminded all present of Albi: 'They tend to forget that one.'

But it's one worth remembering for it was this display that was honest and pure, fast and impressive. It was this sort of character who could win the Tour de France. He didn't win a lot in 2007, but he was always there. He missed out on points in just three of the ProTour races he contested, but he still had enough to take out the title with 252 points in total. The next best that year was Davide Rebellin, a rider who finished in second place in the Olympics the following September, a rider who had won Flèche Wallonne and Liège–Bastogne–Liège, a rider who – you guessed it – would later fail a doping control for CERA. But that wasn't until 2009.

Still, Cadel beat him in the ProTour in 2007; 252 points to 197. In third place was Alberto Contador with 191 points.

Going into the Tour, neither of these two were the favourite. Quite simply, there wasn't really one. There wasn't even a number '01' in the peloton. The sequence for the 2007 Tour de France began at '11'. The legacy of Floyd returned. Oscar Pereiro began the race with the lowest number, but at the start of July that year he still hadn't been formally notified that he was the winner of the previous edition. Cadel would later be formally notified that he finished fourth, but it would come in September.

With the number 1 *dossard* absent in 2007, the Tour would begin with several considered good chances but it was also widely acknowledged – by Pereiro as well – that the 2006 result, while eventually legitimate, was also a strange sequence. And in a lucky break, the one which initially earned the Spaniard a taste of the yellow jersey was what yielded the ultimate prize. He'd escaped. He'd gained time. At the end, he was the first rider in the general classification not to have failed a drug test. He was the winner. But that didn't make him a favourite again.

In London, it was the city that made the headlines for the *Grand Départ* rather than the appearance of any one rider at the obligatory pre-race medical control. The fact that the Tour had gone to the British capital for an ambitious foreign start was what made the race popular. But before the race, there was a dark cloud lingering on the sport. The UCI had issued an ultimatum: riders who wanted to participate in the ProTour had to sign a pledge that if they were caught violating doping regulations they would tender a year's worth of their salary to a fund established by the governing body. This unwanted contribution would be used to fund future anti-doping education campaigns and to improve testing procedures. It was a publicity stunt then and remains that today. There were plenty of men who were caught by the clause, but to date not a single euro has been exchanged as part of the pact.

However the promise of clean cycling remained the focus of the headlines as the start of the Tour got closer. Then when racing finally began the action could be considered. There were impressive displays; strength and courage were rewarded. Cheats did prosper but were also evicted. Liars did continue and fraudsters infiltrated the results, but an honest guy continued to be consistent. He was later that year rewarded for this when he was presented with a jersey that represented all that the UCI could hope for: a white jersey. In 2007 he was the ProTour champion. It was important then and will remain significant in the history of cycling. This was an impressive achievement, but the crowds care for one race more than the entire series. The Tour de France is the one that matters. The man who would become the best rider in the world that year was there; he was amongst those listed as possible candidates, but this was a race to be won at a curious time for cycling. And he was ready!

Cadel Evans was the most consistent performer in professional cycling in 2007. His focus was on achieving the objectives he set for himself at the start of the season. That included racing in March in the Paris–Nice, France, April in the Vuelta al Pais Vasco, Spain, May in the Romandie, Switzerland, June in the Dauphiné, France, and July in the Tour de France. In his sights was the yellow jersey.

But on the final day of the Tour de France in 2007 there was just 23 seconds separating first from second in the general classification. In theory, victory was still attainable by the man who was 23 seconds behind. In theory it was possible for Cadel to win the Tour de France on the last day. With two intermediate sprints both offering six, four and two seconds off their aggregate time at each, a win at both intermediate sprints and Cadel would have been in with a shot at victory. Even if the leader Alberto Contador was second at each, the difference for the final dash – which offered 20 seconds, 12 seconds and eight seconds to the first three over the line – would have been 19 seconds.

Cadel's *directeur sportif,* Redant, was adamant that defeat was not accepted until the final time the riders emerged from the tunnel leading to the left turn onto the Rue de Rivoli. The yellow jersey was still within reach. Twenty-three seconds. Not a lot can happen in that time. Redant explained the only possibility as far as he could see it:

> *The only way you can do it is winning the last stage and having 50 metres in advance. And the only way you can do this, is get out of*

that tunnel and go like a madman and just explode. There is always a chance you can make it. All you have is that little tiny chance and you have to take it.

In 2007 life had been breathed back into the Tour. It was exciting again. That's not to suggest that Lance's years were not good for cycling but it was different now that the difference was so little. New champions were emerging. But when Cadel arrived in Paris he still had the deficit of 23 seconds and he came second.

'Experience,' wrote Oscar Wilde, 'is the name everyone gives to their mistakes.' Cadel didn't lament his loss to Alberto Contador. The gap was so tangible that he could recount the actual instances when time slipped away, such is his experience. At the age of 30 he'd been a pro athlete for half his life – and there had been many chances. He could list the moments when the Spaniard got the better of him: 'It was Astana not chasing over the Peyresourde, Contador and Rasmussen working together, and that one acceleration up the Aubisque when I couldn't follow Leipheimer.'

That was the day he lost 12 seconds to Contador. His nemesis is a man who can outsprint anyone in the peloton when a gradient is presented; a rider so strong that when he lost over half a minute due to a chain problem, he was not only able to catch the lead group but attack them again.

Evans had none of that luxury. He can match pace, follow wheels and also attack. But that's hard to do when valuable energy has been spent doing the work that others have team-mates for.

The Australian held his own but couldn't respond to the vicious accelerations of the Spaniard. Evans recalls one of several crucial days:

The stage to the Col d'Aubisque was all about not losing time to Contador. Of course, if the opportunity came to take time then I'd go as hard as I could, but not losing it was the main objective. It wasn't the only day of the Tour I had to fight that. I know exactly the moment I lost the Tour: it happened as we went over the [Col de] Peyresourde. After that stage I was absolutely furious. Not many people understood why I was so angry about 56 seconds.

His reference was to the final climb of Stage 15. He was in a group of ten that included Carlos Sastre, Alejandro Valverde, Leipheimer and three Astana riders – Andrey Kashechkin, Andreas Klöden and Serguei Ivanov. They finished 56 seconds behind a group that included Contador, and six minutes 47 seconds after the stage winner, Alexandre Vinokourov.

A turning point of the Tour happened on 24 July. A bulletin was posted on the *L'Equipe* website stating that Alexandre Vinokourov had failed the doping control for the time trial he had won. Within a matter of seconds everyone in the press room had heard; it may have been the fastest spreading news in the race's history.

Did that mean Cadel had won a stage? Technically, the answer was yes. But it was a minor consolation. Evans reflected on his achievements in 2007:

It's different from winning a one-day race in a sprint, where you are losing the race until maybe the last 20 metres, then all of the emotions come in a rush. In the Tour, you start doing well in the first 20 metres of the prologue. You don't stop losing the Tour until you cross the finish line three weeks later. It is an emotional release that extends over a three-week period.

When asked what he considered when he heard about Vino – and the fact that he had won a stage – Evans related a story about his good friend and team-mate Chris Horner:

I couldn't believe it. Chris hadn't gotten out of bed all day and he jumped up and said, 'Yeah! I moved up a place on GC!' To gain a place without getting out of bed is pretty good, I think.

It wouldn't be the last time either, thanks to the Rabobank team's decision to send Rasmussen home.

In 2007 though, second place in the Tour de France was recognised for the great achievement that it was, even at home in Australia where the mainstream media had never taken much interest in cycling. Evans enjoyed a surge of media interest after that July. It was the first time an Australian had stood on the podium in Paris at the end of the Tour de France as part of the general classification presentation.

Cadel was pleased to see his sport finally gaining some media attention because he appreciated the chance it presented for him to introduce others to the sport that he loves so much:

To see that change and be a part of it is something I'm proud of. I like to promote our sport, and sport in general. A satisfying aspect of my result at the Tour is the number of people in Australia who had never watched cycling, but they saw every night of this year's Tour and loved every minute of it. People are discovering cycling and I'm excited about that happening.

In October 2007 Cadel won the ProTour, confirming his place as the most consistent rider in a series that, in 2007, still included all the major races on the calendar – including the three Grand Tours as well as the collection of one-day Classics. At a gala function beside Lake Como, with the rest of the cycling elite, Cadel celebrated the end of a season that spanned March to October. Cadel's string of high placings – first in the Beijing Olympic test event, second to Vinokourov in Stage 13 of the Tour de France and second overall in the Tour de France, Dauphiné Libéré and Tour of Poland, fourth in the Vuelta a España and Tour de Romandie, sixth in the Giro di Lombardia and seventh in the Paris–Nice race – accumulating enough ProTour points to make him the highest ranked rider in the world.

In the 2008 Tour de France history would repeat itself, only this time Carlos Sastre stood on the top step of the podium in Paris at the end of the 95th Tour de France. But it was the combined effort of the CSC–Saxo Bank team that got him there.

CSC–Saxo Bank had the strength of numbers and dominated the race at all the critical moments. The Spaniard had been sheltered by his colleagues until the base of the deciding stage to L'Alpe d'Huez. Until that final ascent of Stage 17 of Le Tour 2008, Carlos Sastre had been riding in the shadows of team-mates without having to exert himself more than necessary. He was relatively free of any pressure. He had not crashed, nor had he faltered badly at any phase of the race before arriving at the base of the celebrated climb. He was ranked fourth overall, 48 seconds behind another CSC–Saxo Bank rider, Fränk Schleck, who was the sixth rider that year to wear the *maillot jaune* but he would not be the last. That honour was left for Carlos Sastre – 'Carlito'.

'We wanted to explode the race at the bottom of the climb. Carlos just went. He was strong and ... that was the plan.' Bjarne Riis had tears in his eyes as he spoke at the summit of the mountain that Sastre used to climb into the overall lead. 'I'm very, very proud,' continued the Danish team manager. Gone was the frustration of 2006 when Ivan Basso who was to lead his forma-tion in France that July was found to have had an association with a dubious doctor. A shy, humble Spaniard became the team's reluctant leader in 2008.

On that day, he grew wings, but Riis knew all too well that more was required. What about the final time trial? Was Bjarne confident that his quiet crusader could cope? With a coy laugh at the knowledge that there was still work to do, Riis nodded. 'I will make him fly.' He didn't need to. After the 53-kilometre penultimate stage Riis was glowing. 'We were united and very strong,' he said in Saint-Amand-Montrond. 'Today, Carlos found the will-power to win the Tour de France.'

Carlos Sastre became the third Spaniard to win the Tour in three years. His win was the result of a master plan by Riis. The rider who was fourth overall the previous year was to be protected in a team acknowledged almost universally as the strongest in the world. But that didn't mean the race was just his for the taking.

Sastre had been close to the yellow jersey after Stage 17 in

2006 when he was ranked second overall, just 12 seconds shy of the lead. On the final Thursday of the Tour in 2006, he crossed the line five minutes 42 seconds behind Floyd Landis. On that day Sastre was, in fact, really the winner. It's a sad reflection of the times that retrospective victories are relatively common.

That's how it was for Cadel Evans and Kim Kirchen in 2007; the reason? Alexandre Vinokourov. He won stages, but he cheated. The Australian, Cadel Evans, and the Luxembourger, Kim Kirchen, would eventually receive an email from the head of cycling's governing body to say 'You won.'

Amidst the racing in the 2008 Tour there was all sorts of intrigue to contend with. A cast of villains on miracle elixirs were up against others who were trying to resuscitate the sport's reputation with clean, honest competition. Alas, the 'baddies' were still beating the 'goodies'. Of the 21 stages in the 2008 Tour de France, five were won by riders who would end up failing doping controls.

But Sastre had nothing to do with the tainted shenanigans that took place on the roads between Brest and Paris in July. Before the action got under way, Riis presented his team to the media in Brest in the far west of France:

> *The team is very homogenous and very strong. The team is prepared in the way that we wanted, the best way to be 100 per cent for the Tour. And, of course, our leader will be Carlos Sastre. We believe he can be one of the best in the* classement *but we also have Fränk and Andy Schleck who are both in very good condition ... everybody knows them and what they're capable of. I feel very comfortable and confident that we can be competitive in all the stages – especially in the mountains.*

Looking only at the opening week of the 95th Tour de France – which, contrary to tradition, began without a time trial to establish a pecking order of those men actually capable of aiming for victory – there was reason to be satisfied. Cadel came close to winning stages but never did; still, he was the most consistent of all in the general classification standings. Cadel is consistent; it's one of his many strengths and he was the only rider who remained in the top 10 of the GC standings all the way through the 2008 Tour. His stage placings would vary although he was always in the top 40, even when the sprinters were battling it out for the day's spoils on flatter terrain.

In the general classification for three weeks his statistics were impressive. Broken down after each day it was: sixth, fifth, ninth, fourth, second, second, second, second, first, first, first, first, first, third, third, fourth, fourth, fourth, fourth, second ... second. His luck ran out at the halfway mark but he lost the Tour with just one day to go.

Many other stories would be written during the 95th Tour but the tale of Carlos Sastre's surge near the base of the ascent to L'Alpe d'Huez is what most will remember it for. It was emphatic and effective.

'I was suffering a lot, man,' Sastre said following Stage 17. 'When you suffer that much you can't really enjoy it.'

There were many others on the mountain that day who appeared to be in a lot more trouble than Sastre. Perhaps the secret to his apparent composure lies in what he was actually achieving. 'If you're gaining time, it's a big satisfaction inside and you're pushing, pushing … as much as you can and you try to go as fast as you can.'

The three CSC musketeers – Fränk Schleck, Andy Schleck and Carlos Sastre – arrived at the climb primed to create havoc. The only one of the team not present at the head of the peloton was Stuart O'Grady. Instead of being part of the lead-out train for Sastre's epic and ultimately successful sprint to the summit, the Australian had emptied with a turn of pace setting that lasted almost 100 kilometres. And Fabian Cancellara had the honour of leading the bunch onto the early slopes and as soon as he peeled off, it was … Game On!

On that final Thursday of July 2008, CSC hoped to take control of the Tour. Fränk explains the plan: 'He should go first,' said Schleck of Sastre, 'then I was to attack and then Andy was to have a go. We would keep going in that order until we made the other team leaders tired.'

That was how they cracked Cadel Evans, and how Fränk squeezed out a nine-second gain on the Australian who had led the Tour for a week. Cadel later commented:

The rest of us have to watch for splits or be aware of the crosswind or whatever other problems may occur. With Carlos and that team, it's different. He could relax a little more because he knew he had such strong support. An enviable position to contend the Tour from.

Cadel has plenty of praise for Carlos. He admires many of his traits:

He's got a really good eye. He can sit in the middle of the bunch, keeping out of the wind, and seems to sense when it's time to move forward and mark his rivals. Secondly, chances are that if a group is going to split it's highly likely that it's going to be his team that's creating the carnage.

When that happens, obviously he's going to know well before the shit is gonna go down and he is not only prepared for it, he's part of the reason for it happening.

He's someone I've always spoken to. I think 'amicable' is a good description. He's always someone I've gotten on well with. Everyone seems to appreciate him and he's never a rider who's caused problems for anyone.

When he was riding for Basso and I was doing my first Tour in 2005, Carlos was always there for Ivan to get bottles and do his domestique *duties. One day, when he was returning from the team car with a jersey full of* bidons, *Carlos said to me, 'Look, if you ever need a bottle or whatever when you're alone, just let me know and I'll get you one. If I can help, you let me know.' He knew I was a little isolated. To do that for a competitor is a sign of the person that he is, and also his sportsmanship.*

The Australian warns that it will be different for Sastre in the future. 'Having now won the Tour once, he won't be able to ride the race as he did this year to win it again.'

CSC's riders knew they were going to go one, two, three … one, two, three until one of them got away. Did the rider they feared most, Cadel Evans, expect that Carlos would be able to take as much time as he did?

No, but he was lucky having done that attack, because having Andy Schleck with us – who, in my estimation, was the strongest climber in the race – meant that we couldn't go after Carlos without taking him with us; their advantage was having two behind, and a Spaniard in front. The Spanish press would have crucified Sanchez or Valverde if they rode their own race and assisted me in the chase.

On L'Alpe d'Huez there was only one team there that had more than one rider and that was CSC. If you look at the composition of the chase group you realise how strong Sastre's team was. Caisse d'Epargne had one rider (Valverde); Rabobank had one rider (Menchov); Silence–Lotto had one rider (Evans); Garmin had one rider (Vande Velde) … I think CSC deserved to win the Tour.

'Relief' – that's it; relieved.' That's all Cadel Evans had to say at the end. 'Relieved.' He repeated it when prompted again. Was there anything else to add? Surely there was more going on in his mind after finishing second in the Tour de France. But he wouldn't budge. There were no excuses. The then 31-year-old sighed, wiped himself down quietly just minutes after finishing seven seconds ahead of Carlos Sastre in the stage to Paris, but 58 seconds slower than the Spaniard in the Tour's race for the yellow jersey. He was less than a minute behind. It was the second year in a row that the winner was less than a minute ahead of him.

As well as being relieved, he was distracted, this time by a small Australian flag being presented to him to take onto the podium. 'He was behind the split? Oh …' It interested him but what could he do? A minute. Why not 10? The difference was irrelevant. It was all over.

For that moment, briefly catching his breath before climbing the steps leading to centre stage on the Champs-Élysées, he wanted to be calm. There was a distinct lack of any showmanship. He is criticised for being coy, abrupt, sometimes snide; at other times he is accused of being angry, placid and temperamental when he is the centre of attention. He understands that it's part of his job but doesn't understand why he should tolerate being pushed and shoved while catching his breath and gathering his thoughts after racing up a mountain or three. When you're at the point of exhaustion, how do *you* feel?

Under pressure, in pain, people lash out. A television reporter triggered the rider's wrath after he grabbed Cadel's damaged shoulder in what was meant as a congratulatory gesture. It was on Stage 10, the day Cadel became the fifth Australian to wear the Tour's *maillot jaune*. It happened as Cadel was talking to a reporter from Norwegian television. He was explaining his emotions on claiming the lead by one second: 'Yesterday I thought my Tour was over and today …' He was in yellow. He was also very sore. He crashed badly in the ninth stage; skin was torn off his back and the left side of his body with bruising that sank much deeper. Ligaments were damaged and he raced the stage wrapped in bandages. Despite the setback, he had lived up to pre-race expectations. The favourite for the title – the runner-up in 2007, the rider with the number-one *dossard* – was in the lead. The journalist didn't mean to cause harm. Cadel didn't mean to lash out.

Apologies were later exchanged and the world kept on spinning without any consequence.

But his brevity during question times had many weary journalists poised with venomous pens. 'So far, so good.' It was the centrepiece of many of his musings up until Stage 9. Things had been going well when he wasn't the centre of attention; that responsibility went to stage winners and the consistent Kim Kirchen who led the general classification as the first rendezvous with the high mountains loomed. Evans used these four words to sum up his emotions on what would turn into more of a roller-coaster ride than he would have liked.

He arrived at the Tour relatively fresh. He was runner-up to Alejandro Valverde in the Dauphiné Libéré at the beginning of June, claiming the same position he'd earned a year earlier in the crucial lead-up race. He illustrated that, despite the opinion of some pundits, he was willing (and able) to attack. He just couldn't shake the Spaniard, who would sprint to stage honours on Day 1 at the Tour. Still, Evans could be satisfied with his progress. So far, so good.

The relief he talked about so insistently on the final day softened the blow of what might have turned into bitterness. For the second successive year many believed Cadel Evans was the strongest rider in the Tour de France, but that he lacked the good fortune and team support of his Spanish rivals that was required for success in the race for overall honours.

He eventually opened up to journalists waiting beside the red carpet to the podium on the Champs-Élysées. After stepping down from centre stage, flag in hand, it was time to explain his emotions:

To wear the yellow jersey after such a selective week of racing was really something special. It was an experience I think every bike rider wants to have. I've never worn a world championship jersey but it was quite incredible to be in yellow. I've learned things that will stand me in good stead for future Tours.

Only a few minutes after a stint beside Carlos Sastre and Bernhard Kohl to accept the accolades for his second place, Cadel had begun considering the 2009 Tour. First, however, he vented about one bout of bad luck.

I'm cursing one Spanish rider, Number 29, who brought me down by accident. To come back and finish second and be able to hold off the rider in third … that's something I'm happy with.

Gorka Verdugo is the man known to Cadel by number, not name. It could have been anyone. Accidents happen and the Australian acknowledges that it wasn't a malicious move by the Euskaltel–Euskadi rider. A touch of wheels is all it took for Number 29 to crash. Evans happened to be right behind and had no time to react.

I'm pleased that I was able to continue after the crash. To come back and get yellow was a bonus. There's always room for improvement, otherwise I might have walked away feeling content with an eighth place Tour debut. But I've done a lot in the last four years to improve on that result.

It wasn't Cadel's plan to take the yellow jersey so early. The team support he had was better than the three previous times he'd started the Tour. The management of Silence–Lotto realised that the rider who claimed second place last year deserved all the backing they could conjure. No longer would they divide their cast between helping Robbie McEwen win stages and Evans in his quest for a high GC placing.

This year it was all for one. 'Yell For Cadel.' This was the working title of a documentary about his 2008 Tour campaign. Serge Borlée was recruited as the bodyguard. Yaroslav Popovych ('Popo') – who had served both Lance Armstrong and Alberto Contador when they won – was enlisted as a super-*domestique*. All riders who were shortlisted for the Tour were happy to join Cadel at training camps in the lead-up to July. But they were not the most formidable crew in the Tour.

Borlée did his best to protect the rider but admitted that Cadel did a pretty good job of it himself and, through it all, the pair became friends. 'Popo' served a purpose but he was far from the freight train force he had been during his tenure at the Discovery Channel squad. The Ukrainian wasn't useless but he certainly didn't offer the protection that Evans needed.

> *The team do everything they can and that's all I ask of them. I think the performance of the team correlated with my effort on the bike … they lost a bit of morale after the crash and that, coincidentally, was when all the mountains started and where the team's weakness lies.*
>
> *There are other riders and other elements I would battle once my passion became my career. But I don't lament lost races. What's the point? Second is a place. It is what it is.*

15
2009: Finding a solution

Moral fortitude

There had been trying times, professional frustrations and personal tragedy leading up to his fifth Tour de France but upon arrival for the *Grand Départ* in Monaco in 2009, Cadel appeared to be in a sea of tranquillity – relaxed and content.

Equipment difficulties and race schedule confusion plagued his pre-season training, difficulties that would have been insurmountable except for the dedicated support of good friends and family.

On 7 February 2009, a week after he left Australia for the start of the European season, bushfires of unprecedented ferocity tore through huge parts of Victoria. One of the worst-hit areas was the valleys and hills of the Kinglake Ranges just north of Melbourne. Early reports out of the chaos were that the community of Arthurs Creek was destroyed. It would be twenty-four hours before he would learn that his mother was safe. But with relief at that news came the tragic news that Danny Shepherd, one of his closest high school friends from his early teenage mountain biking days, and a big part of the pleasure during summers at Barwon

Heads, was killed in the fires. The Kinglake Ranges were Cadel's 'country', the place where he grew up and developed the passion that would take him to the other side of the world. Just as his family still lived in the area, so did many of his friend's families. The small communities in the area remain devastated; many people lost family, and everyone lost friends.

By July on the morning of the opening stage of the 2009 Tour de France, it was a considered and controlled person who warmed up on the rollers on the west side of the harbour of the rich little municipality of Monaco. Of course he was distracted. But he smiled at the sight of familiar faces – his stoic façade cracked a little and he allowed a glimmer of humour to emerge once all the formalities that led to race day had been completed. Cadel had come to race. But this time he was adamant that he was not just there to be part of the peloton. After two years finishing second, he was intent on improving. He was insistent about his approach:

> *To me, it was to win it and nothing else. A bad 2009 Tour would have been to finish second or third.*

There had been changes forced upon his support cast only three days beforehand. Investments in the team had continued to be made where possible to ensure the best possible crew arrived in Monaco in 2009 primed to take on whoever turned up for the 96th Tour. Of the nine men who had been named as part of the Silence–Lotto line-up, the Dutch candidate had to forfeit his place.

Thomas Dekker had been part of the Rabobank line-up since

the beginning of his career. He joined the Dutch squad's development program as a teenager, and had achieved such success early that he was promoted to the senior team within two years. He enjoyed immediate success, becoming national champion in both the road race and time trial in 2004. The next year he would contest his first Grand Tour, finishing 75th in the Giro d'Italia. A year later he won a ProTour stage race, the Italian season opener from sea to sea, Tirreno–Adriatico. By 2007, he was part of the stellar cast that took Michael Rasmussen from the Alps to the Pyrenees in the yellow jersey.

Then Dekker's glory years were over. He started fast but his end was swift. Rested from competition from April onward, he did line up for one showcase criterium in August, beating Danilo Di Luca and Bernhard Kohl in the 100-kilometre set-up fixture with the rhyming name, Draai van de Kaai. But all three failed a doping control: Kohl for the new-generation EPO, CERA, after finishing third in the 2008 Tour de France; Di Luca for the same substance after finishing second in the dramatic centenary edition of the Giro d'Italia in 2009, and Dekker became a casualty of retrospective testing. Silence–Lotto's PR people issued an explanatory statement after Dekker's dismissal:

> *He found out on Wednesday morning that fresh analysis, carried out in May at the behest of WADA on urine samples from a random doping control, had turned up positive for EPO.*

Had the news about Dekker come three days later, the entire Silence–Lotto team ran the risk of being eliminated before even a pedal had been turned in its major appointment of the season.

Cadel attacks the Col d'Aubisque in Stage 16 of the 2005 Tour de France. He wears a black band on his left arm in memory of his compatriot, Amy Gillett, who was killed in a road accident while training the day before. He finished the stage in fourth place and moved from 11th overall to seventh. He finished the 2005 Tour de France eighth in general classification. (*Yuzuru Sunada*)

Cadel (at right) congratulates fellow Australian and team-mate Robbie McEwen after his third stage victory in the Tour de France. (*James Startt*)

Chiara Passerini and Cadel Evans raise a glass on the day of their wedding in Gallarate. The reception was in 'Cascina dei Brut', a farm house that has been converted into a restaurant in Chiara's hometown in the Lombardia region of Italy.

The three musketeers: Chiara, 'Manneke' and Molly up on the hill just behind their Swiss apartment in Stabio, just three kilometres from where he would win the world championship road race in 2009. (*Daniele Venturino*)

The off-season lasts just a matter of weeks. He takes a break from the bike for less than a month each year and enjoys the time he gets to spend at his home in Barwon Heads. (*Jess Vreulink*)

Cadel and his beloved 1966 Mustang coupe, which he proudly declares, 'looks like it's just been driven out of the showroom, but there are hidden extras like the CD and MP3 player under the dashboard'. (*Graham Watson*)

Cadel's position on his time trial bike is extreme, so much so that he had to modify his 2009 team-issue Canyon to attain the low position he craves to minimise wind resistance. This photo is from the opening stage of the 2009 Vuelta a España, a race in which he would finish third overall. (*Graham Watson*)

In 2007, after he first finished second in the Tour de France, he was invited by organisers of the Melbourne Cup to carry the famous trophy onto the race track. (© *Sport the library*)

A day after his crash in the ninth stage of the 2008 Tour de France, Cadel was bandaged and a severe shoulder injury restricted his ability to stand while riding, but he still had the tenacity to fight to the first 'hors catégorie' summit of that year's race at Hautacam. It was on this mountain that he took the lead of the general classification and received his first yellow jersey. (*James Startt*)

Hendrik Redant has been one of the pivotal people in Cadel's cycling career. The Flemish *directeur sportif* assists the rider after a mechanical problem early in the 2007 season. (*Graham Watson*)

Cadel receives the yellow jersey after the stage to Nîmes during the 2008 Tour de France. This was his third taste of the podium protocols during the race and – after an initial faux-pas when he forgot to shake hands with the dignitaries waiting in the wings – he had learned not to make the same mistake again. (© *Sport the library*)

In the yellow jersey, Cadel follows the wheel of his Silence–Lotto team-mates Christophe Brandt and Robbie McEwen with British sprint sensation Mark Cavendish on his left. (© *Sport the library*)

Second for a second time: Cadel stands, Australian flag and toy kangaroo in hand, as the Spanish national anthem is played for Carlos Sastre, the winner of the 2008 Tour de France. Bernhard Kohl finished third and wore the polka-dot jersey as King of the Mountains, but would later be exposed as a cheat who used EPO–CERA to falsely achieve this conquest. (*Yuzuru Sunada*)

Lance Armstrong entertains Cadel before the start of a stage of the 2009 Tour de France. (*Graham Watson*)

The winning attack...! Going over the final climb of the circuit in Mendrisio, Cadel surged ahead of his escape trio – that also contained Alexandr Kolobnev and Joaquim Rodriguez – and onward to the gold medal. 'I've ridden that climb hundreds of times, but this was the only time I did it with the chain in the big ring ... I knew this was the chance to win the world championship!' (*Graham Watson*)

One dirty rider can spoil the image of an entire team.

Bernhard Kohl, the Austrian crowned the King of the Mountains of the Tour de France in 2008, finished third overall and appeared to have emerged as a bright hope for future editions. He had signed a contract with Silence–Lotto for 2009, but, like Dekker, he would not be in Monaco. He too would be exposed as a cheat and admit his culpability.

However Dekker's omission, or that of Kohl, didn't rate a mention in Cadel's appraisal of the race:

> *In summary, the Tour started well. In Monaco I was happy, healthy and content. I had pretty good results just beforehand and things were going well leading in to the race. Everything was under control. The results from the Dauphiné were promising.*

In Monaco, Cadel was content. He didn't care about Dekker. He dismissed the case, relegated it to memory and moved on. It's what he did after Kohl was exposed. And he knew that he had a troop behind him who, although it wasn't the strongest in the peloton, was a group with no shadows of doubt.

Dekker was replaced by Charlie Wegelius, and that fact alone broadened Cadel's smile. The Finnish-born, British-registered racer who lived in Italy was another key off-season recruit by Silence–Lotto. He is a linguistics freak, who already spoke English, Swedish, Italian, French, Spanish and German, then recognised that Flemish would also be useful. It seemed only right that he take on another language. 'When we signed the contract in August, he had already picked up a few phrases and he surprised me with his accent already,' observed Hendrik. 'By the time he turned up for a team meeting at the start of October, he was virtually speaking Flemish. He'd even mastered some dialect.'

Wegelius was admired for his proficiency with languages but that's not the reason he was hired. Roberto Damiani had worked with him at other teams, first at Mapei when he made his pro debut, and again at Liquigas in the year before Damiani signed on with Silence–Lotto. Damiani explains why he values Wegelius:

He is the perfect domestique. He doesn't like to be in the spotlight. I don't even know if he's ever won a race but I've seen him set things up for others to win. I can say, 'Charlie ... we work now.' And 100 kilometres later he will still be on the front of the peloton setting the pace. He can pull back escapes. He can climb. He can suffer like a dog! But if you tell him, 'Charlie, it's your turn to win now ...' he doesn't know how to respond. It's not in his nature. Charlie works. He likes to do it. He is an asset and I'm proud that he's part of this team.

Forget Dekker. The ghosts of what might have been were no longer relevant. Cadel was quite clear about how things stood at the start of the 2009 race:

It was all under control. It was going all right when everything was considered. But then the team time trial came and went; from that stage onward ... well, losing two and a half minutes put me a bit too far behind.

In my mind, it was too much time to lose. From there on it just went downhill for me.

There are few instances in his riding life that have been a setback. In his four previous attempts at the Tour he had progressed: eighth in the 2005 debut; fifth to fourth in 2006 after the Floyd Landis' testosterone 'error', second by just 23 seconds in 2007; and second again in 2008, 58 seconds behind the winner. He had been close to the top step and it was the place on the podium he coveted in 2009.

Just three days after concluding his racing program in 2008, Cadel found himself in the French capital for the unveiling of the route for the 2009 Tour de France. It was an exercise in generating hype that his team had asked him to attend. Almost as soon as one season ended, he was presented with the route that would occupy his mind until the next July. Cadel was typically succinct with his responses to journalists who were looking for insights into how he thought he'd fare in his fifth attempt.

I have to race whoever turns up. The race decides who is the best. All I have to do is prepare properly and do the best I can.

His appraisal of the 2009 route – from Monaco to Paris – was characteristically summarised in one word: 'Interesting'. When plied for more information he offered enough for a sound-bite but little more. 'It suits a strong team. Twice I've finished just off the top step of the podium, so I have to believe I've got a chance.'

The comment came after the ceremony that displays the *parcours* on an enormous screen in the Palais des Congrès in Paris. The audience is treated to a montage of images from the previous year's Tour. It has become an interesting exercise for the organisers to portray the action that had unfolded the preceding July. Needing to be culled from the 2008 review were some pivotal players, men who raced with the assistance of CERA in their veins – delivering more oxygen to depleted muscles – and propelling them ahead of their clean rivals who were trying to complete the race honestly.

Bernhard Kohl was occasionally seen on the screen. His positive result had only recently come to light. Stefan Schumacher, a team-mate of Kohl who won both time trials and wore the yellow jersey for a day, was also missing. So too was Riccardo Riccò – a 'winner' of two stages before departing the race after becoming the first to fail a new test for the new-generation EPO. In total seven men would appear in the Tour's 2008 records with asterisks beside their names. Like Dekker, Kohl, Riccò, Schumacher, Leonardo Piepoli, Manuel Beltrán and Moises Duenas Nevado, the six who failed controls in 2008.

The auditorium was full. The seats were filled by dignitaries, cycling personalities – former Tour champions, stage winners, young hopefuls, also-rans, *directeurs sportifs,* race staff, journalists, town planners and mayors, politicians and royalty. It presented quite a crowd. Prince Albert II of Monaco made a speech before Christian Prudhomme explained the 21 stages and an itinerary for 2009 that would include a team time trial (for the first time since 2005) and the imposing Mont Ventoux, a climb that's synonymous with suffering. This monster that emerges out of the flat landscape of the Vaucluse department is not part of a mountain range. It's a giant that stands alone casting shadows over Provence. Ventoux has been part of the Tour on 13 previous occasions and evokes fear and trepidation from those who must scale it if they want to complete the Tour de France; it has taken the life of a cyclist during the race. Never before had a mountain like this come after the final time trial. It's one of the famous climbs of the race and its presence always earns gasps when it's revealed that it will be part of the itinerary.

From the moment the route is plotted there's discussion about what could come of the next Tour. The calendar is packed with road racing events that litter dates from January until December so that – if a rider was sadistic or stupid enough – he could compete 12 months a year. For the GC Guys it's all about timing: finding form at exactly the right moment and trying to hold onto it for the duration of the event they target.

Cadel has learned to pace himself. He understands pragmatism and avoids the temptation to race more or less than he needs to. If he's to achieve his ambitious objectives, he must get the recipe of events just right:

Peaking for a three-week event isn't like you just turn up on Day 1 and ride through to the third week and make sure you're always at 100 per cent and just put yourself in a bag for the rest of the year. Everyone has to ride the same stages. The race will decide the winner. I have to be ready.

Commentary about what *could* happen annoys Cadel. For him it's little more than empty words. Being ready involves more than just honing his body. Everything must be considered: the riders need to be measured and fitted for clothing, both casual wear and cycling kit. The new recruits need to introduce themselves to their future team-mates. Representatives of the new bike supplier,

Canyon, need to be on hand to answer any concerns the riders might have about their equipment. A new wheel supplier, Mavic, had come on board at the behest of Cadel who wanted to improve the aerodynamics of his bikes, particularly the ones he would use for time trials.

He had been impressed by Canyon. 'There are amazing developments in materials and I'm surprised by the size of this company,' said Cadel afterwards. But he was already plagued with a problem that was distracting him.

'I can't get low enough at the front,' he said about his position on the bike. He's one of the most flexible riders in the peloton and years of diligent stretching exercises and pragmatic use of pilates have helped him tuck into a stance that minimises the frontal area which is exposed to the wind. The less he has to push against, the faster he can go with the same wattage pushed through the pedals.

It became obvious that a solution had to be found. Canyon's road bikes had a higher head tube than Cadel wanted and his time trial frame was 'just not right; we have to get them to build a new one for me'.

When he returned to Australia he was without a bike to train on. His new team bikes were not available and had still not arrived by the time the brief rest period was over. Two renowned local frame builders came to the rescue, producing training bikes for him to use during his time at home in Barwon Heads. Peter Teschner was responsible for a temporary time trial bike that provided the rider with the ideal position. And Darren Baum crafted a titanium frame for the road, and painted it Canyon white to ensure the sponsorship investment wasn't put in jeopardy.

Teschner and Baum can command several thousand dollars for their work on one bike, but for the two who wielded the welding torch it was a labour of love; they both tended to every one of Cadel's many requests without fuss. They wanted to help him with his campaign. With a little bit of planning and the cooperation of people who cared about what he was trying to achieve, a solution was found. He could train and set himself up for another assault on the Tour.

There would be other races to contest and thousands of kilometres would pass under his wheels before he arrived at the Tour de France, but it's this contest that consumes him.

Once it's over, however, he hates talking about it. Even when he finished second, he was frugal with words. 'Relief.' That's all he offered about his thoughts on reaching Paris in 2008.

In 2009 he had even less to say; he was not interested in talking. He opted to keep it all to himself and although he insisted there was nothing of interest about the race, he couldn't disguise the fact that he was still thinking about every element.

Cadel admits that the hardest aspect of the 2009 Tour de France was the ability to come back from what he considered a slump in form and health problems at Verbier. It was at this Swiss village nestled high above Martigny that he finished seventh. It was Stage 15 and already enough had unfolded that Cadel was no longer in the top tier of general classification. The main cause was the team time trial. Silence–Lotto failed. That happened on Day 4.

As expected, Astana was more than formidable with the strength of men who, between them, shared eight Tour titles and a wealth of other impressive results. The man the squad insisted was the leader when the race began in Monaco – Alberto Contador – had won the Tour de France the last time he contested it in 2007. Contador had also added the titles of the Giro d'Italia and Vuelta a España to his list of achievements. He is an agile rider with a display of speed on a climb such as we've not seen for years. The Italian cycling star Marco Pantani could fire off into the distance but even he didn't have the immediate acceleration of the Spaniard who beat Cadel by 23 seconds in his second attempt at the Tour.

Contador is now as complete as a cyclist can be. He weighs 62 kilograms and stands 176 centimetres tall. The scar of brain surgery with a horseshoe-shaped keloid shows through his crop of short dark hair. It's the same thing that interrupts Cadel's hairline.

The two have risen to the fore of a new generation of cyclists but at a time that it seemed the sport couldn't get any darker. Their arrival at the top of the classification at the Tour de France in 2007 coincided with the removal of the rider who won what ultimately became his farewell stage while wearing the yellow jersey. Michael Rasmussen's lead on Contador was three minutes and 10 seconds, and over five minutes ahead of Cadel when he was pulled out of the Rabobank roster.

No one wore the yellow jersey in Stage 17 of the 2007 race because the man who had it was no longer there. Rasmussen became a ghost. In 2007, by Stage 18 Contador wore yellow. He would take it again in Verbier in 2009. This time he did so convincingly. It happened as the Silence–Lotto team displayed a bout of mountain tactics.

On the approach to the climb at Verbier, the second mountain top of Cadel's fifth Tour de France – Contador's third, Lance Armstrong's twelfth – the Astana team was one of the dominant forces at the front of the peloton. There was a pursuit of sorts going on, but really the capture of the escapees didn't matter as much as making sure that the right people were positioned well for the ascent. It would prove to be the deciding moment of the Tour.

During the frantic dash to the foot of the mountain the name of Matt Lloyd was often heard over the airwaves of Radio Tour. He was one of the loyal workers who put himself at the service of Cadel, and roomed with Cadel during the Tour. Lloyd has a calming effect on people. His personality is complex and his conversation often obtuse but it's his whimsical indifference that helps mellow the mood. No one needs a sedative when they're trying to win the Tour de France but if anyone was able to help Cadel chill, it was Matt. 'Matt is like Valium,' observed a mechanic from the Silence–Lotto team. 'When he's around, it's difficult to feel stressed.' Lloyd explains his own approach this way:

There aren't a lot of things that upset me. I like to think that I'm fairly adaptable. Even when things get awkward because of a stressful situation, then I try to manage it.

In a bike race there are a lot of things that can go wrong but it also works in the reverse. One day you might have some good luck, the next it could be bad. That's life. But since my accident, I've been careful to remind myself about all the good things of the career I have.

That Matt was at the Tour at all was a remarkable achievement. The Belgian team had recruited him for the 2007 season, as his strength is climbing. In his second attempt at a three-week race, the Giro d'Italia in 2008, he finished 30th overall. It was a result he could be proud of, especially as he endured the effects of a knee injury which hindered him a little.

He was the Australian champion that year and he wore the green and gold jersey denoting this status in both the Italian and Spanish Grand Tours. His season began in January and ended on the same day as Cadel's: with a showcase two-man time trial the day after the Giro di Lombardia at the end of October. He had paced himself well throughout the year and continued his steady progression of learning how to live the life of a professional cyclist.

He was selected for the Olympic team for the road race in Beijing, and the Tour de France was the obvious next step for the one-time ice hockey player and former triathlete. But before taking that step, he first had to overcome adversity of his own. In the Amstel Gold Race in April his season stalled. He describes what happened:

I was with Fränk Schleck and the race was starting to hot up, about 60 kilometres from the finish. There were a lot of groups going off the front. From what I remember, we came around a corner and were actually going up a small hill. It was not a big climb, more of a false flat, and there were two guys in front of us who locked handlebars. It was just something stupid that can happen when you put over 200 riders together on a road and prompt them to scurry along for over 260 kilometres until determining who is the fastest. We had to take evasive action.

Fränk hit these dudes and smashed his head. It looked like he was dead.

All I remember was my front wheel hit the gutter, I went into the air, and then I had one of those moments that passes by really slowly. I had time to consider exactly what was unfolding but there was nothing I could do to change the outcome. 'Oh fuck! That's a tree!' And then all I remember is 'Snap!' That was it.

Fränk remained in the middle of the road and while he was being tended to, I waited. It was frantic and there were medicos beside me in an instant. And then my team car arrived. It all happens so quickly, but when you're living it, the sensation is slow motion.

When my directeur sportif *leaned down to try and get some sense out of me, I made sure I had his full attention and said, 'Just make sure, when I get to the hospital, that they x-ray my back. Something is wrong with my spine.'*

He said I was so relaxed. I was just lying there without panic. I was on the ground and already thinking, 'What good is panicking going to

*do?' It's not like I could run away from the situation. By the time I
was in the ambulance my mind started to wander. I wasn't sure if I
would even ride again.*

*If you can somehow find the motivation to really pick yourself
up, I think making a comeback is almost made easier because you're
not thinking about the actual work; you're just in a happy place. If
you can move, be happy. If you can ride your bike, cherish it. If you
can race the Tour de France, recognise how special that opportunity
is. I'm blessed. And I want to remember that. I have found a happy
place and it may not last forever, but the weeks in hospital gave me
new spirit. To just have the chance to get back on again – to ride my
bike – that's a beautiful thing.*

Matt Lloyd had come back from breaking his sacrum and
fracturing six vertebrae. The Dauphiné Libéré in June was his first
race since the crash. He had no pressure from the team to perform
and that helped him; during the opening rounds of the eight-day
race he hid in the bunch, followed wheels and got to the finish
without much fanfare.

Cadel, who had finished second in this French event the two
previous years, got the perfect start in 2009 when he won the
opening time trial, beating Alberto Contador by seven seconds.
In the scheme of things, the lead of a prestigious pre-Tour contest
was confirmation that his body was responding well and that he
was reaching peak condition at exactly the right time.

In the Dauphiné he had proven that his time trial form was
good. Victory on Day 1 was the perfect remedy to doubt; that was

raced over 12 kilometres and he was the fastest. Three days later there was another individual test, this time over a far greater distance: 42 kilometres – him, his bike, taking on the wind and terrain; a man against the world. Cadel had a point to prove and the fourth stage of the pre-Tour bout provided him with the platform to demonstrate his consistency. An escape artist, Niki Terpstra, had stolen the yellow jersey but the Australian took it back with an emphatic ride in the time trial around Valence. He didn't win, but he came very close. Seven seconds behind the world champion in the discipline, Bert Grabsch of the Columbia team, and he had every reason to feel satisfied. He finished well ahead of Alberto Contador who was fifth, and that put the Australian GC Guy back in charge of the *classement*.

The Dauphiné provided an opportunity to witness strange shenanigans between rival Spanish teams, and Cadel seemed to be the target. Spanish allegiances on Mont Ventoux would rob him of a victory in the Dauphiné, but Cadel wasn't finished. Jean-François Quenét, a respected French journalist who specialises in cycling, summed up the sentiment of what unfolded in the event held at the start of June. The itinerary of this warm-up race included Mont Ventoux and other elements that combined to give it a feel of being an event somewhat of a Tour de France style, albeit in a more concise format: two time-trials, plenty of mountains, the heat of summer and riders who were finding peak condition.

Quenét wrote about the obvious allegiance between the Astana rider and the defending champion who took the yellow jersey after the stage up the Ventoux:

> *The Australian didn't hide his irritation about Contador putting himself at the service of [Alejandro] Valverde. 'There was no more I could have done against two Spanish guys racing together,' [Cadel] said …*

Such collusion between riders from different teams is prohibited by the sport's regulators, although *commissaires* rarely want to take any action on the matter as it's often difficult to prove a coalition. Valverde was being ridiculous when he denied any deal by saying, 'Contador rode to keep his third place'. That explanation would have made sense had Contador chased riders who threatened his standing, but he actually only chased the rider who was one place ahead of him on GC.

It was in the Dauphiné and the stage to Mont Ventoux that provided a glimpse of possible challengers for the Tour. But that came on Day 5. Matt Lloyd was still riding into form. By the crucial Stage 7 Cadel's roommate became a key contributor to the race. Lloyd recalls the situation:

> *Every day I started to feel better. But I couldn't read into it too much because it's not often that your body feels too great after a significant time frame off the bike – when you're trying to remind yourself that it's all part of the recovery process … but eventually I found myself with a bunch of 25 to 30 guys at the end of a stage.*
>
> *In the simplicity of it all, I turned around to Cadel and said, 'I'm*

going to get on the front and I'm going to ride.'

And 25 minutes later, with six kilometres to go in the stage, there were four guys left on my wheel, all of whom were pretty much the biggest climbing names in the sport: Contador, Valverde, Robert Gesink and Cadel.

I had heard on the radio some normal encouragement and it then went quiet for a while. I gathered that something had unfolded – that I might have done my job …

I felt incredible. I really didn't turn around for the whole last portion of the stage. I just listened to the things that Cadel was relaying to me as he followed my wheel and also to what the direc-teurs were saying over the two-way radio.

We had Hendrik in the car and for me – and I think most of the team – he's not just a special person, he's unique in cycling with his ability to motivate people. When you have someone that influential behind you in the car saying, 'You're tearing the field to pieces here!' You don't need to turn around. You just assume that something is unfolding. And it's large.

Once Matt Lloyd had reduced the field to just four men on the penultimate stage of the Dauphiné he peeled off and let the respective team leaders duke it out. This is when Cadel opened up. Time and time again he surged forward trying to open an advan-tage on the slopes of the Saint-François-Longchamp climb that concluded the stage. Each acceleration was ferocious, spiced with the venom of a man trying to prove a point: I Do Attack!

Some commentators had taunted him over the years with the

suggestion that all he did was mark his rivals, follow wheels, watch the peloton diminish and ride for a good result but never attack for the win. It became a hobby for a few journalists, some who should have known better, others who will never fully comprehend the nature of bike racing. This is not motor sport; the engine is finite. Energy must be spared so that it doesn't run out before the finish. Cadel demonstrated what happens to a rider when all the fuel is burnt back on Passo Coe in the 2002 Giro d'Italia. A collapse can cost dearly: 14 minutes in less than seven kilometres can be the result of inexperience – combined, of course, with fatigue and honesty.

Throughout the Dauphiné, Cadel had been an aggressor. He didn't have the allegiances of the Spaniards who finished first and third. The organisers relished how he animated the action, and chastised the collusion between Valverde and Contador, but they couldn't do anything about it. Nicolas Cazeneuve, the son of event director Thierry Cazeneuve, told it as he saw it:

> *Evans made the race exciting this year. He was bold and daring. It might have been training for the Tour de France but thanks to his animation, we had an exciting race from start to finish.*

Cadel was grateful for the praise he received because of his attacks. He was pleased that it was noted not just by the Cazeneuve family but also by the media in general. But his policy remained unchanged: 'My job is to win,' he reminds people often. 'The only thing that is remembered about a rider in the Tour is the results they got.'

He did the Dauphiné because that's the race he did in the lead-up to the two Tours in which he finished second. And although the prelude event was used mainly to test his legs at race pace, he also excelled in it. For three successive years he has been the runner-up in the Dauphiné. All the while, his mind is on what's yet to come: the Tour de France. That's the race that matters most; that is what his year is judged by. It is the only race which accounts for bonus payments from his team if he excels.

My job is to ride a good Tour. Competing in other races helps to maintain or increase my value as a professional but that's all.

In the 2009 Tour the escape group that formed at the 40-kilometre mark of Stage 15 – Pontarlier to Verbier in the Swiss Alps – were 10 men including Jurgen Van den Broeck from Silence–Lotto. The Belgian was making his debut in the Tour but he was a strong rider who had prepared for July alongside Cadel. He had attended the training camps in the Sierra Nevada mountain range in the south of Spain, 'where there are no distractions, no journalists, no other riders but plenty of the right conditions: good roads to ride, long climbs to test the legs and accommodation at altitude'.

Jurgen was another of Cadel's support cast. He had ridden for the Discovery Channel team before joining Silence–Lotto and had some opportunities to expose his talents in the past, but the Tour is a different league to all other races. He had finished seventh in the 2008 Giro d'Italia, his second three-week race. He was more a climber than a time triallist but he has the capacity to become a GC Guy. This 26-year-old debutante was still doing his apprenticeship. Hendrik Rendant explained how he saw Jurgen's role:

> *It's good to have Jurgen in the move. He's not going to do a lot of work but we want him to contribute to the pace to help put some pressure on Astana and force them to chase.*

Mikel Astarloza was also part of the group that contained Van den Broeck. At the 125 kilometre mark they reached a maximum gain: four minutes 40 seconds.

> *If the group stays away then we may get Jurgen to ride his own race but there's also the option of having him drop back to help Cadel if necessary.*

Redant was employing more traditional tactics now. Here is how he saw it:

> *Cadel is fine after the first two weeks. He's in really good shape and now the challenge is to try and find a way for him to make up the time in general classification. We expect he will move up today. He's ridden the course just after the Dauphiné in June, so it's fresh in his mind. The last climb suits his strengths.*

It was true. But it suited Contador better that day.

Van den Broeck was impressive. He had recovered from a crash that happened on the day Silence–Lotto suffered the most – when they finished 13th, two minutes and 35 seconds behind Astana in the team time trial. He put himself in the escape, saved something for the finale and, when the general classification gathered halfway up the final ascent, he attacked.

It was his first true attack in a stage of the Tour de France and he quickly gained an advantage on a group of 12. And effective it was, for he immediately distanced the others in what was, until moments earlier, known as the 'yellow jersey group', except that Rinaldo Nocentini had just been dropped. He couldn't handle the pace; days of defending a coincidental leadership had taken its toll. He limited his losses but his yellow days were over.

All that remained in the selection that Van den Broeck attacked were two who had been part of the early breakaway – Fabian Cancellara and Mikel Astarloza. They were joined by the nine men who would finish the Tour at the top of the general classification: Contador, Andy Schleck, Armstrong, Bradley Wiggins, Fränk Schleck, Andreas Klöden, Vincenzo Nibali, Christian Vande Velde, Roman Kreuziger … and Cadel.

Jurgen Van den Broeck moved ahead. But at the business end of a bike race, not even the most efficient mountain man can accelerate away from the elite men of the Tour de France without having to wrestle his bike and fight the demons of fatigue. Still, Van den Broeck did manage to gain some momentum; metre by metre he worked his way ahead. It lasted long enough to be noted by Radio Tour. He had been identified. He had shown panache. He had his chance at the front of the race. But almost as soon as it started, it was to end.

The focus quickly returned to the group of 12, for there was movement of another kind. Alberto had decided it was time to fly. This was no ordinary display; it was brutally effective. Not even the television motorcycles had time to respond to the acceleration.

While everyone else was struggling up a mountain, the Spaniard seemed to be on flat roads.

Rising from the saddle, accelerating out of the shadows of his team-mates, Alberto shot ahead of the 12 and within a breath was alongside Jurgen. By the time the Belgian realised what had happened, Astana's leader was gone – off into the distance, never to be seen again until he crossed the finish line with his traditional salute. Fuelled by frustration with Armstrong – which would become a battle before the end of the race and a full-blown war of egos after the final presentation – he fired a shot that killed the hopes of every other rider in the race. Contador had these comments at the end of the stage:

I thought I'd attack between four and five kilometres from the finish, but when I saw the work that was done by Saxo Bank, and the fact that the group was already reduced to a handful of favourites, I decided to move into action earlier than planned.

I did everything I could. I put all my strength into the climb. I needed this stage to happen like it did, to make a big difference against my rivals. The only thing that concerned me was that I had good legs. I felt very good, but there were still some doubts before I went into action.

Contador found the answer to his doubts. The rest now knew who was in control of the general classification.

Some would continue to maintain optimism for they knew that the Ventoux was on the horizon. The eventual runner-up, Andy Schleck, declared that day that he would never concede.

'Tomorrow is a rest day and we'll try until …' He hesitated because he knew that it sounded a little fateful, but then let his ditty slip: 'We'll try until we die.'

This was a day when Silence–Lotto had laid its cards on the table. Just like every year he'd raced the Tour, Cadel was well positioned for the mountainous finale. He lost a little bit of time and finished seventh but was demoralised. Van den Broeck had obeyed team orders; he'd put himself in an escape, waited, attacked, got caught … and then limped to the line in 17th place. Lloyd served his last drinks before reaching the imposing ascent and then crashed on a roundabout.

While Astana stamped its authority – winning the stage, taking the yellow jersey, and igniting a fire that took careful political manoeuvring to manage – Silence–Lotto had suffered a blow. It wasn't the knockout punch but the bruising went deep.

Verbier; the thing that was strange there was that I was just not myself physically. I did everything possible to finish as best as I could on that climb. From the day that the route was announced it was obvious that this was going to be a pivotal stage. We visited the area after the Dauphiné and I rode the course as part of our reconnaissance efforts. It's an area where a close Australian friend lives and I have trained, raced and driven the 8.8 km climb many times. It was one of just three mountain top finishes for that Tour and I looked forward to what it presented. It's steep enough to ensure the elimination of all but the best.

The climb to Arcalís came too early and was not selective enough; in Stage 7 there would still be riders willing to wait, to mark their rivals, bide their time, play the patient game. By the time we got to Verbier, the race was going to be wide open. Those who were out of contention could mount an attack and maybe, with a bit of luck, muscle their way back into the top order of GC. But it was destined to be a stage suited to those few who were really able to challenge for the yellow jersey.

I was seventh and lost a minute and 26 seconds. That put me over four minutes down in general classification. At that point I was like, 'Shit! I'm not just not good; I'm bad.' Physically, something was not right. And I certainly felt well down on my usual level. My performance was good considering my level, but my level was at the worst in my Tour career.

Cadel was furious with himself. This was the place he could have reclaimed some of the deficit from the team time trial, perhaps even win the stage. At the very least he knew he was capable of not losing time to the main contenders ... but it didn't turn out that way. He fell further down the rankings at Verbier but the real damage was yet to come.

The 2009 Tour did not end how he had planned it. In fact, it was never right. From well before the start it was a race he believed he could push for the win, but his downfall had become apparent after four stages. There was a chance of resuscitation but at Verbier he began to concede.

We had a rest day and I thought, 'Okay, we've made it this far. I'll have a break.' And we'll just hope that whatever is going on heals itself. I could have been tired, or sick, or maybe I had a physical problem that I didn't know about. But I thought I'd be able to recover and be a bit better.

The following day, to Bourg-Saint-Maurice, as it turned out, I wasn't good. I was not even at the same level as before; I was worse. At that point, when they started attacking I was struggling to follow and I was already four minutes down ... I could see that I was riding up against a very impossible task.

Well before this realisation dawned on Cadel, members of his team had read the signs. Matt Lloyd was the one who, in theory, could have got closest for he was the one who shared a room with the leader. But even 'Matty' – the rider Cadel has been known to call 'his little brother in the bunch' was worried about his room-mate:

By the time he had tended to all the things that needed doing after each stage, Cadel had worked himself up into such a state that there were times when I couldn't understand what he was talking about.

He would come into the room staring at the result sheet and mumble a few words in English about the GC rankings. He was so distracted by the standings that he failed to articulate what was on his mind.

There were many aspects that had caused him frustration but at the heart of it all was the fact that another year had passed and the opportunity to find fulfilment had escaped him. Despite arriving at the start with arguably the best form of his life, there were other distractions that cost him energy.

His relationship with Roberto Damiani had suffered a blow. The Italian was part of the inner sanctum but it was his idea to have Cadel race the Giro d'Italia as part of the program of lead-up events. The Australian had not returned to the Italian Grand Tour since 2002 when he became the first from his country to lead the general classification. He admits that the idea offered some appeal. He may live in Switzerland but Stabio is just across the Italian border for a good reason: he loves the country where his wife is from. The culture suits his sensibilities. He enjoys speaking the language, and although Chiara enjoys the chance to correct him when he gets some terms wrong, she also admits that he's got a good command of Italian.

But riding the Giro d'Italia as training? No thanks. He's too competitive to just turn up, go through the motions and reach the finish with better form but without leaving an impression.

When the team announced that I would be riding the Giro d'Italia in early December, I had to change my whole mental approach towards the Tour. This, to a certain extent, changed the way I did all my work. At this point, in my mind, I was saying we may as well give the bouquet of flowers and congratulations to Contador now. You cannot win the Tour alone, and without Roberto's help, I was on my own!

The announcement that I was in the Giro d'Italia team was a bit annoying; it was made without my knowledge. They didn't consult me directly about it. We had talked about the possibility, but it was going back and forth and, in the end, I went back to Australia knowing that I had to give the idea some serious thought. The next thing I knew, the team declared that I'd be in Venice for the start.

Considering that, not even 24 hours earlier, I'd done an interview saying that I would not be doing the race, it all became a bit of a strange situation.

At Silence–Lotto though, there was the support of a group who had his interests at stake. The Tour de France eluded him for many reasons. The numbers can be reviewed in the result sheets, but the main time losses accrued were in Stages 4, 7, 15 … and then came the bomb.

Detonation came on slowly. The fuse was lit even before the start. He didn't recover on the rest day as he thought he would. His body wasn't responding as he expected. His mind was in all sorts of turmoil.

Since 2006 he had never been so far behind the leader of the Tour de France. He was ranked 14th in the general classification and for a GC Guy – someone who thought of little else, during work hours or idle time – this was a burden which weighed heavily on him.

'I was physically really down and that was very disappointing,' he explained.

He races a bicycle. He's paid well to do it. He gets to see a lot of the world. And Cadel recognises that these are benefits that come along with the calling he's answered. Damian Grundy was the first coach to really try and tap into the psyche of the future star. He admits that, once victory in the Tour de France started becoming a possibility, he was well removed from the life of the rider he invested a lot of time in. 'I'm the equivalent of the little kid watching the scary movie,' is how Grundy explains how he now watches Cadel race:

I'm hiding behind the couch. I've got the television on and the race is being broadcast. I'm there, but it's too scary to watch.

But in my heart I hope that it will turn out for the best. It would be a tragedy for him to finish his career without that victory. But, equally, there are already a lot of achievements in his career.

An Australian will win the Tour de France one day, whether it's Cadel or somebody else, and I believe Cadel is sowing the seeds of that potential victory.

It's hope that keeps me watching. It's belief that forces me to peek over the lounge and see the race unfold and wonder when his time will come.

While Grundy was there at the start of the career, Charlie Wegelius – Cadel's team-mate from Mapei and, years later, Silence–Lotto – assesses him this way:

Cadel is blessed with exceptional talent. I think that this is some-thing that passes many people by in cycling, especially the public.

The guy has an amazing engine and an ability to suffer that is way past the norm, even for a cyclist. And believe me, even average riders like me can take quite a bit of pain. I think that there is something about his mind, his way of seeing the world, that allows him to ignore pain or tolerate it in an unusual way.

———————

Chiara had come to Paris to be there for the final stage for the fifth year in a row and on the Monday after the 2009 Tour de France, Cadel was due to fly back to Stabio late in the afternoon. He was dressed like any other guest and was trying to blend into the crowd, but his facial features are prominent and he's easily recognisable.

He's a lot smaller than he appears on television; most bike riders are. The images on television screens seem to bulk them up. The ripple of muscle on legs does exist; it's just that there's no excess on the professionals. By the end of the Tour the level of fat clinging between bone and skin is negligible. Even faces become drawn and withered by the effect of the racing. But Cadel's chin dimple remains, and a few autograph hunters approached him in Le Méridien. He happily obliged, signed photos or postcards issued by the team, and posed for photos with a few in the lobby.

He was getting back into the rhythm of life, training for his next race (the Vuelta), thinking of the world championships, savouring the memories of a brief few days away from phone or internet connections.

He has his quirks. He has a unique ability on the bike. He attracts admiration from those who follow him but can frustrate those who are close to him because of his perpetually stubborn attitude. But he is focused and driven; he's committed to excellence and annoyed if he cannot achieve it. 'Even if I was at my best,' he says about Verbier, 'I would have lost time to Contador. There's not much doubt in that. From then onwards it got rough.'

His mother had this to say after the 2009 Tour:

The problem this year is that it's the first time that he hasn't been able to achieve his ambition. He's been beaten before but he always was able to extract the best out of himself. That eluded him in the Tour this year, and that's hard to cope with.

He doesn't manage self-defeat easily. It is a foreign experience for him.

Never mind the documentaries, retrospectives, books and magazine that will be filled with information about the race. They keep the dream alive in the endless cycle of hype that breathes energy into the event for the full calendar year. The Tour happens in July but the rest of the year it's either reviewed or previewed.

For the riders, the days that follow offer a brief respite from the pressures of what their real job is. Many dart out of Paris as quickly as possible in pursuit of the healthy doses of euros that are on offer for showcase criteriums – fixtures that usually last 100 kilometres and take place at various spots around the continent. Successful Tour riders command large appearance fees, pocketing up to €50,000 per race – for the yellow jersey – and significant sums for others who performed well. During these 'crits' riders wear their prize jerseys from the Tour and the crowds turn out in great numbers just to catch a glimpse of the freshly crowned stars of cycling. It's a cryptic tradition that continues, even though the set-ups are well known and an agreed winner crosses the line.

Who cares? It's part of the show. *Une fête d'été.* Cycling has its clichés and the criteriums are one of them.

The next big event for Cadel would be the Vuelta a España. Like the Tour de France, the Vuelta is three weeks and 3500 kilometres of pain. The unseasonable wet and cold added another layer of suffering for the riders. Frustratingly, though Cadel was perfectly positioned on Stage 13 and poised to take over the lead, the loss of valuable seconds stretched into diabolical minutes over a botched tyre change at a critical point of the race. Despite the setbacks, Cadel and his team fought back and the result was another first for Australian cycling, a podium position in the Vuelta a España when Cadel finished third. There would also be the World Championships at the end of September in Mendrisio, Switzerland, with another chance at that elusive rainbow jersey and the pride and pleasure in the opportunity of riding to represent his country.

Cadel usually rides the Giro di Lombardia, a 242-kilometre one-day race that starts in Varese, Italy, loops around Lake Como and concludes in Como. It's a picturesque event known as The Race of the Falling Leaves. As Chiara says, 'Lombardia perfectly marks the arrival of autumn. My father loves this time of the year; it's risotto for us every night. And in the daytime he goes hunting for funghi.' October is funghi season.

I never knew much about cycling before meeting Cadel, but I always knew that the Giro di Lombardia was on. Sometimes I would join Dad when he was searching for funghi and in the distance we could see the commotion. There were times when we planned it so we could see the peloton; other years I remember being held up because of the road closures.

'My season ends at Lombardia,' Cadel says after the Tour de France. There's little time for a rider with the hopes and objectives Cadel has set himself to rest or relax. He promotes the sport he fell in love with, encourages people to ride their bikes, and spreads a message about road safety. His achievements in other races – the steady progression from the early days in the bush in Bamyili on his first bike, to the realisation of how mountain biking could take him around the world, to the conquests off-road and on it – meant that he has a voice. There were plenty of successes during the first 15 years of his racing career but it is the Tour de France that has made his more of a household name in Australia than any other rider in recent times.

16
The rainbow glow

Reaching the podium's top step...

After Le Tour came La Vuelta a España. And a week later came the world championships contested in Mendrisio, Switzerland. The first race was one he'd rather forget. The second, another frustratingly close call. The third, the perfect remedy for a season of mixed emotions. Ultimately, it became a season of success.

For Cadel, the theme for 2009 had been 'Working on a dream'. In June, as the Tour approached, his osteopath, confidant and friend David Bombeke made a video montage of the rider training on his time trial bike to the soundtrack of a Bruce Springsteen track. At that stage, the yellow jersey was all they thought about. It was set as the quest: the attainable prize that was worth working for; a dream for every cyclist but one that can only remain in the mind for all but a rare species. True GC Guys are few and far between. Over the years they come and go, rise up the rankings into the lead of grand tours and – if they're lucky – onward to victory. But for these highly motivated individuals, once a win is achieved it's time to start working on another goal.

Cadel has been working on his dream since he was 16. Back in his senior year of high school he admitted his intentions, bold as they were, with clarity: 'to be the best mountain bike rider in the world'. He achieved just that, although the title of world champion eluded him during that phase of his career. He would win nine World Cup races, and take victory in the season-long series twice, but then it was time to shift focus, swap disciplines; to move on and dream up a new objective.

Since his high school days, the words 'mountain bike' had been struck from his mission statement. He now wanted to be the best rider in the world. After having been a professional cyclist for 15 years, now was the time to prove something greater.

His dream for July wasn't achieved and he laments that, yet despite the emotions he experienced after arriving in Paris in 30th place, it wasn't the end of the world. He was still working on a few things, he wanted to get the dreams out of his head and make them a reality, and a rainbow jersey could remedy this.

Late on a Sunday afternoon, on a road three kilometres from a small, simple apartment in Switzerland that he calls home, he raced ahead of a pack and into unknown territory. Even for GC Guys, there are dreams that extend beyond the *maillot jaune*. In cycling, five horizontal stripes – blue, red, black, yellow and green – translate to what many consider the ultimate prize.

These stripes are not the true spectrum as it appears in nature, but these five lines denote the rainbow, each colour representing one of the world's continents. And for cyclists, to achieve the honour of being able to wear these colours on a jersey is a humbling experience. It represents so much – two words that are universally acknowledged: World Champion.

There's one for each discipline but the rainbow jersey for elite men's road race is widely considered as the pinnacle. Winning it can often seem like the right numbers have come up in a lottery, for there are so many variables to consider in a competition which is contested one day each year on circuits that can be more favourable to one style of rider than to another.

On 27 September 2009 the strongest rider was also the most cunning. He had superb support from a cast of Australian riders who had committed to helping the team leader put himself in the best possible position to win. He had motivation, first-class form and the strength to finish the work done by his colleagues. This time he also had some luck on his side, and Cadel seized it.

After 255 kilometres of racing he was in the winning selection. A moment of hesitation from others in the elite group prompted Cadel to push the thumb of his right hand down on a lever that, in turn, clicked the chain to a smaller cog. With a harder gear selected, he surged ahead.

From when I got a gap after my attack, and onward to the finish, it was like I was living out a dream.

He would ride the final seven kilometres on his own. Out of the saddle over the closing climb, the Torrazza di Novazzano – 1750 metres long with a gradient as steep as 10 per cent – he surged.

He built an advantage and never looked back. He didn't want to see what was behind. All he considered was the finish. It would come soon, but there were still unanswered questions. Would others sprint past and wake him from this dreamlike trance? Would his equipment cope with the force he applied on the pedals? Would cramp seize him and halt his progress after almost seven hours of racing? Would tyres, pumped to 130psi, resist all the debris on the road? Would he collapse or triumph?

I wasn't getting any time checks over the radio once I attacked. I didn't know if I had a lead of five seconds or 50. And, having been so close before, even looking like the win was in the bag I refused to celebrate too soon. I've lost world titles before because of a puncture or a crash near the finish. In my experience, it's never over until you cross the finish line, so I was taking no chance.

He explains the closing sequence of his victory in the world championships with pleasure, but eventually – only two days after being crowned world champion and receiving his stripes – returns to the reference of it being like a dreamlike trance.

Once I got a gap at the end of the race, from then onwards it just seemed like being in a dream. It was my 15th world championship. I've got seven medals from those races and none of them were gold. To win on the biggest of them all, three kilometres from my house and to wear the jersey for a year ... compared to that, what would winning three junior world titles have done for me?

He laughs when he realises that he raced to the line in the style he's become accustomed to since becoming a road cycling professional: like a GC Guy, when every second counts for the classification. But in a one-day contest a win is a win – and it doesn't matter if you're one millimetre better than second place or one kilometre. The time is arbitrary; it's only the result that matters.

What he was coming to terms with was that he had proven he was a winner. Not the 'guy who had the potential'; not the runner-up. He finished first. His dream was no longer a work in progress, it was a reality.

It is my first win in a professional one-day road race on the asphalt.

I've finished close in a lot of one-day races. I've won plenty of stage races. But this was the only world championship that I've won … and it's the one that matters most.

I was second in the Commonwealth Games (2002), second in Flèche Wallonne (2008), fourth in Giro di Lombardia (2007), fifth in Liège–Bastogne–Liège (2005), and fifth in the worlds (2007). I have often been there for the win but in our sport it's not about being close; it's about either winning or losing.

I look back on it. I saw it replayed on television. This time I wanted to watch. And I started thinking, 'What the hell are people going to think of this?' After riding for 255 kilometres and then, even going to the finish on your own, it's not like I wasted time thinking about a salute.

He arrived at the line with an advantage of over half a minute. He was on his own and had time to throw his arms aloft and allow all the pent-up emotion to escape, but he refrained. He is a champion, the world champion, yet even in the time of his greatest conquest he remains an atypical cyclist, preferring a simple aesthetic rather than a gesture with great fanfare.

Metres from the finish, he lifts his body from the aerodynamic racing tuck position, raises his right hand and gently kisses his finger tips. A wave to the left. Another kiss on the fingers and a wave to the right. A clenched fist out of which a thumb raises before he offers a soft punch to the air. A touch to his heart and another wave to the left. He was now the world champion.

I had so much personal satisfaction from that result that I didn't need to be exalted.

The thing that people may not have understood is that I touched my heart and I pointed to the left, which is essentially where my house is. That was the big significance of it all.

I think that's what's so nice about the book, it helps to explain all the steps – the various stages – of the process that have gone into this.

If we go back to 1994, my first world championships when I came second to Miguel Martinez in Vail, and the feeling – which I explained again to Chiara when we were watching the footage of me winning in Mendrisio – returned to me. You can't understand the sickening feeling that you have on the podium, when you're standing there in second place and the guy next to you is putting on the rainbow jersey. I've had that often. After always just missing out and then for it to come now made the 16 year wait worthwhile.

I look back at all those people who beat me – even in my first junior world road championships – and even there I didn't have as good a lead-up as I could have. I'd just come out of a mountain bike race in Italy and I rode a time trial and I had the legs to win, but because my training wasn't as specific as it could have been I ran third. I look back and realise a lot has happened since.

Missing out all those times kept me hungry. The more I look back on it as my career has progressed, the happier I was that I didn't win earlier. This is the scenario that has helped keep my hunger for longer.

Really it's funny to look back on the season. I've had so many obstacles to overcome, setbacks that just kept coming through the year – one after the other after another. It felt like, for as many weeks as there are in a year, I had setbacks. And there was always Chiara telling me how she saw it: 'One day, your honesty will be repaid.' Boom! All of a sudden, it was.

You can be physically gifted but winning the world championship cannot happen unless the form is there. Cycling doesn't simply shine on fortunate souls, the work must also be done to ensure the legs can turn the pedals and the heart can handle the strain. There were better riders than Cadel in the Tour de France and he accepts that. Fate could have given him a little bit of a reprieve and allowed him some gains rather than losses but it didn't happen in July 2009. He would have to wait a few months for a touch of luck to come his way. Before that happened, however, he had to endure a sequence of errors by others that might be laughable were they not so ludicrous and costly for what would have otherwise almost certainly have been a winning result.

My goals for this year were Tour de France and world champion-ships. My best preparation for the world championships was to ride the Vuelta. My best result came from riding the Vuelta and finish-ing third on GC.

Despite those around me. I just stuck to that. I eventually got it to be the way I wanted and the result tells the story. I came pretty close to winning both the Vuelta as well as the worlds. All along I had to fight for that and it puts a bit of pressure on to perform: 'Shit! I've got to win this grand tour and the world championships!'

He almost did just that. But the Spanish race became a good way to hone form, demonstrate his strength and experience an exercise ... in frustration.

For the first time that I can remember I cried about my cycling in Sierra Nevada after Stage 13 of the Vuelta. There was just too much build-up and I finally let it out but it took some prompting. I didn't just start sobbing; I waited until what had only just happened began to sink in. I'd lost the chance again. I lost the Vuelta a España because of a flat tyre at the wrong moment.

Nearing the top of the penultimate climb, the Alto de Monachil, his rear tyre punctured. He was riding with the leaders of the general classification, often off to the far right of the road and weaving through crowds that had lined certain sections of the course very closely, forming just a small thoroughfare fenced in by hands applauding – or taking photos – and a corridor of voices in a myriad of languages.

Cadel had been in the lead of the 64th edition of La Vuelta.

The rainbow glow

This was a race created to commemorate the birth of a new Spain after the departure of the monarch King Alfonso XIII and the establishment of democracy with what was called the Second Republic – a New Spain. The first Vuelta, in 1932, was as much a political event as a sporting spectacle.

You could form conspiracy theories and ponder some antics that made up the drama of Cadel's journey from an opening time trial on the race track in Assen – normally used for motorbikes, but this time the site of a foreign departure of the Spanish grand tour – to the end on Madrid's Plaza de Cibeles. The execution of a rudimentary wheel change by a neutral service motorcycle was so poorly done that blame could be thrown at those responsible: it was like Basil Fawlty and Manuel were in charge. Throughout the ordeal, Cadel stood still while his rivals charged away.

One hand on the saddle, he patiently waited for service. Any service would do. Finally, it arrived in the form of a neutral squad that essentially turned up and declared: 'qué?'

If you weren't involved, it would have seemed like a comedy. It was ridiculous. Compelling, if you're into seeing what should have been a professional swap of wheels become a farce that would ultimately lead to the loss of a chance.

This was it: a real opportunity to win a grand tour. Everything was right. I'd worn the leader's jersey, had a deficit of just eight seconds, I felt fine and everything was under control. It was presented as a race to win.

But then I stood there and saw it all ride away from me. The wheel change took one minute and 23 seconds. Okay. I changed

279

*bikes. That cost me time. I then had a bike with no drink bottle, so I
got one from the team car. They penalised me an additional 10 seconds.*

I lost one minute and 33 seconds that day.

I lost the Vuelta title by one minute 32 seconds.

He never gave up. The chase after the repairs were finally
effected is one of the great scenes of the season. It showed a
man at the height of his powers with a quest he felt obliged to
fulfil. Finally, with a new bike after the comedy had milked its
last laugh, he was riding again. He clicked into the pedals, dipped
his hands into the drops, and set off. A high speed pursuit for 20
kilometres! First challenge: the dying kilometres of the Monachil
pass and then onward to the 2520-metre summit on the mountain where Cadel stayed and trained to get in climbing work at
altitude before the Tour de France – the Sierra Nevada.

*It's a climb I've done what seems like hundreds of times. Martin
Whiteley lives only 20 kilometres from where I had my puncture.
When I visit him, I do these climbs. This is the one part of Spain
that I know really well. These were roads I'd ridden, climbs I'd done.
I knew my form and the Vuelta was mine. But instead, I was
chasing.*

Ahead was Ezequiel Mosquera, Alejandro Valverde, Robert
Gesink, Ivan Basso, Samuel Sánchez and Joaquim Rodríguez. All
these riders, with Cadel dropping from second to fifth – made up
the top seven places in the general classification standings after
Stage 13.

In years to come, when people search for information on those days when Cadel Evans became the second Australian to wear the leading colours of all three grand tours – first the Giro in 2002, then the Tour in 2008 and finally the Vuelta in 2009 – the result sheet will remind them that, at Sierra Nevada, Cadel was over a minute and a half behind the Spaniard who would go on to win the title. There'll be no asterisk to denote the fact that with 20 kilometres to go the Australian was forced to lose the race because of a sloppy example of mechanical support.

But when he spoke about the event, he explained it. Remembered it. Discussed it. And dismissed it. 'That was the Vuelta,' he would say only 10 days after it finished and he was wearing a rainbow glow.

This is what saved him a little. It provided the relief and the opportunity to purge himself of the feeling of not living up to his expectations. This time he had achieved something truly special. Does the title of World Champion not say it all? This is what he now is and it is proof of the most prestigious component of what cycling has to offer. As the final editing work was being completed on this book Chiara was inspired to write some additional notes expressing her very personal recollection about her husband's magnificent performance in the race at Mendrisio, for this was not just the race that turned Cadel's jersey into a spectrum of colours, but it happened on the doorstep of their adopted home. It was the chance for him to perform on roads he knew and in front of people he cared about. Chiara takes up the story:

I had been getting organised with family and friends for days. We were all looking forward to that day for a long while. You can wear the yellow jersey in Paris if you win the Tour, but you'll get dressed in the rainbow colours for a whole year if you win the championships.

The worlds were held just three kilometres away from home. Mendrisio is at the south of Lake Lugano, in the Canton Ticino, the Italian part of Switzerland also known as 'terra di ciclismo' – 'land of cycling'.

Getting organised wasn't difficult; the race virtually passed our village, Stabio. With family and friends – a total of about 20 people – we left home at 7.45 in the morning to catch the bus that took us closer to the start/finish; then we had to walk to where we wanted to stay for most of the day. Destination: La Torrazza! It is the second climb of the circuit, the one closest to the finish.

After about 45 minutes, we got to the top of La Torrazza and we started setting ourselves up in the best spot. We had a lot of Australian flags, huge 'CADEL' signs, horns and all sort of things that would be useful to cheer on Cadel. I went up there the night before with my choir friends and a couple of spray-paint cans! It was past midnight and we were so excited; we painted a huge sign: 'Cadel we love you!' I sprayed out a large a 'Cadel' with a big heart. I could spot it during the TV coverage when Cadel made his solo attack.

The atmosphere on the circuit was like one giant festival: people from all over the world having fun, getting drunk and playing music loud, day and night. I wish I had slept in a campervan on the circuit the night before the race, it was such a great atmosphere.

It's different to the Tour de France. You get used to that after three weeks; the special thing of the worlds is that it's just for one day and people are cheering with national pride.

We were there to support Cadel throughout the race, no matter how he went; we were there to say, 'Hey, we're having fun with you. Just keep on riding because you love it!' What happened later was just the beginning of a confused period that lasted for a couple of days.

There were so many people that day, about 120,000 on the circuit. You could hear all of them. We heard what was going on in the race over the speakers but I was distracted and nervous. I remember the listing of all the cyclists in the leading group. 'Cadel ...' he was there. Then I remember 'Evans solo ...'!

My family started screaming. He attacked! At that point, I wasn't sure what was going on, but I knew I needed to get away from there. The crowd was going mad; my family was going mad! Everyone started screaming. I moved from there and I went to sit by myself on the grass a couple of metres behind; I had to shut my ears to not hear.

All of a sudden, everyone went quiet. My family didn't speak for a couple of seconds, but it felt like an eternity. Why the silence? What has happened? Then I saw Cadel coming alone up the Torrazza, just a few metres away from where we were standing. Everyone exploded with noise as they went past. Then it went quiet again. The cheers turned to statements and questions – everyone was offering their version: 'He'll make it.' 'He's got more than 15 seconds.'

'Chiara, he'll make it!' 'No one follows him!' 'Only one kilometre to go!' 'He's still alone!'

I could only hear some pieces of sentences, but it all sounded good. It was happening. And then it did happen. He won! He did it! My dad was crying and hugging me tight, screaming: 'He made it!' I couldn't stand. I was falling. I lost control of movements and emotions. I ran to the road crying. I was stopped by people asking if I was okay.

My husband won!

All the Torrazza went mad too! But I had only one thing on my mind: getting to the finish. We were three kilometres away, and the road was full of people. I would have never made it on time for the podium ceremony. I was crying and asking policemen, but they didn't want to stop one of the cars to help me. The fans chimed in and told the story, so they told me, 'Just climb the fence and stand in the middle of the road; someone will have to stop.' So I did.

Eventually someone stopped. I remember the cheers from the Torrazza – everyone clapping and yelling, 'Bravo Cadel!' The car that stopped was one of the photographers; I jumped in and when we left I found my sister Ilaria by my side. My dad was worried that I might faint, so he sent her after me.

Still crying, we got to the finish. I wanted to get closer to the podium as much I could, so, with the help of an official and a photographer, I jumped the last fence and I found myself at the base of the podium.

After a minute, I saw Cadel. I never thought it would be possible to cry so much. It came out and it was because of happiness, because *winning the world championships is the perfect victory for a cyclist wanting to prove he is the best in the world. I cried for those who have always believed in Cadel, not just those who were interested when he was going well. I cried for our little kid in Kathmandu, who I'm sure now is the most envied at school. I cried for my grandma, who would have turned 100 that day. And I wasn't the only one feeling like that. I turned and I saw a lot of people crying. It was very emotional.*

What happened later, was just the start of a long evening of celebrations. While the world around us was moving quickly, we were still sitting and staring at the rainbow jersey, hoping that it was real and not just a dream. We hung it on the wall before going to bed; if it was there the next morning, that means it must be true. But we didn't get to sleep that night …

He's been a marked man since he first started racing. His strength and ability propelled him into a career racing a bike. It opened doors for him that allowed him to traverse the globe. On two wheels he became an ambassador for a sport in a nation that, until his arrival, had struggled for the general public's acceptance. Thanks to Cadel, cycling is becoming mainstream in Australia.

He has won the MTB World Cup series twice and the UCI's ProTour. And he has twice stood on the podium of the Tour de France as the runner-up. He has had many more wins and places, but it's not always the result that tells the full story. There are so many variables in cycling and unless all the elements align, the strongest rider in the race may not also be the one who becomes the champion. In both the instances in which Cadel finished second in the Tour, he was widely acknowledged as the best, and was the centre of attention.

He has captivated the crowds, kept people awake, polarised opinions of aficionados, succeeded, spoken out and became a pivotal player in the world's biggest race. He has lost, but won at the same time. He has appealed to a nation that is only just understanding what it takes to win the prize that matters most in cycling.

There are just two riders from the 2009 season who have worn the leader's jersey in all three grand tours – the *rosa* of il Giro, the *jaune* of le Tour and the *oro* of la Vuelta: Alberto Contador and Cadel Evans have done this. The Spaniard has won all three of them, but the Australian has led them, all at crucial phases. Were it not for the collapse on the Passo Coe, the crash in Pujos or the stupidity of mechanics on Monachil, Cadel too would most likely have been a Giro/Tour/Vuelta champion.

He has the consolation of knowing that he is consistent. If it's a battle of bragging rights, Cadel can take on the best in the world. He is the only man to have been the world's number-one ranked cyclist in mountain biking and road cycling. He is the only rider to have worn the five most coveted jerseys in cycling; the three grand tour leader's jerseys, the ProTour jersey and the rainbow jersey.

My undoing has not come from the way I am or the way I go about things. In the races, my undoing is not because I'm not strong enough or not good enough.

If I go in a break, the two or three strongest teams in the race panic and close the move down straight away.

Being strong and talented and having so many years of consist-ently good results, everyone is watching me everywhere I go. That's something that has held me back on the winnings count.

But it doesn't get him down. Cadel still has more to offer. Per-haps he hasn't even taken off yet. There's still energy in those legs; there's still pure blood flowing through his capillaries and spirit in his emotion-charged mind.

17

Deep blue ocean

The honesty of the journey

The one trait Cadel cannot seem to avoid is 'honest'.

His honesty is often blunt in delivery and is open to be misinterpreted as dismissive. But he does care and he does listen. He does see the beauty in how much people care. He loves to ride and he gains a lot of enjoyment from the fact that a chance exists for him to show Australia what cycling is all about.

There have been formidable riders from his country who have become stars on the world cycling scene before him. From Phil Anderson to Stuart O'Grady, Brad McGee and Robbie McEwen – all men who have led the Tour de France on at least one occasion – to what is yet to come from a program that has been integral in producing superb talent. Australian cycling has a lot to be proud of. Cadel Evans has, however, been able to raise the level of awareness of cycling in a nation that is starting to appreciate the beauty of the simple notion: riding a bike is good. Cycling is fun. It offers benefits that extend beyond attaining a smile and getting somewhere. Ride a bike and savour what it offers. That's what Cadel wants to remind people.

Those who have been part of the journey have taken something from his experience – and it doesn't matter if they've cheered from the sidelines, tuned in late at night from the other side of the globe, been in his teams or are fellow national representatives, or followed in the car behind him as he pedals around races full of history and prestige.

What Anderson, O'Grady, McGee and McEwen did at the Tour alone – winning stages, wearing yellow jerseys, winning green ones, taking on international rivals as part of cosmopolitan teams – has drawn the crowds. Australians enjoy the Tour de France. And, from the year that it was first shown live for each stage, it was the fifth Aussie to wear the *maillot jaune* who exceeded what any compatriot had been able to achieve.

There are many who truly do care about him.

Damian Grundy watched the 2008 Tour de France from behind the couch. 'It's too scary to watch at times but in my heart I hope that it will turn out for the best.'

After the final time trial of Cadel's fourth Tour, his beloved *directeur sportif* Roberto Damiani stopped chewing his fingernails. He walked away from the team compound and found a patch of grass in Saint-Armand-Montrond. Sitting down with his knees bent in front of him, he dropped his head into his hands and cried. Everything went according to plan and there was belief right until the end but when Cadel's body called 'enough!' that's how it had to be. He couldn't give any more of himself.

'Poor Cadel,' said a lot of people after he came so close to being the winner of the Tour de France but was less than one minute slower than the actual champion of two editions. It's a shame, but he's not poor; of course he wanted to win but he's a richer man for having tried.

Martin Whiteley watched and admired a prodigious kid come up a mountain faster than anyone else, wondered about the pronunciation of his name, and then became his friend. One of his first confidants in the cycling world still has occasional contact with the rider and he's proud to have witnessed the never-ending development of a man who insists on being the best at what he does. But Martin also appreciates the quirks that others find frustrating. 'When he cracks up and has a great laugh he's still that junior rider that I remember,' says Whiteley years after they stopped having regular contact. 'He's still a kid at heart in many ways as a lot of us are. When you hit on something that's funny to him, it's usually quite cryptic to others. I used to do comedy radio and I would love an audience of Cadels because he tends to laugh at the stuff that you don't have to work hard at, it's kind of silly humour.

'I love to see that side of him because the Cadel I see in the Tour de France is just a part of him, but there's a lot more to it than that steely façade that few can crack.

'He's aware of his shortcomings and tries to deal with them as much as he endeavours to manage his immense talent. Some athletes like being in the centre of attention but a lot of these guys have no soul. Some of the guys are like robots when they talk to the media, they're so careful of what they've got to say and they're so worried about losing a deal. They can be so nervous or precious that all you get is this automaton, robotic response to everything. You can almost write the answers before they are spoken because you know what they're going to say.'

Helen has seen the full evolution. From a broken nose baby to blond infant; from being in a coma with a fractured skull to patting horses in the paddock upon his recovery; from a cycling adventurer around the hills of Plenty to a bike racer succeeding on the world stage. She's been there and she has shed a tear or two, but she is just happy to be there to give her son a hug when he crosses the line.

But it's Chiara who matters most. She is the perfect companion for Cadel Evans. The two make a great couple. In photos of the pair – with Molly on an elegant leash at their wedding, or when he's reached the Champs-Elysées after finishing his five Tours de France … no matter the occasion – they are happy. His smile can, at times, seem laboured. As though it's pulled by thoughts somewhere in the back of his mind for the benefit of the prying lens. But when he's around Chiara it's always natural. Joy is on display. It's lovely to see.

As I see it, I'm just getting better as a rider – physically and mentally. I'm as motivated as I ever was. I enjoy it as much as I ever did. When you're a good rider on a good day, the bike doesn't rattle and bounce. You're smooth. Even if it's rough you can find a way to make the bike float.

At first I didn't have that ability. I worked on my technique and, over the years, it came. It's what happens to anyone when they're passionate about what they do. You ride – you enjoy it. You ride more – you get better at it. Ride more – perfect your method and technique; it's a natural progression when you're having fun.

It's like the 'speeder bikes' in the chase scenes on the forest moon Endor from Return of the Jedi; *there's a sequence of close proximity to nature in a surreal setting. In Mendrisio I felt it – the exhilaration of what the bike has to offer. It's a simple machine that conjures a vast mix of emotions. It can evoke the senses and raise the spirits of people who watch. For those who ride it can seem like the perfect vehicle for transport. For those who race, there's no better sensation than being on top of your gear making mountains feel like flat roads. Cycling throws up plenty of obstacles, unknown territory, high speed split-second considerations. Where to next? What's around the next corner? Who cares? You're flyin'!*

Thank you

A lot had already been written about Cadel Evans before the notion of this book was considered. And during the process of writing this book – which began with an informal chat, one of many between Cadel and me during the course of the past decade or, dare I say, even longer. On the day that Norman Mailer died we spoke, I told him the news and he recalled me giving him a copy of *The Fight* at the beginning of 2002. He had suffered taunts from the media and tried to respond in the only manner he knew how: honestly.

It was around the time that he started his career that I embarked on mine and we've followed a similar path since, him on the bike and me at the keyboard. I've written a lot about a rider, an ambassador, a pioneer, a champion – an enigmatic man who has achieved great things and in the course of that happening has become a friend.

Little did we know, but we led lives that paralleled each other from the mid-1980s until we first met in 1994.

He rode a bike and lived on a property north of Coffs Harbour, the town where I was born. Cadel started formal schooling in nearby Woolgoolga. I spent three years in the country of my father, the Netherlands, but returned to the NSW north coast for high school. Cadel rode a bike and so did I; not a lot of people did at the time. At least, not as many as those who do now, 25 years on from when we started riding.

I raced BMX. He found mountain biking, and the rest you've read about. I started publishing cycling magazines in 1991, around the time he was first taking medals home. Then he started winning, and it was inevitable that I would meet him. That happened a few years later, at Thredbo in 1994. It was a brief encounter, one I remember but he doesn't.

In 1996 we rode what was a very early incarnation of what would become 'Fairfield Farm – home of the MTB course for the Sydney Olympics'. He was flying. I was riding. And he followed my lead down a trail and I set the pace to the base of the real climb, with him complimenting me as we rode. Then he was gone.

He waited at the top and we talked. I was out of breath so he recalled the downhill and he offered his take on technique. He did most of the talking. He was young and enthusiastic on the eve of his first Olympic appearance and we were out enjoying riding our bikes. What more could you want?

The first magazine I published was in conjunction with a race promoter, Phill Bates, who put on the Commonwealth Bank Cycle Classic. It was the longest naming-rights association of a corporate sponsor and a sporting event in Australia. It was a race that began in 1982 after the staging of the Commonwealth Games in Brisbane and, in stages, aimed south. For 19 years, it would pass through Coffs Harbour – even starting there later in the event's history. I wagged school to watch it and became hooked on road cycling. Cadel was too young to care.

Years later, he would understand the attraction. He stopped mountain biking for competition – but cherishes the chances he still has to ride the trails and enjoy it for recreation. Many others do too, and for some of those it's Cadel who introduced them to the idea. He first enticed people to ride when he did well off-road, but he became a world champion on the road.

By the time he started his first Tour de France, I'd already covered the race eight times, seven as the person responsible for writing the content of the event's official site. I'd followed every minute of the racing by writing the 'live' ticker that has been part of a portal that has attracted record numbers in the 13 years that I have now been doing the job. I've written millions of words about cycling.

The magazine I publish, *RIDE Cycling Review*, celebrated its 12th year in the season that ended with an Australian success in the world championships. Cadel's face has appeared on the cover at least once a year since he started riding the Tour de France. In the last five years, there have been frequent appearances in my magazine, on the Tour de France website and in thousands of other media outlets around the world of the name of a rider, a racer, a contender – a runner-up – and a friend.

Cadel Evans eventually found road cycling. Or, like mountain biking before, it found him. He rode a bike and he did it well. And because of what he did for a job and what I did for a job, we talked.

And so, on the day Mailer died – 10 November 2007 – Cadel

recognised something had happened during the course of years of discussion. He realised that perhaps there was, after all, a story to be told about what he does.

This wasn't a highlights reel of a list of sporting conquests – for if we listed all that came along the way, those who beat him or those who lost to him, it would take another volume of race-related writing. But the notion was to make people realise what gave him the fight to be who he is and what he's become. 'It's hard to read through the manuscript,' he told me in the dying days of production, 'because I'm taking a look inside a life – my life – and it's quite daunting. It's personal.' And it's honest.

Cadel, we know you're a fabulous bike rider. That is what you were but you wanted to be a world champion. You are that now. Bravo, my friend. Thanks for giving this book the fitting conclusion. With every pedal rotation, the bike can steer the rider in a new direction. For Cadel it's usually been 'up'. Higher on the podium, higher up the rankings, to the top of his game, the best of the best. The final chapter is certainly not the final phase of a career that's all about stages, but it provides an end that helps people to appreciate what has come from the journey from Bamyili to Mendrisio. The ride from the place of his birth to the site of conquest has been an amazing one already. I look forward to writing many more words in a story that is still being told.

Throughout the process of writing the book there are many people to include in the 'thank you' list and at the top of the list is Helen

Cocks. Without her support this book would never have come even close to flying. She kept it together when it felt as though it was falling apart.

Pam had the patience to wait until it was finished. It just so happened that the deadline came after the high point of a career that is ongoing and still captivating. I'm so pleased to have prolonged the process.

Telling the story of anyone's life is an interesting challenge. To have the chance to do this about a person with such rare ability and a unique outlook on the world meant that it became a cathartic experience that simply would not have been possible without the support of Helen. But there were many other people who deserve praise for their contributions. Chiara Passerini deserves pride of place in the credits; she is the Queen of Cadel's world, someone who helps to manage his daily routine and share his varied passions. Her friendship and grace have helped put a smile on the face of not only her husband but all who know her. A person with endless energy and a perennial problem solver, Chiara is a pleasure to have on your team and I'm forever grateful for the influence she had on both Cadel and this book.

To the others in 'The List of Five' – Martin Whiteley, Damian Grundy and Roberto Damiani – thanks for sharing your time and thoughts on a most enigmatic man who you've praised, cursed and admired over the years.

If there was ever to be an addition to 'The List', then I would nominate Hendrik Redant to become the sixth member. He has become a friend of mine in the time that he's known Cadel and it's been a pleasure to have his support over the years. He is a true believer, a man who has helped guide a special person at an amazing time of his life. Even if he was speeding down a mountain pass – foot on the accelerator, *'volle gas'*, in pursuit of a peloton – he always had the courtesy to answer questions, discuss tactics and explain his take on a most intriguing rider and a sport that can be confusing even for those who have followed it for over 20 years.

To the guys who have sat beside me in my office throughout the course of writing this book, thanks for listening and sorry for my outbursts of emotion over the years: Shane Lovejoy, Toby Shingleton and Rob Rixon. Without any real volition, you became my sounding board and I'm grateful that you always had the patience to listen.

To the many who have been team-mates of Cadel – riders, *soigneurs*, mechanics, managers and more – thanks for sharing your stories with me and allowing me to get a greater insight into a subject. Robbie McEwen, Matt Lloyd and Charlie Wegelius have all earned even more admiration from me because of their honesty, willingness to express their opinions and their achievements as colleagues of the GC Guy.

To the team who helped him win the rainbow jersey, thanks for making this moment happen. Goosebumps will always appear when I see the footage of those final kilometres in Mendrisio and the presentation of the rainbow that followed, but it's you who delivered Cadel to the line and it's essential to acknowledge your contribution, for cycling might be a sport in which an individual wins but it's the team that allows that to happen.

On a personal level, I'd like to acknowledge the support of a few people who were always prepared to help, read or listen, even though they had plenty of other things to do: Louis Doucet, Kathie Stove, Greg Chalberg, Mike Cotty and Geoff Schmidt; thanks for your support and friendship.

To the third musketeer, Molly: *mille grazie* for making Cadel happy when he wondered if there was anything to smile about.

And finally, to the two most important people in my life, Nicola and Louis – thanks for loving me always. This book would not have been possible if the two of you didn't allow me to write it. Thanks.

Palmarès (achievements)

1994

2nd   World Championships (junior), Cross Country (MTB), Vail, USA

1995

3rd   World Championships (junior), Cross Country (MTB), Kirchzarten, Germany

3rd   World Championship (junior), Time Trial (road), Forli, Italy

1996

5th   World Cup (elite), Cross Country (MTB), Cairns, Australia

3rd   World Championships (under-23), Cross Country (MTB), Cairns, Australia

9th   Olympics, Cross Country (MTB), Atlanta, USA

1997

1st   World Cup, Cross Country (MTB), Wellington, New Zealand

2nd   World Cup, Cross Country (MTB) St-Wendel, Germany

2nd   World Cup, Cross Country (MTB), Budapest, Hungary

1st   World Cup, Cross Country (MTB), Vail, USA

3rd   World Cup (elite), Cross Country, (MTB), Overall Results

2nd   World Championships (under-23), Cross Country (MTB), Château-d'Oex, Switzerland

1998

1st   Mount Buller Classic (road), Mt Buller, Australia

2nd   Stage 2, Geelong Bay Classic Series (road), Portarlington, Australia

2nd   General Classification, Redlands Bicycle Classic (road), California, USA

1st   World Cup, Cross Country (MTB), Silves, Portugal

2nd   World Cup, Cross Country (MTB), St-Wendel, Germany

1st   World Cup (elite), Cross Country (MTB), Plymouth, UK

1st   World Cup, Cross Country (MTB), Canmore, Canada

3rd   World Cup, Cross Country (MTB), Bromont, Canada
1st   World Cup (elite), Cross Country (MTB), Overall Results

1999

2nd   Stage 2, Mount Buller Cup (road), Mt Buller, Australia
2nd   Prologue, Tour of Tasmania (road), Launceston, Australia
1st   Stage 3, Tour of Tasmania (road), Mt. Wellington, Australia
1st   General Classification, Tour of Tasmania (road), Australia
2nd   World Cup, Cross Country (MTB), Napa Valley, USA
2nd   World Cup, Cross Country (MTB), Sydney, Australia
1st   World Cup, Cross Country (MTB), Madrid, Spain
2nd   World Cup, Cross Country (MTB), Big Bear, USA
2nd   World Cup, Cross Country (MTB), Canmore, Canada
3rd   World Cup, Cross Country (MTB), Houffalize, Belgium
1st   World Cup (elite), Cross Country (MTB), Overall Results
2nd   World Championships (under-23), Cross Country (MTB), Åre,
        Sweden

2000

3rd   Australian National Championship (elite), Cross Country (MTB),
        Kooralbyn, Australia
1st   World Cup, Cross Country (MTB), Mont Sainte-Anne, Canada
1st   World Cup, Cross Country (MTB), Canmore, Canada
3rd   World Cup, Cross Country (MTB), Swansea, USA
7th   Olympics, Cross Country (MTB), Sydney, Australia

2001

3rd   World Cup, Cross Country (MTB), Grouse Mountain, Canada
2nd   World Cup, Cross Country (MTB), Kaprun, Austria
1st   A Travers Lausanne (road), Switzerland
1st   Stage 4, Österreich Rundfahrt (road), Kitzbühler Horn, Austria
1st   General Classification, Österreich Rundfahrt (road), Austria
2nd   Stage 2, Brixia Tour (road), Lumezzane, Italy
1st   General Classification, Brixia Tour (road), Italy
2nd   Japan Cup (road), Japan

2002

1st   Stage 5, Tour Down Under (road), Tanunda, Australia

2nd	Stage 6, Paris–Nice (road), Col d'Eze, France
3rd	General Classification, Settimana Ciclistica Internazionale Coppi-Bartali (road), Italy
3rd	General Classification, Tour de Romandie (road), Switzerland
2nd	Stage 13, Giro d'Italia (road), San Giacomo, Italy
3rd	Stage 14, Giro d'Italia (road), Numana, Italy
1st	Stage 4, Uniqa Classic (road), Grossmaning, Austria
1st	Commonwealth Games, Time trial (road), Manchester, UK
2nd	Commonwealth Games (road), Manchester, UK
3rd	Rominger Classic (road), Engelberg, Switzerland

2004

3rd	Stage 4, Vuelta Ciclista a Murcia (road), Alto Collado Bermejo, Spain
3rd	General Classification, Vuelta Ciclista a Murcia (road), Spain
1st	Stage 2, Österreich Rundfahrt (road), Kitzbüheler Horn, Austria
1st	General Classification, Österreich Rundfahrt (road), Austria

2005

2nd	Stage 5, Paris–Nice (road), Toulon, France
4th	Stage 16, Tour de France (road), Pau, France
1st	Stage 7, Deutschland Tour (road), Feldberg, Germany
2nd	Mountains classification, Deutschland Tour (road), Germany

2006

3rd	Stage 3, Tour Down Under (road), Yankalilla, Australia
3rd	Stage 3, Tour de Romandie (road), Leysin, Switzerland
3rd	Stage 4, Tour de Romandie (road), Sion, Switzerland
1st	Stage 5, Tour de Romandie (road), Lausanne, Switzerland
1st	General Classification, Tour de Romandie (road), Switzerland
2nd	Points classification, Tour de Romandie (road), Switzerland
3rd	Stage 8, Tour de Suisse (road), Ambri, Switzerland
2nd	Stage 9, Tour de Suisse (road), Bern, Switzerland
4th	Stage 11, Tour de France (road), Val d'Aran/Pla-de-Beret, France
4th	Stage 16, Tour de France (road), La Toussuire, France
5th	General Classification, Tour de France (road), France
3rd	Stage 6, Tour de Pologne (road), Karpacz, Poland
3rd	Stage 7, Tour de Pologne (road), Karpacz, Poland
2nd	General Classification, Tour de Pologne (road), Poland

2007

1st	Stage 1, Part b Settimana Ciclistica Internazionale Coppi-Bartali (road), Misano Adriatico, Italy
3rd	Stage 7, Critérium du Dauphiné Libéré (road), Annecy, France
2nd	General Classification, Critérium du Dauphiné Libéré (road), France
3rd	Points Classification, Critérium du Dauphiné Libéré (road), France
3rd	Stage 9, Tour de France (road), Briançon, France
1st	Stage 13, Tour de France (road), Albi, France
4th	Stage 16, Tour de France (road), Gourette–Col d'Aubisque, France
2nd	Stage 19, Tour de France (road), Angoulême, France
2nd	General Classification, Tour de France (road), France
3rd	Wiesbauer Rathauskriterium (road), Austria
1st	Castillon-la-Bataille (road), France
2nd	Marcoles (road), France
3rd	Gouden Pijl Emmen (road), Netherlands
1st	Stage 2, Test Event Beijing 2008 (road), China
2nd	Stage 10, Vuelta a España (road), Andorra (Vallnord/sector Arcalís) , Spain
2nd	Stage 18, Vuelta a España (road), Avila, Spain
4th	General Classification, Vuelta a España (road), Spain
1st	General Classification, UCI ProTour (road)

2008

1st	Stage 2, Vuelta a Andalucia (Ruta del Sol) (road), La Zubia, Spain
3rd	General Classification, Vuelta a Andalucia (Ruta del Sol) (road), Spain
1st	Stage 4, Paris–Nice (road), Station du Mont Serein Mont Ventoux, France
1st	Stage 3, Settimana Ciclistica Internazionale Coppi-Bartali (road), Pavullo, Italy
1st	General Classification, Settimana Ciclistica Internazionale Coppi-Bartali (road), Italy
2nd	General Classification, Vuelta Ciclista al País Vasco (road), Spain
2nd	Stage 6, Vuelta Ciclista al País Vasco (road), Orio , Spain
2nd	Waalse Pijl (road), Huy, Belgium
3rd	Stage 3, Critérium du Dauphiné Libéré (road), Saint-Paul-en-Jarez, France

2nd	Stage 5, Critérium du Dauphiné Libéré (road), Morzine, France
2nd	General Classification, Critérium du Dauphiné Libéré (road), France
3rd	Points classification, Critérium du Dauphiné Libéré (road), France
4th	Stage 4, Tour de France (road), Cholet, France
3rd	Stage 6, Tour de France (road), Super-Besse, France
2nd	General Classification, Tour de France (road), France
2nd	Bavikhove (road), Belgium

2009

3rd	Stage 3, Vuelta a Andalucia (Ruta del Sol) (road), Benahavis, Spain
4th	Stage 6 Paris– Nice (road), La Montagne de Lure, France
4th	Stage 2, Settimana Ciclistica Internazionale Coppi-Bartali (road), Faenza, Italy
2nd	Stage 3, Settimana Ciclistica Internazionale Coppi-Bartali (road), Serramazzoni, Italy
1st	Stage 5, Settimana Ciclistica Internazionale Coppi-Bartali (road), Sassuolo, Italy
2nd	General Classification, Settimana Ciclistica Internazionale Coppi-Bartali (road), Italy
2nd	Stage 3, Vuelta Ciclista al País Vasco (road), Eibar, Spain
4th	General Classification, Vuelta Ciclista al País Vasco (road), Spain
5th	Waalse Pijl, Huy, Belgium
1st	Stage 1, Critérium du Dauphiné Libéré (road), Nancy, France
2nd	Stage 4, Critérium du Dauphiné Libéré (road), Valence, France
3rd	Stage 7, Critérium du Dauphiné Libéré (road), Saint-François-Longchamp, France
2nd	General Classification, Critérium du Dauphiné Libéré (road), France
1st	Points classification, Critérium du Dauphiné Libéré (road), France
5th	Stage 1, Tour de France (road), Monaco, France
4th	Stage 8, Vuelta a España (road), Alto de Aitana, Spain
3rd	Stage 19, Vuelta a España (road), La Granja. Real Fábrica de Cristales, Spain
3rd	Stage 20, Vuelta a España (road), Toledo, Spain
3rd	General Classification, Vuelta a España (road), Spain
1st	World Championship (elite), Road, Mendrisio, Switzerland